LEADING WITH DEPTH

LEADING WITH DEPTH
The Impact of Emotions and Relationships on Leadership

Claudia Nagel

PHOENIX
PUBLISHING HOUSE
firing the mind

First published in 2024 by
Phoenix Publishing House Ltd
62 Bucknell Road
Bicester
Oxfordshire OX26 2DS

British Library Cataloguing in Publication Data

A C.I.P. for this book is available from the British Library

ISBN-13: 978-1-80013-229-0

Typeset by Medlar Publishing Solutions Pvt Ltd, India

www.firingthemind.com

To ISPSO

The International Society for the Psychoanalytic Study of Organizations

My professional home base

Contents

Acknowledgements

This book is presented as a gift to commemorate the fortieth birthday of ISPSO, the International Society for the Psychoanalytic Study of Organizations. While writing and compiling this book I was the president and CEO of this society, but my term will end soon; hence this book is not presented as the work of the ISPSO president, but as the personal work of myself and the contributing members and experts.

This society is a very special community of like-minded people who study and work with all kinds of organisations with the aim to understand the unconscious dynamics within them. Therefore, I would like to sincerely thank, first of all, my case contributors—experts in their field and personal and professional friends—who were willing to share their own experiences in our field of work, followed by all my friends and colleagues from ISPSO and around it. I have learned so much from you and with you and I am incredibly grateful to you and to be part of our community.

I would also like to express my deep gratitude to my publisher, Kate Pearce, who accompanied me on this short-term journey and whose trust and belief brought this book to life. It was written in half a year but contains almost twenty years of thinking and working in the field of leadership and psychodynamics.

Two very dear friends and artists in their field have written forewords from their respective position. The first one, my very dear Bolko von Oetinger, who has a strong background in management and strategy, is one of the best thinkers I know, clear, concise, curious and always ready to discuss and reflect further. His mind is ready to question what is happening in the world and to incessantly pursue new ideas and approaches. It is always a great pleasure to be the counterpart of these conversations. Thank you, dear Bolko, for your deeply reflective preface from a leader's perspective.

My wonderful friend and colleague Anton Obholzer has written a fabulous foreword which made me blush, but then I think I was not alone in writing this book. Anton represents one of the pairs of giant shoulders I stand on. Thank you, dear Anton.

Finally, I am extremely grateful to my beloved partner, Heiner, who is always encouraging me and relentlessly supporting me in many different areas of life, not only letting me write any time I need to but also cooking for me. He is always willing to give me constructive feedback. I learn a lot from his own professional entrepreneurial experiences and deeply enjoy our conversations.

About the author and contributors

Author

Prof Dr Claudia Nagel is a consultant, coach, author, and senior advisor to international organisations and their board members. She is a full professor at the Vrije Universiteit Amsterdam holding a chair in change and identity. As an economist (MBA), organisational psychologist (PhD), and chartered psychoanalyst (ISAP), Claudia is an expert on strategic management, leadership, and change processes. She runs her own consulting business, Nagel & Company, and is past president of the International Society for the Psychoanalytic Study of Organizations (ISPSO). She talks and publishes extensively on behavioural strategy, and recently wrote *Psychodynamic Coaching* (Routledge, 2020) and can be contacted at claudia.nagel@nagel-company.com.

Contributors

Gilles Amado, PhD (in psychology), is emeritus professor of organisational psychosociology at HEC Paris (École des hautes études commerciales de Paris). He is one of the founding members of the International

Society for the Psychoanalytic Study of Organizations (ISPSO), of Le Centre International de Recherche, de Formation et d'Intervention en Psychosociologie (CIRFIP), an associate member of the Research Centre on Work and Development (CRTD) at the Conservatoire National des Arts et Métiers (CNAM), a member of La Société Française de Psychothérapie Psychanalytique de Groupe (SFPPG). He was the co-chief editor of the *Revue Internationale de Psychosociologie* (1994–2005), then of the *Nouvelle Revue de Psychosociologie* (2005–2018). His articles and books deal with group dynamics, organisational change, work psychology, leadership, and the use of the systems psychodynamics approach. He conducts international interventions and supervision sessions within the private and public sectors.

Birgitte Bonnerup holds an MA in psychology, University of Copenhagen. She is a registered psychologist, and a qualified specialist and supervisor in organisational psychology. She is a partner in organisational psychologists Bonnerup & Hasselager in Copenhagen, where she works as a therapist and organisational consultant. She holds a position as an external lecturer on the master's degree course in organisational psychology at the University of Roskilde, Denmark. She has been a member of ISPSO since 2008. In 2019 Routledge published *Love and Loneliness at Work*, her book co-written with Annemette Hasselager. In 2022 she contributed a chapter to *The Covid Trail* edited by Halina Brunning and Olya Khaleelee, published by Routledge. She can be contacted at www.bonnerup-hasselager.dk.

Philip Boxer BSc MBA PhD brings many years of strategy consulting experience to developing clients' capabilities for leadership within highly networked environments subject to the effects of digitalisation. He uses approaches that enable clients to scale learning across networked organisations and develop the agility of supporting business platforms. Philip is a member of the (Lacanian) Centre for Freudian Analysis and Research and the International Society for the Psychoanalytic Study of Organizations. His research and writing are focused on ways of understanding and working through the maladaptive responses of client systems to the demand for one-by-one responses within turbulent business ecosystems.

Halina Brunning is a chartered clinical psychologist, organisational consultant, and executive coach. Halina has published extensively on clinical and organisational issues, has edited seven books for Karnac, including *Executive Coaching: Systems-Psychodynamic Perspective* (2006). She conceived the idea of a trilogy of books which examined the contemporary world through a psychoanalytic lens. This approach continued in her latest books co-written with Olya Khaleelee: *Danse Macabre and Other Stories: A Psychoanalytic Perspective on Global Dynamics* and *The Covid Trail: Psychoanalytic Explorations*, both published by Phoenix Publishing House.

Annemette Hasselager is a psychologist and a specialist and supervisor in organisational psychology. She is a partner in Bonnerup & Hasselager where she works as an organiational psychologist and therapist with individuals, groups, and organisations. She is an external lecturer at MPO, a master's degree course in organisational psychology at Roskilde University, Denmark. She writes books and articles on organisational psychology. In 2019 Routledge published *Love and Loneliness at Work*, her book co-written with Birgitte Bonnerup. She has been a member of ISPSO since 2004. She can be contacted at www.bonnerup hasselager.dk.

Manfred F. R. Kets de Vries is the distinguished clinical professor of leadership development and organizational change at INSEAD in France. He is also a psychoanalyst. He is the author, co-author, or editor of more than fifty books and hundreds of articles. His books and articles have been translated into twenty-five languages. As an educator and consultant, he has worked in more than forty countries. In addition, he is the recipient of many awards, including four honorary doctorates. The *Financial Times*, *Le Capital*, *The Economist*, and El País have all judged him as one of the world's leading thinkers on management.

Olya Khaleelee is a corporate psychologist and organisational consultant with a particular interest in leadership and organisational transition and transformation. She was director of OPUS: An Organisation for Promoting Understanding of Society from 1980 to 1994, is a professional partner of the Tavistock Institute, and was the first female director of the Leicester Conference on the theme of authority, leadership, and organisation. She has published extensively in the areas of leadership and system psychodynamics in organisations, and beyond, in society. Recently she has co-authored two books with Halina Brunning: *Danse Macabre and Other Stories: A Psychoanalytic Perspective on Global Dynamics*; and as co-editors of *The Covid Trail*.

Fiona Martin, MA, is an organisational consultant, coach, and researcher. Her research interest is the impact of disruptive environments, including climate change, on management, and group dynamics especially in relation to the capacity of organisations to remain focused on purpose and their ability to learn from their experiences. Her current research is into barriers and enablers to research utilisation, organisational learning, and animal–human relations. Her findings have practical application for the understanding of group dynamics in contemporary organisations. She has authored and co-authored academic papers, is a member of the editorial board of *Socioanalysis*, a director of Group Relations Australia, and a member of the organising committee of the NIODA (National Institute of Organisation Dynamics Australia) Symposium 2017–22.

Dr Ajit Menon is currently the head of people and organisation at Investec PLC. He has more than twenty years of experience working in the areas of culture, organisation development, change, and HR. Prior to joining Investec, Ajit was a strategic leadership and organisational consultant. He built and ran his own organisational consulting practice, Blacklight Advisory Ltd., delivering strategic people and organisation solutions to companies across multiple industries and geographies. Ajit has a doctorate in organisational consulting, has been a visiting faculty member at Tavistock and Portman, London School of Economics, and University College London, and recently co-authored a book, *What Lies Beneath: How Organisations Really Work* (Phoenix, 2021).

Dr Rose Redding Mersky has been an organisational development consultant to a wide variety of private, public, non-profit, and professional organisations for more than thirty years. Her many publications have focused primarily on the practice of consultation and the utilisation of socio-analytic methodologies in both organisational and research practice. She is a Distinguished Member of the International Society for the Psychoanalytic Study of Organizations, and she served as its first female president. She is an honorary professor at the National Research University: Higher School of Economics in Moscow, where she teaches master classes. Her new book, *The Social Dream-Drawing Workshop: A Handbook for Professionals* has just been published by Routledge. She is an American citizen living in Germany and can be contacted at rose.mersky@dream-drawing.com.

Malachi O'Connor, PhD, principal at CFAR (Center for Applied Research), a US management consulting firm, has worked for more than thirty years with senior executives and managers across a broad range of for-profit, non-profit, and public sector organisations. Mal's approach to consulting combines his training as an ethnographer with a psychodynamic, systems thinking model. He applies this framework in his work with clients on strategy and system-wide strategic change, board and executive development, mergers and acquisitions, and making the business case for cultural diversity. He is co-author of *The Moment You Can't Ignore: When Big Trouble Leads to a Great Future*, published by Public Affairs Books in October 2014.

Larissa Philatova is an executive and team coach and HR consultant. Larissa has twenty years of experience in talent recruitment management and offers professional advice on career, education, and HR solutions for corporate and small business clients, focused on advising clients on building a more reliable and well-suited business and HR policy. Larissa explores the negative capability of a leader; the basis of the study was her master's thesis "Leadership through the prism of psychoanalysis: negative cability as a key skill in the pre-uncertainty" at Moscow Higher School of Economics.

Martin Ringer, BE (Hons), MEd, is an author and artist who has a passion for understanding human behaviour in groups, organisations, and communities. His work history includes engineering, directing a bi-cultural adventure therapy programme in New Zealand and management consulting and coaching, as well as lecturing at a number of different universities in social work, group dynamics, psychodynamics, psychotherapy, and experiential learning. His publications include a book on group dynamics and experiential learning and he is lead editor of a recent edited book, *The Collective Spark: Igniting Thinking in Groups, Organizations and the Wider World.*

Rob Ryan is a psychoanalytically informed organisational consultant, executive coach, facilitator, writer, and director of wisdom+work—a boutique consulting firm based in Melbourne, Australia. He provides consulting services in individual and team leadership development, analytic coaching, strategic thinking, organisation and service reviews, and governance. Working in government, business, and not-for-profit sectors he has designed and led many leadership development programs with a focus on systems psychodynamics and strengths-based approaches. Rob's work is informed by his extensive experience in roles including consultant, CEO, educator, board president, regional ISPSO co-convenor and, until recently, Director of Administration of ISPSO.

Kalina Stamenova, PhD, is an academic, researcher, and consultant working at the University of Essex, UK. Her current research interests include the psychoanalytic understanding of online dynamics in teams and organisations working in virtual environments. She has co-edited with R. D. Hinshelwood *Methods of Research in the Unconscious: Applying Psychoanalytic Ideas to Social Science* (Routledge, 2018). She is also a book review editor for the *Journal of Organisational and Social Dynamics.*

Preface—The magic mirror on the wall

Bolko von Oetinger

Rarely have I read a management book so intensively in one go, and rarely did the reading make me so thoughtful as *Leading with Depth* by Claudia Nagel. I asked myself what spirit breathes from this book and why it is decidedly worth reading for managers. As so often with complex matters, at first glance the answer seems to be simple: it is about the performance of managers. But behind this lies an almost impenetrable intricacy. For Claudia Nagel, it is about the leader as an emotional human being, about his or her relationships with other people and within organisations that are supported by individuals or other organisations.

From important management meetings we know the significance of the so-called "elephant in the room". Like all dead metaphors, this says it all, but doesn't ask any new questions. That is exactly the starting point of the book: we have to have the courage to look in the mirror and ask ourselves what emotions are driving us and others involved when we argue about supposedly factual issues. We know that something in the deep unconscious exists within us and affects our actions as decision makers. We may have a vague idea of what it might be about, but we cannot operationalise it and consciously block it out. The book takes us into this mysterious land.

You can't read the book without asking yourself, what does my deep inner self look like? Wouldn't I myself have to get more clarity about my emotions and their causes in order to understand myself and then put myself in the shoes of others? Fortunately, Claudia Nagel does not offer a checklist, the complexity and respect for the individual is too great for that, but she wanders through so many fields that a voice in the reader stirs: "Watch out, this could also be the case with you, you have experienced this before, here you need to know more about yourself, this could help you ..."

This voice of the reader, that is, one's own voice, which becomes louder and clearer in the course of reading, is the great value creation that the book evokes. The voice tells me that I should not stand in my own way, that I should not avoid self-exploration of my emotions when it comes to big decisions with which we associate many hopes, but also many fears. The fact that the exploration of one's own emotions is often fruitless has to do with the concern that we might learn something about ourselves that instils fear. Claudia Nagel therefore talks at the end of the book about the courage to look into one's own "abyss".

Readers learn how experiences from the past, perhaps from their early youth, which they are no longer aware of, influence their current performance. Of course, it is very reassuring to gain more insights of what strongly influences us unconsciously. Equally important, these insights are very helpful to run our daily operations, for example to convince our employees to follow us, to make better strategic choices or initiate innovations more courageously. The prerequisite is to better assess the elephants that have been riding us for a long time. It would not do the book's seriousness and academic depth any good to put it under the journalistic category of "How to become more successful" guidebooks, but there is no doubt that knowledge of the largely unknown territory within oneself is an important prerequisite for more effective leadership.

The current accumulation of distortions such as climate crises, energy crises, pandemics, technological disruptions, wars, and inflation requires an assessment from a variety of perspectives in order to define the space of possibilities that is constantly shifting. As leaders, we must lead our own organisation to explore this space without fear—on the contrary, with an appetite for ambiguity—and to catch the faint signals that hint dimly at the new. The power to lead thousands of employees into a new space is not genetically given; Claudia Nagel constantly points out that leadership can be learned and changed and that, however, one has to start with oneself. She demands that we must be in contact with ourselves. Self-awareness can be promoted through self-reflection and self-discovery.

The image of the leader that emerges here is the opposite of what can be called the "Davos man". The "Masters of the Universe", who fly into Davos every year, seem to know everything, believe they have everything under control, and mutually confirm each other. They already have all the answers. With Claudia Nagel, on the other hand, we discover leaders who are quite different, men and women who ask themselves questions about themselves, who are not free of fear, who know that their view of the world is shaped by their implicit emotional assumptions, their life experiences, personality traits, their organisations, and the situation in which they are placed, and who are sufficiently aware of this.

Reading the book inevitably raises the question, do I really want to take this arduous path, to know more about myself? This is where hope and fear come into play. However, the hope of discovering undreamed-of possibilities should be greater than the fear of finding out things about oneself that seem scary. Claudia Nagel uses a pedagogical trick to show the reader that the world of the unconscious can be explored step by step. Each new important thought in the book is followed by a small case study written by colleagues of the author. These case studies show that problems cannot be so easily traced back to a few causes; we humans are too complicated and too different to fit into a few boxes. The case studies include personal background (parental home, siblings, partner relationships, etc.) and organisational conditions. You get a feeling that the person we are dealing with is not only a functioning manager who manages his or her tasks rationally, but also an individual with his own personal family history, her burdens, his emotions, and everything else that influences him and her consciously and unconsciously. This makes the individuals in the case studies sympathetic; they become a kind of colleagues of the reader.

The book is divided into two parts. The first part focuses on the individual, the second on the organisation. Both are closely linked: it is individuals under a unified leadership that form the organisation. Traditionally we measure organisational success in financial figures, customer satisfaction, innovative strength, or whatever the organisation defines as success. A manager is only successful if, in addition to assessing the factual tasks, he or she mobilises the organisation to achieve demanding goals. The higher the position in the company, the more the ability of social coordination comes to the fore and thus the management of human relationships and emotions. Particularly in major change processes, the manager is required not only to have the highest level of personal performance but also to be able to respond to the fears of the employees, the depths of which are largely unknown.

Nothing is more uncertain than the future. The illusions that we can guess the future ("illusions of foresight") are fed by the fear of the future. Everything that can be estimated falls under calculable-risk decisions. Ambiguous surprises, on the other hand, belong to decisions under uncertainty. There are no management tools for them. Business leaders must therefore be required not to fear ambiguities, ambivalences, surprises, crises, but to feel a pleasure in the resulting potential opportunities. Claudia Nagel recommends that managers create a thinking space in which those concerned can examine and reflect together their thought patterns and implicit assumptions based on their emotional history. In this way, a potential solution space is jointly developed in the strategy process, in which the conscious and the unconscious, fantasy and reality intermingle. Strategy is thus not only a rational process, but a process that is shaped by a few individuals and their conscious and unconscious assumptions. Practitioners are aware that strategy is much more person-bound than strategy concepts suggest, but what the deeper drivers are is hardly ever explained. This is what one learns in Claudia Nagel's book.

Most business books describe what happens on the surface of the actors, with references to psychological factors, but what happens behind the stage of the actors is largely left out because access to this is difficult without appropriate training and experience at the border between business and psyche. Claudia Nagel has this access and has made the visit backstage extremely readable.

Prof Dr Bolko von Oetinger
Co-founder and former chairman, BCG Germany
Professor for Strategic Management at the WHU-Otto
Beisheim Business School of Management

Foreword

Anton Obholzer

When Claudia asked me to write a foreword, I had no hesitation whatsoever as I valued and respected her work and felt honoured to be asked! It was only when the book arrived on my doorstep that I realised what I had let myself in for. I had expected a traditional paper such as happens among colleagues in the brotherhood and sisterhood of coaching and consultancy. What had arrived was an encyclopaedia such as has never existed since time immemorial.

I had expected to write an informative introduction to the work and perhaps propose a toast to the author-editor of the work about to be launched! The work as it exists left no gap whatsoever for my intentions, for it covered the entire field of knowledge past, present, and future in as much as one can look into the unknowable developments on the distant horizon.

So, what is to be done?

Calm down, something is going to turn up, but then again that eventuality is already in the text along with a plethora of other ways out of the emotional Sargasso Sea. For those not familiar with sailing, it is where all ships are becalmed, there is no breeze to sail away, and the ships are marooned, growing seaweed on their hulls that slow them even more should a breeze arrive! So, how to comply with the requirement of writing a foreword to this unique and detailed volume of information covering the field of leadership, management, coaching, and organisational processes and realities?

I remembered when as a medical student we all got massive textbooks detailing the world's illnesses. All of us found that we had symptoms of just about every serious disease in the universe. It struck me that anybody looking at this book might fall into the same trap that I have just mentioned: namely, that every possible dynamic as described in the text, both personal- and work-wise, might be seen as being present in the reader's life and occupation.

The other image that came to mind occurred when, after a long-term business school event, every student called the local transport service to ship large boxes of lecture notes back to their home or work addresses. And what have you done with them since, I asked one graduate? "Oh, I use them to prop up my office door." I thought he had done well to not let the supposed "proper" learning blight his personal growth and development.

As far as doing your work, my view is that "properness" must come from your inner-world consciousness with appropriate inclusion of new ideas and concepts, and the awareness that there is a risk of throwing your traditional work baby out with your bathwater. This book is the finest one to be found in the field and its encyclopaedic contents make for excellent opinions and facts for incorporation in your work. But it must be recognised as encouraging further growth, not as a device to diminish your personal experience and learning.

For you, the result must be based on ongoing insight and monitoring your inner-world reaction to everything that makes its appearance in your professional performance. In addition the whole operation must of course take into account social and community factors, the nature of the industry to which you are consulting or belonging to, and the risks and benefits of the relevant interactions. You should be present as a thoughtful and observant visiting anthropologist, entitled and expected to share your observations in and with the individuals and the setting in which you are conducting your work.

And most importantly, retain your right and capacity to ask stupid questions. Your observations and stupid questions are the only antidote to the common institutional dynamic of being drawn into the institutional state of mind that exists in the setting that you are supposed to observe and comment on.

A colleague of mine told me how his grandmother always put dummy plugs into power sockets to stop electricity leaking into and interfering with the atmosphere in her house. It is a good metaphor for "This is the way we do things here" leaking into the institutional atmosphere and the observer, to the detriment of objectivity and insight.

A word of "warning" about this book: under NO circumstances read it from cover to cover! It would leave you with a whirlpool of ideas and uncertainty about your work and professionalism.

This advice is followed with a recommendation that I strongly support: you could not find a better and more informative response, if you need to pursue an idea that is firmly lodged in your mind and needs a helping nudge, than to look it up in this volume—but nothing more than that at any one time.

You need to allow yourself time for reflection, playfulness, and fun. This book will heighten your self-awareness and your confidence in your professionalism. But beware—do not make it your Bible. You need other reading material, poetry, etc. to balance your life. Beware of falling into the trap of only having mainly work friends in your personal circle! There must be a non-professional side of your life that is actively pursued. That side is an essential counterweight to your work! Without it you are at risk of boredom and loss of creativity.

So by all means have this book by your bedside along with a notebook and pencil to record your dreams. They might very well shine a light that this book misses out on! The book also acts as a magnetic marker of your personal valency, what strengths you bring to your work, and what your Achilles heel is that undermines your work competence and life. I rest my case!

Anton Obholzer
Emeritus psychiatrist and psychoanalyst
Chief executive, Tavistock and Portman NHS Trust and
faculty member, INSEAD

Overview

This book is about the hidden influences that emotions and relationships have on leadership. It explores their impact on the lives of leaders as individuals and as part of larger units such as groups, teams, organisations, and all other kinds of systems. It is written for incoming and experienced leaders who want to learn more about their own inner emotional life while being in a leading role. It will help you to explore and deepen your self-awareness and your personal way of executing leadership.

The book consists of two parts: the first part deals with the leader as an individual, whereas the second part takes the organisational and thus systemic context of leadership into account. Each part develops from a theoretical perspective to more practical and method-oriented questions and chapters. The first chapter of each part is purely theoretical, whereas the following chapters are complemented by case studies.[1] The case studies are written by well-known experts (coaches, consultants, or academics) in the respective field and, referring to their own experience, explore and apply some of the theory or phenomenon explained in the respective chapter. It makes sense to read each chapter as a whole to develop a full understanding of the depicted subject matter. Each chapter concludes with a brief overview of the key learnings.

In the introduction I give a very basic overview of the ground from which the hidden aspects of leadership emerge, that is, the unconscious and its different notions and understandings. I would recommend reading the introduction before diving into any of the other chapters.

The first part, which explores how emotions and relationships develop and by that present how you as a leader develop, comprises eight chapters. Chapter 1 is about the development of your inner emotional landscape from infant to adult and the subsequent patterns of relating with other human beings; it provides the theoretical framework upon which our entire understanding of the world is built. In Chapter 2 we look at the key tasks of the leader—holding and containment. Both are important prerequisites and part of negative capability, which is the capacity to manage difficult feelings in decision-making moments to let new thoughts emerge instead of prematurely jumping into action. The case of Larissa Philatova describes how a leader finds his negative capability over time. The capability to create hope and identity is the result of the interplay of these three different "leadership ingredients". How dysfunctional leaders can be is the subject of Chapter 3, and Manfred Kets de Vries shows us the functioning of a narcissistic leader. We also look at what is needed to become an effective leader.

Chapter 4 summarises recent scientific insights and neuroscience research into our seven basic emotional systems and discusses their importance for leadership. Fiona Martin and I analyse a firefighter case from this perspective.

Chapter 5 delves into our family bonds and the role siblings play in the development of the individual as a leader. In the following case study we look at a young CEO to understand how his family ties shape his professional reactions. Chapter 6 to 8 are devoted to more practical subjects. Chapter 6 investigates whether and how women lead differently. In his case study, Rob Ryan analyses how a coaching client falls into some of the "female leadership traps". How leaders emerge, are made, chosen, and what you need to do to develop into a leadership role are depicted in Chapter 7. Here, Olya Khaleelee shares a few of her secrets about how she selects leaders and what she looks for. In the next chapter we examine whether leadership coaching will benefit you and what it may contribute. In her case study, Halina Brunning illustrates how leadership coaching may work.

The second part of the book looks at you as a leader in the surroundings of a system, be it a group, team, or organisation.

Chapter 9 investigates organisational and social defences which help us manage our fear, anxiety, and other difficult feelings in the realm of work. It is a basic theoretical introduction to this extremely important field of knowledge since it is almost always at play when people come together to work.

Chapter 10 provides an overview of decision-making, especially strategic decision-making, and explains why it is so difficult. In his case study, Mal O'Connor shares with us what happens when not all strategic options are carefully considered and no real decision is taken. Here we also look at the moral impact of having to make choices.

In Chapter 11 we focus on the difficulties of developing creativity and innovation in organisations and what you as a leader can do to overcome this challenge. Gilles Amado describes in his case study how a tennis player found his inner, creative space to overcome his likely loss of the match. The locker room is the symbol for this space.

Chapter 12 explores the essential demands that strategising makes on organisational leaders, that is, thinking together. This should be a leader's basic requirement, yet this is often not fulfilled because it is more difficult than it seems. Martin Ringer demonstrates in his case study the development of a thinking-together process in preparing for a joint venture. In Chapter 13 we delve into organisational culture, how it develops, and how to understand it from a symbolic perspective. Rose Mersky's use of social dream-drawing explores what an applied symbolic perspective can contribute to overcoming group conflict. We also take a look at deep roles and organisational archetypes.

Chapter 14 is the pivotal chapter in this second part and is both theoretical and practical—it drills down into systems thinking and its different facets as well as what it means to lead a system. The second half explores how leaders can support collaboration between organisations and how to overcome the inherent fallacies. In the case study I share some research results on collaboration in hybrid organisations.

The last four chapters are focused on the more practical questions of leading (in) systems.

In Chapter 15 we look at the clashes of cultures when organisational mergers and joint ventures take place and the subsequent emotional journey that needs to be understood and managed by you as a leader. Ajit Menon analyses the failing case of a merger and the reasons behind it.

In Chapter 16 we examine the role of two important emotions for all of us and what they have to do with you as a leader: love and loneliness. In their case study, Annemette Hasselager and Birgitte Bonnerup showcase how a professional friendship develops, how this is a form of expressing love, and the impact it has on a business. Chapter 17 explores the emotional questions around the digitalisation of our world of work. It also looks at the emotional effect that artificial intelligence has on us. Phil Boxer leads us through one of his digitalisation projects in his case study. The closing chapter focuses on a very current subject—how to lead hybrid teams and how to lead virtually. Kalina Stamenova then shares with us her research insights on working together via Zoom.

Finally, I summarise my reasons for writing this book and I give an outlook on the key competencies and capabilities that will be needed by future leaders.

And now let us get started!

Introduction—Hidden forces

What makes you move as a leader

What first comes to mind when you think about leadership and performance? You may think about the results you want to achieve for your company, the time frame, the underlying strategy, productivity, a functioning IT and communication system; maybe you want to create a good organisational structure, or be a successful leader? You may even ponder what your personal success might look like.

But you might also think about motivating people, aligning them behind a goal, making them willing to work and to enjoy their work, supporting them, giving them advice, controlling them, telling them what they must do and so on.

In any case, you must work together with people. At the beginning of their career, most leaders think that if you tell a person exactly what to do, they will do exactly that. Well, this idea is swept aside after a while (hopefully), as you begin to understand how different people are and quite how different their understanding of what you tell them can be. How come, you might think? How can that be? I have explained everything so clearly, concisely, and several times with different words—and yet, the other does not understand what I say in the way I understand it and as I want him or her to understand. Something is lost in the transmission. The reasons for this aren't complicated: the way people listen to you (not very well, with a subjective individual focus), the way you say something (your behaviour and your attitude, the words you choose—we will talk about that), the person's personality and character and, of course, their cognitive intelligence.

Yet there exists more than what you perceive from this conscious and obvious perspective. There is a world beneath the carpet, behind the curtain, beyond rationalism and reason. Something that is influencing us, something which one could describe as what lies underneath the visible part of an iceberg. We call it the *unconscious mind* or the *unconscious.*

There are two main scientific approaches to making sense of this invisible part of the iceberg—one takes place through philosophy and psychology[2] and the other through the neurosciences. We will look at both over the course of this book.

The unconscious

The idea of the unconscious mind[3] is considered to have come into being around the beginning of the twentieth century, when psychoanalysis was developed—within neuroscience and psychology—as a fashionable way to understand the psyche and psychological pathologies. The unconscious was part of the zeitgeist.[4] Freud and Jung were important founding fathers of the new field of psychoanalysis, which developed quickly into a method of helping people get to know themselves better. The first ideas around a dynamic psyche and of suppressing perceptions had already appeared a century earlier.[5] Hartmann wrote a bestseller in 1869[6] synthesising the ideas of Hegel, Schelling, and Schopenhauer in *Philosophie des Unbewussten* (Philosophy of the Unconscious), which connects the cognitive, irrational, and volitive aspects of the unconscious.

However, long before this development, mind and soul were linked and universally used in art and literature—think of the age of romanticism, or Goethe, who used it in much of his work, for example in *Elective Affinities.* In animistic religions and in Christianity, the soul was understood as the mediator between the spiritual world (God or the gods) and the material world (the body of humans). Later, the link between the mind and the soul, its metaphysical and spiritual connection, was lost, and today the word soul is not used as much as it once was, although it conveys clearly a deeper and more emotional level in us humans. Consequently, the mind was stripped of its rich network of connotations and history. Mind seems to sound more digestible, more abstract, and not so far detached from a rational, reason-based understanding. Esoteric movements have unfortunately added to the bad reputation of the word soul.

Nevertheless, Freud did use the word *Seele* in his writings (soul, psyche), yet this was mostly and wrongly translated as "mind". Freud was not only the first self-styled psychoanalyst, he was also a great writer whose works are a pleasure to read. Most people know of his model of the psyche that differentiates the ego, the id, and the superego; it has entered mainstream and day-to-day language. For Freud, the unconscious is the realm of suppressed memories and emotions, and also of socially unacceptable wishes, desires, and ideas. These suppressed drives are always looking for fulfilment and entail a longing for what once was, or a "paradise lost".[7] Following Freud, many more thinkers further developed and applied the notion of the unconscious—C. G. Jung, Anna Freud, Neumann, Ferenczi, Kohut, Bion, Melanie Klein, Lacan, and many others.

Advances in the neurosciences have seen this field invest more and more research into the unconscious mind, and there is an attempt to apply some of the insights gained to all kinds of concepts, such as neuro-leadership, neuro-marketing, neuro-finance, neuro-coaching, and what have you. These approaches seek to explain how biases work and how they influence our decision-making. *Thinking Fast and Slow*, the famous book by the Nobel Prize winner Daniel Kahnemann,[8] describes how the brain uses two different ways or levels of thinking: the fast system, automatic and impulsive, is based on emotions and biases (which are always connected to emotions), and the slow system, our conscious and thinking system, which is rational, reflective, and helps us stay focused and in control. Kahnemann and Tversky[9] were together building the foundation for discovering biases when developing their new prospect theory. They found out that the pain of loss is stronger than the joy of gain, the hurt of losing a euro is greater than the pleasure of finding one, for example. This cognitive bias is known as "loss aversion". Kahnemann won the 2002 Nobel Prize for his work on integrating psychological aspects into what were previously considered "rational" choices. Based on his notion of biases, the "homo economicus" lost ground in economics and the focus shifted to the fact that humans have the tendency to make so-called non-rational decisions which are influenced by things such as loss aversion, priming, their perception of the messenger of a message, and other influencing factors.

Yet the unconscious is more than biases, and biases cannot only be understood as negative and irrational; they are also a shortcut that enables our brain to arrive at decisions more quickly, which in many life situations can be quite helpful. This can be called, as many people would also think of the unconscious, "gut feeling". Gigerenzer[10] (2007) views the intelligence of the unconscious as a synonym for "gut feeling" in which quick and simple heuristics play a key role. Heuristics follow their own rationality, and instead of the term "gut feeling" one can speak of intuition as "affectively charged judgements that arise through rapid, non-conscious and holistic associations".[11] Intuition is, although affectively charged, itself not emotional, yet it can be negatively impacted by feelings of fear, anxiety, pride of authorship, and wishful thinking.[12] Intuition helps with preparing a decision, by directing attention to external stimuli which only later will be categorised as opportunities or threats. "Affectively charged" here means, for example, that discomforting information can be rejected because it threatens self-esteem and self-identity, and can thus be connected with fear and anxiety.

However, the neurosciences have developed their insights much further than biases and heuristics. We will take a more detailed look at this in Chapter 4. For the time being, we understand that feeling, thinking, and acting are influenced by factors that lie beyond our conscious understanding of the world.

This means that in every action, in every thought and decision, and in all kinds of more or less conscious feelings, the unconscious plays a role—there is no thinking without feeling, as Damasio puts it,[13] and there is no conscious reaction without the influence of the unconscious. We can imagine the effect of the unconscious as a big filter through which all external and internal (bodily) information flows (see Figure 1).

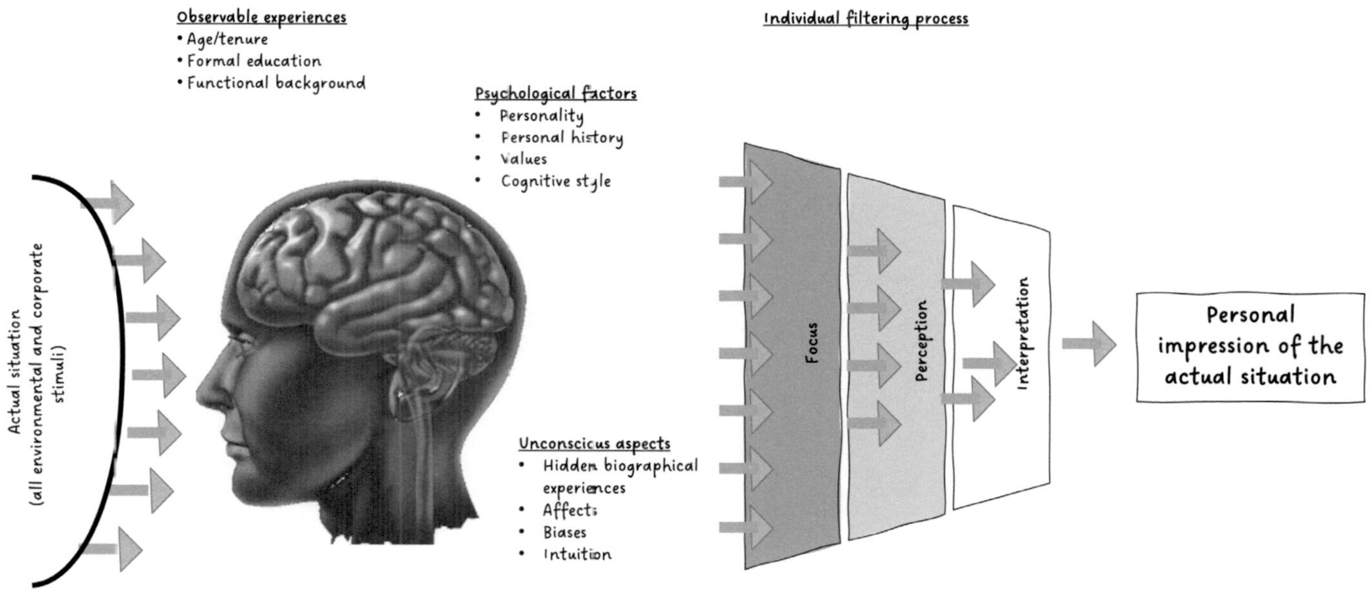

Figure 1: The leader's unconscious filtering system (author's image)

The best illustration of the unconscious and conscious was developed by Jonathan Haidt.[14] He imagines the unconscious forces as an elephant, being ridden by a man that represents the conscious part. "I'm holding the reins in my hands, and by pulling one way or the other I can tell the elephant to turn, to stop, or to go. I can direct things, but only when the elephant doesn't have desires of his own. When the elephant really wants to do something, I'm no match for him."[15]

The rider wants to achieve something and of course wants to do it together with the elephant, but very often the elephant either does not do anything, runs in the opposite direction, or just sits still and eats. The elephant is not to be managed and controlled so easily, if at all. Over the next few chapters, we will explore the "elephant" to better understand how we can improve cooperation and influence other elephants and their riders.

Part I

The personal

In Part I you as the individual, with your personality, your character, your strength and weaknesses as a leader are in the focus. We will explore how your emotional reactions and your way to enter social relationships come to be shaped. In the next step we look at dealing with unpleasant feelings. Since I assume that you also want to read how to become a better leader, we will look at the choosing and making of leaders as well and will figure out the (non) needs for leadership coaching.

CHAPTER 1

Setting the tone

Early development

As adults, most of us underestimate the influence of the very first years of childhood. Even these very early years have a huge impact on how we become who we are today. The brain is key to that process. And we know much more about how the brain interacts—not only with its owner, but also with the brains of other people.

Four factors influence early child development and by that set the tone for who we are and who we become:

- Genetics, the individual DNA set
- Epigenetics, the control over the functioning of the DNA
- Relationships with caregivers (mostly parents)
- Context (family, country culture, economic situation, etc.).

These factors are mutually influencing each other, especially relationship experiences and context experiences, which via epigenetics influence the expression or suppression of genes, which then affect body and brain development and, by that, psyche and behaviour (see Figure 2).

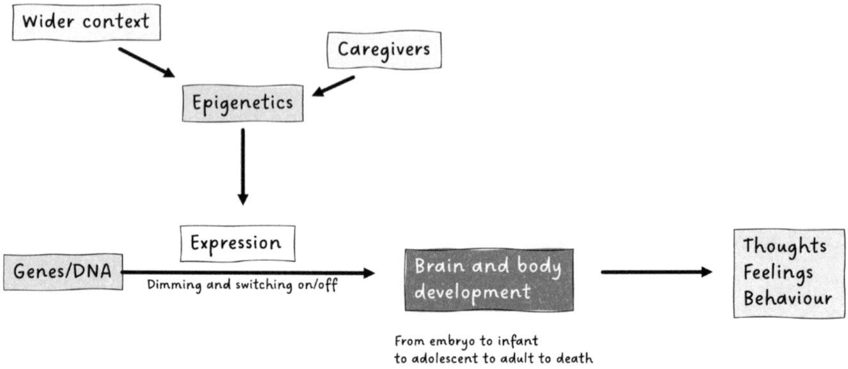

Figure 2: Factors influencing brain and body development and, by that, thoughts, feelings, and behaviour (author's drawing)

Epigenetic mechanisms influence the expression of the genes by regulating the transmission from DNA to RNA, which mirrors the DNA and then continues to produce (or not) the respective proteins. Epigenetics therefore control the genes and their expression, switching them on or off or dimming them. One often-used analogy describes the genes as the hardware and epigenetics as software. Yet, epigenetic research on human beings is difficult, and many insights are not yet fully experimentally proven.[16]

The embryo in the womb reacts to the mother and her mood. It is assumed, for example, that antenatal depressive and anxious mothers have a negative impact on not only the weight of the newborn, but also on the baby's reactivity to stress and stress regulation, which might then lead to depression later in life.[17]

The infant develops via the emotional relationship with the parents.[18] The fine attunement of a newborn baby, his or her capacity even to initiate intimate conversations, and the quality of the rhythm and the dance which develops between the infant and the caregiver are essential for the development and the later well-being of the child.

> In healthy families, a baby forms a secure attachment with her parents as naturally as she breathes, eats, smiles and cries. This occurs easily because of her parents' attuned interactions with her. Her parents notice her physiological/affective states and they respond to her sensitively and fully. Beyond simply meeting

> her unique needs, however, her parents "dance" with her. Hundreds of times, day after day. There are other families where the baby neither dances nor even hears the sound of any music. In these families she does not form such secure attachments. Rather, her task—her continuous ordeal—is to learn to live with parents who are little more than strangers. Babies who live with strangers do not live well or grow well.[19]

This "dance" between the parent and the infant creates an affectionate and playful companionship. The attunement and mutual understanding foster development. "The biggest mystery concerns the ability of a newborn to share by imitation acts of attending, as well as delicate expressions of feelings about what is perceived together."[20] But babies not only imitate, they already have their own things to tell.

What we also know from research is that babies even but a few months old are able to perceive the depression of the mother through their emotional non-responsiveness and try to cheer her up by aiming for attention and smiling. These early disturbances in the infant–caregiver relationship can lead in later life to psychic disorders. Even worse is for children to be completely deprived of paternal care, especially when also deprived of physical care and holding; children in such circumstances develop hospitalism syndrome, which has entered the everyday narrative as Kaspar Hauser syndrome. Love, care, attunement, and play are, from the very beginning of a child's development, crucial. Fast-changing emotional interchanges in intense relationships give rise to the development of thinking.[21] One could also say: "I am loved therefore I (develop myself and) think" to quote Simon Cohen-Baron with a small addition.[22]

A newborn baby is not a tabula rasa to which drives are taught and by that imprinted, as it was thought at the beginning of the twentieth century. For thirty years or so we have talked about the competent infant which co-designs relationships and acts out of his or her own creativity and ideas. The baby is born and ready and predisposed to actively interact with other humans. The child is also capable of self-regulating, as all living systems are, to build the necessary physiological homeostasis (to a certain degree).

Further, the infant is rather resilient and returns from deviations and pathological events to the original course of development (again to a certain degree). Also, the neonate is from scratch capable of differentiating between what is pleasurable and unpleasurable and wants to return to the pleasurable.[23] With this basic innate package, the ground is laid for the psychosocial development of the child.

Attachment styles

Early childhood relationship experiences determine our social life as adults. They create the basic pattern and the basic reactions we form to make sense of our social world, of encountering other people, of being with them, working with them, loving or hating them. We form so-called attachment patterns which can be healthy or disturbed.[24] These early attachment styles influence all our social relationships later on in life.

When a child grows up in a home environment of love and care, of playfulness and understanding, the chances are very high that he or she will develop a secure attachment style. A positive attachment style contributes to shaping the brain for growth, regulation, and immunological functioning, whereas negative attachment styles have the opposite effect: lifelong physical and emotional illness. Negative, unresponsive, and insensitive caring leads to chronic high stress and high levels of cortisol (stress hormone), the neurotoxic effects of higher level of cortisol which are believed to result in a smaller hippocampus.[25]

A secure attachment style is based on a feeling of security, warmth, and trust in the attachment figure, the caregiver. It can be best described as the capability of being open and honest with other people, trusting them, developing lasting relationships, and having a generally stable and positive image of oneself and of others, which also entails self-confidence. Such people do not typically have problems with long-term relationships.

The other three attachment styles are: anxious–ambivalent, fearful–avoiding, and disorganised/distressed. The anxious–ambivalent attachment style is the result of non-stable, unpredictable behaviours from caregivers. Such caregivers are distrusted, yet the child seeks their approval and constantly fears being abandoned. In adulthood these people often feel unloved by their partners; they also have difficulty expressing their love and commitment and feel emotionally dependent.

Fearful–avoidant attachment stems from the experience of their emotional needs being unmet—they feel unloved and insignificant. They have difficulty understanding and expressing their emotions and later on in life avoid intimate relationships.

A combination of these two attachment styles is called disorganised/distressed attachment. These children show deep anger and rage and might destroy other children's toys. Their relationships with their caregivers are obviously very difficult from the beginning; these children are neglected, unloved, abused, separated from their caregivers for a long time, or have had to undergo other very difficult early life circumstances. In adulthood they tend to avoid intimate relationships. They have difficulties controlling their emotions and might easily explode.

One interesting study[26] shows that the model of self and other are crucial to explaining how we relate to other people (see Figure 3).

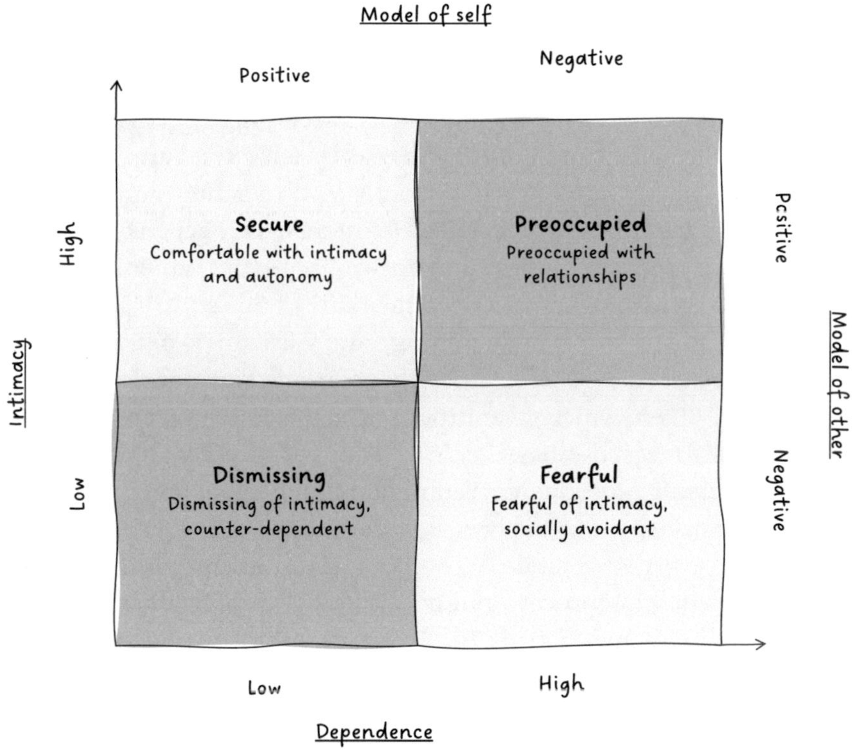

Figure 3: Relationship styles depending on model of self and other[27]

The "model of self" determines whether the abstract image a person has of her- or himself is viewed as either likable/lovable or unlikable/not lovable, and also depicts how worthy one feels. The "model of other" explains whether a person views and accepts another person as trustworthy and open or as unreliable and rejecting.

While the securely relating type, having experienced secure attachment, does not show any larger or noticeable problems, the other three types have characteristic problems. The dismissive type, who has gone through dismissive/distressed attachment, shows high self-confidence and low emotional expressiveness and is not very interested in closeness and intimacy, yet prefers to be in control of the relationship. I have once experienced a CEO who belonged to this type. Quite intelligent and self-confident, he literally devalued everybody around him while his wife at home suffered from alcoholism. He was not pleasant to be with or work for since very rarely did a word of appreciation escape his mouth.

Those of the preoccupied type, based on the anxious–ambivalent attachment style, are the opposite of the dismissive type on many levels; highly emotionally expressive and overly disclosing, they are caregiving and at the same time use the other as their secure base. They are, for example, highly interested in romantic involvement in relationships and are in general highly dependent on others. This type is not often found in top leadership positions in organisations, but rather in (lower) middle management where they can take care of others.

Those of the fearful type stemming from a fearful–avoidant attachment style avoid close relationships. They fear rejection and do not trust other people either, which means they are unable to rely on any one else. Yet, they have low self-esteem.

For leadership positions, decision-making behaviour and interaction with the management team play a key role and we can observe different styles here. A negative model of others leads to excluding them from the decision-making process and not listening to them. This accounts for the dismissive and fearful type. However, the dismissive type probably could not care less for the opinions or ideas of others. Their insulting and rejecting behaviour usually leads to an overestimation of their capabilities and in the long term to bad decisions. In contrast, the preoccupied type will put little trust in his or her own perceptions and rather rely too much on the opinion of others.

What we have learned from attachment theory and infant research is now also confirmed by brain research. Human beings cannot develop without "an other", and our brain cannot develop without another brain and another human being. We are by nature social beings and our brain is by nature a social brain. From birth and throughout life, survival depends on others. The baby needs to be fed not only physically but emotionally and cognitively. Nurture is crucial for brain development and leads to the integration of the various brain systems. Later, we need others and good relationships with them to build shelter, organise food, and mutually protect each other.

As we have seen above, disruptive relationships with caregivers negatively impact our brain development. Then thoughts, emotions, and immunological functions are not attuned for long-term survival—"what does not kill us makes us weaker"[28] would be a more adequate version of the common phrase. This could also be a hint towards later leadership behaviour—creating anxiety and acting out aggressive impulses do not contribute to a work environment supporting performance, rather the contrary.

Attachment patterns are part of our implicit (social) memory system, which makes them inaccessible for conscious thought or language (only via attitudes, beliefs, and behaviours) that would only be possible with explicit (social) memory (see Figure 4).

Implicit Memory

Categories: sensory, emotional, and procedural memories and conditioning

- Learning to walk, ride a bike
- Habitual emotional reactions e.g. tightening up when others show unfriendly behaviour

Development:

- Early development/subcortical bias

Location:

- Right hemisphere bias (unconscious)
- Amygdala centred/OMPFC

Functioning:

- Context-free, no source attribution

Explicit Memory

Categories: sensory, semantic, episodic, narrative, and autobiographical memory

- Language and stories
- Remembers faces, rules of etiquette, cultural aspects

Development:

- Later development/cortical bias

Location:

- Left hemisphere bias/language
- Hippocampal/dorsal lateral PFC

Functioning:

- Contextualised, known memory source

Implicit social memory

- Attachment schema
- Transference
- Superego
- Background affect

Explicit social memory

- Identity/social information
- Narratives
- Autobiographical descriptions
- Social rules, norms, expectations

Figure 4: Explicit and implicit memory[29]

This implicit memory system "organizes and retains primitive vestibular-sensory-emotional memories of early caretaking, rendering them of permanent psychological significance".[30] Against that sort of emotional background all future relationships and psychic aspects are developed. In healthy people the early implicit and the later explicit memory systems are intertwined. When trauma occurs, these systems can become disconnected, which leads to emotional disturbances such as post-traumatic stress disorder (PTSD); when people experience war or witness or fall victim to a physical attack, they may develop PTSD.

The results of these attachment patterns are also found in everyday interactions with other people, in the sense of how they influence our projections onto them and how we see them. By projection, I mean the psychic process of attributing an aspect to a person which either does not belong to them, or is exaggerated, because we wear a psychic lens which promotes that perspective. Such projection is also called transference and, very often—when we have a first and immediate gut feeling of whether we like someone or not—this is linked to a projection which stems from past attachment relations. (Projection and transference will be discussed in more detail in Chapter 5.) The implicit social memory, having developed in the past, is activated in the present and thus influences present relationships. Transference is used as a tool in leadership coaching and also in psychodynamic psychotherapy to better understand a client and his relationship pattern. It helps to explore the unconscious struggles of a client and makes them available to the coach and, although they are not part of the explicit memory, they can be worked on together. The time it takes for this information to be processed is extremely short; that is the advantage of implicit memory. In less than 100 milliseconds we are able to make judgements on first impressions about trustworthiness, likeability, competence, and attractiveness.[31]

When we really dislike something in somebody or we get overly excited, aggressive, or furious, these aspects that we dislike in the other are in fact something we dislike in ourselves or do not want to admit to ourselves—this is the so-called "shadow".[32] These are reprehensible, dark, and unwanted aspects of ourselves—a simple example would be not being prompt and on time when we have to deliver a task. We can get very excited and angry when another person does not keep a deadline but might not see our own procrastination and unpunctuality.

When we encounter these aspects of our shadow, which are denied and repressed, in the other, this offers the opportunity to become aware of it, to work with and on it, and to integrate it into our personality. This might then lead to more forgiveness for the failures or character flaws of another person.

Life stages

From a leadership perspective, it is also important to see how the child develops over the first twenty years and integrates the basic tensions of life. These basic or paradoxical tensions are the developmental tasks children must undertake to develop a full and mature personality. Yet they are also important for later life stages when dealing with persistent paradoxical tensions. We will talk about dealing with organisational paradoxes from a leader's perspective in the next chapter.

Here I would like to give you a short overview of one of the most influential theories on the stages of psychosocial development, that of Erik Erikson,[33] a German American developmental psychologist and psychoanalyst. Developed in the middle of the last century, despite its long existence this theory has never appeared to become obsolete and is still applied in theory and practice. Erikson's theory describes the development of self and identity and how this leads to the experience of life having a purpose, of being oneself and being united in one person. This occurs within the individual, but also in exchange with the social environment.

In the different developmental stages, a critical aspect of life with two contradictory dispositions—syntonic and distonic—a paradoxical tension must be worked through to build the ground for the next developmental stage. Both dispositions must be brought into balance as, for example, in the first stage, trust and mistrust are both needed in life. When these two dispositions are integrated, a so-called "virtue" develops, which is not so much a moral aspect, more a vital ground for a full and complete way of being in the world. Later in life these contradictory tensions are continually revisited and must be balanced. Balance does not necessarily mean fifty–fifty, but rather finding an adequate balance between the present individual and given social situation.

The next figure gives a comprehensive overview of the life stages, the developmental phases, and later the respective life tasks to be worked on and through (see Figure 5).

Stage	Tension	Virtue	Development	Task in life - Balancing
Infancy	Basic Trust vs mistrust	Hope	Trust caregiver and in turn self and others	Trust and mistrust
Early childhood	Autonomy vs shame & doubt	Will	Be self-sufficient and follow social rules	Letting go vs holding
Play age	Initiative vs guilt	Purpose	Develop peer relations and internalise social rules	Moving onwards vs guilt
School age	Industriousness vs inferiority	Competence	Master cognitive and social skills at school	Productivity vs inadequacy
Adolescence	Identity cohesion vs role confusion	Fidelity	Develop a sense of personal directions re future and awareness re the past	Duplicity vs faithfulness
Young adulthood	Intimacy vs isolation	Love	Achieve love and companionship beyond the family	Connectivity vs segregation
Adulthood	Generativity vs stagnation	Care	Raise and care for children/be productive at work	Being relevant vs inertia
Old Age	Integrity vs despair	Wisdom	Reflect on life as being productive and satisfying	Contentment vs regret

Figure 5: Life stages and tasks in life (author's compilation, after Erikson)[34]

From Erikson's theory, we can learn how essential it is to learn to deal with the basic tensions in life. In the next chapter we will explore the key roles of the leader which are connected with early childhood experiences.

KEY LEARNING

- In our early childhood we unconsciously learn patterns of how we relate to other people. These patterns influence all our social relationships that inform how we relate to everybody and over our lifetime, whether they are constructive and positive or destructive and negative.
- Understanding our own patterns, developing them, and even overwriting destructive ones through new experiences are important for leaders. They are also prerequisites to understanding patterns of the other, be they colleagues, followers, or clients, so that one can react accordingly.

CHAPTER 2

Managing and holding

Leadership expectations

When thinking of the expectations you as leader must fulfil, different perspectives can be chosen—the perspective of the stakeholders (shareholders, clients, suppliers, society), of the organisation as a system, or of colleagues and followers. Very often, to determine what leaders should do, we differentiate between task and management on the one hand and people and leadership on the other. There is also a distinction made between personality and character on one side (what you bring with you) and skills and competencies on the other (that which can be acquired). Another differentiation is made between rational, cognitive competencies and emotional intelligence, or between technical knowledge/expertise/knowhow and social skills. Over the last fifty years, we have observed a shift of emphasis (for executives early on, but now also for middle management) from cognitive-, task-, management-oriented, to people-, emotional-, and personality-oriented leadership. Although this is a simplifying reduction, it still holds true, also with regard to the seemingly new expectations under the title of "agile management and leadership"—"more than ever, companies need leaders who are good with people".[35]

What could it mean, to be good with people? Certainly, this entails aspects of personality and character, which cannot be changed so easily, but it also includes many aspects of being human, which can be explored, learnt, understood, and applied. Leadership of and in organisations is not about abstract principles, it is about human beings and their behaviour within organisations. Effective leaders are meeting their stakeholders' needs, especially those of their followers; they have to listen and communicate well to inspire people, groups, and teams, and create hope and identity as well as calm their anxieties and sorrows—so that they act in favour of the organisation and their goals.

When thinking further about leadership, images of authority and hierarchy come up—despite "new work-ideas". In social systems like organisations which need to coordinate for action and collaboration, leadership emerges always. A leader's main function is to distribute and coordinate work and facilitate collaboration on a task so as to achieve better outcomes than if it were tackled alone. From an evolutionary perspective, leadership arises in all kinds of systems where coordination is necessary—even in a two-player situation, in which the two need to stick together for mutual protection and at the same time look for food and resources. The one who moves first (because he or she is the more hungry or curious) will probably emerge as the leader because he or she will make the second one a follower moving with him/her. The role of leadership also contains conflict solution.[36]

We can summarise that leadership, followership, and, with that, authority and hierarchy emerge naturally in social systems. Leadership and followership seem to be part of a set of psychological mechanisms—in the sense of heuristics and implicit knowledge which we have already talked about. They have developed (or have survived our development) because they have proven to solve problems of survival and reproduction in supporting foraging, self-protection, mating, parenting, collaboration, and conflict resolution. Much of our behaviour is guided by highly automated rules for if–then decisions. The rule "follow an individual that one trusts" is clearly superior to a decision rule like "follow any one individual".[37]

At the beginning, and comparable to other social animals (e.g. honey bees, guppies, hyenas, dolphins, and baboons), group movement was the first task to be initiated and coordinated; later, with increasing system complexity, came conflict resolution, teaching, and social cohesion. Punishment and leading in warfare also became important. For a long time in human history, leadership was built on charisma and personalised influence, which is understood as weak leadership. Only recently (in human evolution) did strong leadership using institutionalised aspects and coercive power develop.[38] From a follower's perspective, leaders are there to actively protect against threats, to give guidance in a shared direction, and to reasonably resolve conflicts.[39]

Holding and containment

We all have our first experiences with authority figures and hierarchy at home with our caregivers. The word "authority" stems from the Latin word *auctoritatem/auctoritas*, which means invention, advice, opinion, influence, and command, and stems from *auctor*—master, leader, author. As we have seen, we are mainly influenced by our caregivers who are our very first authority figures. In their main function of giving care, which equals fulfilling our physical and mental needs, they create an environment for development and growth. An important contribution results from the caregiver's capacity for holding, creating containment, and *Geborgenheit* which is the German word for the feeling of security. Unconsciously, many followers project their experiences of early authority figures onto their leaders. Therefore, it is important to understand the meaning of holding, containment, and *Geborgenheit* for development as a child and as an adult.

The notion of holding alludes to the physical holding of the child in the arms of the caregiver. This holding is an embrace which provides safety, care, and protection. Feeling safe enables the developmental processes of the infant by making the child feel valued and secure. In connection with the concept of the "good enough mother",[40] this results in a psychological development of the self, since she creates a holding environment which, because of her normal human imperfections, exposes the child to partially negative stimuli which we can understand as "the difficulties of life", and thus fosters further development of the self and of identity.

The leader as container

The difficulties of life cause negative, unpleasant emotions, and anxiety. For an infant not yet having developed language, there is thus a need to learn about, transform, and integrate these emotions which he or she is helplessly exposed to. Doing this for the child is the role of the so-called container of the caregiver. The word "container" derives from the Latin *contenire*, and its meaning stretches from a (physical) object which holds other objects, like a shipping container's potential to hold something, to fencing and to keeping an enemy under control, which is important in warfare. Keeping the enemy under control could be translated here as keeping anxiety and destructive aggression under control so that one does not feel eaten up inside. The image of a sealed container alludes to a closed vessel—in Jungian terminology, the *vas hermeticum*—and translates symbolically into a safe space in which something new can simmer, brew, and develop.

Containing and being contained is a relationship between two persons. It usually begins with the mother–child relationship, where the mother/caregiver as the container helps the newborn to digest and transform unbearable anxieties. This is done by tuning in to the emotions of the infant, understanding and relating to them, attuning and reacting in a comforting, soothing way, and also explaining why negative emotions can happen (for example, digestion issues or getting teeth). In doing so, the child can integrate these difficult feelings and learn to live with them. This process is part of developing an identity and a sense of self. A sense of self always strives for coherence, continuity, and integrity.

Part of the containment is also the mirroring done by the caregiver, who looks into the eyes of the infant. The infant can than mirror[41] the reaction and the impression the infant elicits in the eyes or the "gaze" of the caregiver. This mirroring is crucial in that it enables the child to be seen and therefore to feel that he or she exists. Over time, if the containment is working well, the child develops the capacity for self-containment. When a child is not positively or sufficiently mirrored, psychic disorders such as narcissistic injuries may occur. Poor containment and insufficient mirroring may result in an underdeveloped capacity to manage one's own (negative) emotions. These negative emotions can be indigestible on one's own because of traumatic experiences of loss, despair, and the fear of annihilation and death. Splitting off these painful emotions and sometimes projecting them into or onto another is the resultant defence mechanism which can lead to neurosis or more severe psychopathological developments. We will go into these in the next chapter. In any case, the capacity for self-containment will be disturbed or unable to develop at all—later the individual's identity may be fragmented, incoherent, and discontinuous. The healthy process of "giving away" negative feelings and getting them back from the caregiver as digested bits and pieces does not take place because the interconnection between caregiver and child in not working. Thus the positive transformation into manageable emotions does not occur.

Containment or being held in a safe space is necessary all life long and is the factor that differentiates between healthy and destructive relationships. This capacity to contain depends on a receptive and open attitude as well as a capacity for non-judgemental listening and not-knowing. The container function in later life is part of what is expected from the leader (with his protection and direction-giving function) and can also be exercised in groups and organisations.

Negative capability

Both self-containing and containing another are closely linked to negative capability—the capacity to bear ambiguities, ambivalences, and the accompanying emotions of stress and anxiety of the unknown without falling apart or rushing into a split (-decision) in later life. This capacity is needed more and more from today's leaders in a fast-changing, complex, and confusing world in which everything is connected.

The term "negative capability"[42] was first coined by the English poet John Keats in 1817. In a letter to his brothers, he described it as a state in which a person "is capable of being in uncertainties, mysteries, doubts, without any irritable reaching after fact & reason".[43] For him this was crucial—as a genius in literature, especially in poetry. The term itself has moved from religious experience studies to the practice of teaching psychodynamic methods and, more recently, organisation and leadership studies. Eisold defines negative capability as "precisely the ability to tolerate anxiety and fear, to stay in the place of uncertainty in order to allow for the emergence of new thoughts or perceptions".[44] It is the capacity for "reflective inaction",[45] and it does not mean that positive capability, the capacity to decide and act, is not necessary anymore—they both belong to the repertoire of leadership capabilities.

Negative capability entails a number of features:

- The ability to not do something, to resist the tendency to disperse into actions that are defensive rather than relevant to the task.
- To resist the pressure of acting when not knowing and to resist the pressure to give a strong lead.
- To learn to live with doubt, confusion, and not knowing, although it is difficult.
- To realise and manage difficult emotions of anxiety and uncertainty.
- To listen, to stay with the attention to the actual experience, to wait (say nothing, sit, see, and wait for what develops) and, to learn through and from waiting.

The aim is to hear beyond the obvious the hidden meanings which are often covered but also revealed by the words used, and then to choose a good moment to convey them to others. "Through the exercise of negative capability, the leader becomes, like the strings of a lyre, an instrument—not for music or poetry (like Keats), but for organisational inquiry, learning, creativity, and action."[46]

For the leader and the organisation, the two paradoxical sides of the "capability coin" are to embody and be the vision to create and shape their environment, while also being an adaptive listener and being what is needed in the situation. For the latter, leaders must put their egos and themselves aside to be with what is, instead of what was planned or hoped for. It is necessary to be both, and not either/or.

Here, the way a leader experiences his case study will be explored by his coach.

Case study

Negative capability—avoiding premature decisions

Larissa Philatova

The concept of negative capability interested me in the context of my former professional activity as a headhunter. Meeting with many managers, I had a lot of opportunities to observe the development of their careers. I was often preoccupied with the idea that—despite starting with similar skills, knowledge, and requisite personal qualities—some seemed to break down halfway and some burnt out, but there were also those who continued to enjoy life, despite the circumstances. We usually think that such people simply have a plan or that they know some great secret that is hidden from the majority. This has been called "positive thinking", "assertiveness", and even "flexibility" but from studying the phenomenon in the context of organizational leadership, I can say with confidence that what we are looking at is "negative capability".

Negative capability helps people make informed and strategic decisions and be able to correctly assess risk; it's about avoiding mistakes made due to the rush to start doing something, and instead finding innovative solutions that move the company forward. In short, these people have achieved their strategic roles precisely because they can use this skill. Where positive abilities support "decisive action", negative capability implies "reflexive inaction", that is, the capability to resist dispersal into defensive procedures when leadership is at the limit of its knowledge, resources, and trust, creating an intermediate space that allows a person to continue thinking in difficult situations. It is this ability—the ability to maintain stability in difficult situations, despite their own anxiety—that allows leaders to reflect and manage their emotions.

To illustrate the negative capability of a leader, I chose forty-three-year-old Eduard, with whom I started working during the coronavirus pandemic, in mid-2020, when he approached me with a request to work with his team. The company, which he has been at the head of for the last six years, employs more than one hundred people.

Due to coronavirus restrictions, we started our work together online and, although Eduard doesn't really like it, he always gets in touch on time, rarely gets distracted in the process, and demonstrates engagement and open communication. I note for myself the rather simple, even somewhat ascetic atmosphere of his office—businesslike, without any pronounced objects or attributes.

He began his biographical story with a description of his earliest memories—he remembers himself at the age of about two, "sees" himself as a baby lying in a crib, in a small space, and a very bright light hits him in the face. This memory is reflected in him with warmth and relaxation; he responds with very pleasant sensations. Another memory shared by Eduard was a case when, at the age of about three, he was running around the apartment looking for his mother. Angry and crying bitterly, he could not find her. Eventually he fell asleep from fatigue. When he woke up, his mother was present, which brought him calmness. He describes his childhood years as very good; no one watched what he did or where he went, he was largely left to himself; at the same time, there was strict discipline in performing certain duties, hygiene, and self-organisation. He was not afraid to discover the world, and once ran away from kindergarten just to see if he could find his own way home. These memories of Eduard made me think about his negative capability, as they demonstrated his potential to accept the current situation of uncertainty.

After school he furthered his education at a prestigious institute, where he was easily admitted and where he did well in the study of robotics. After graduation, Eduard became interested in programming, and subsequently worked on software implementation projects for a large German manufacturer. He worked in this company for about ten years and believes that this was where he shaped his leadership style. He held several positions in various departments there, and at the end of his tenure at the company worked as top sales manager in the Kazakhstan region. He saw himself as an effective manager—a source of his self-esteem. His immediate supervisor was an Italian, with whom Eduard later became friends, and they still communicate quite closely.

Eduard then talked about "one of the most traumatic periods" of his life, when he chose to leave the German company and at the same time decided to end his first marriage. I noted this sequence was presented in the above order, and Eduard did not return to the topic of his first marriage either then or after. Describing his emotional state at that time, he felt somewhat "strange, although not depressed"—his feelings would more accurately be described as disappointment, fatigue, and surprise at not understanding the situation. It seemed to me that after this depressive episode he learned to better manage his emotions in later life.

It was during that period when his former supervisor, now friend, invited him to stay in Italy and provided him with great support. Eduard did not hesitate to accept this invitation as it gave him an opportunity to take a break for a while, come to terms with his emotions, pain and loss, and then start a new life. According to Eduard, his friend created a very warm and welcoming atmosphere in which Eduard felt constant support, and he believes that it was this unconditional support that allowed him to focus and survive this ordeal. Describing that period of reflection during his stay in Italy, Eduard recalled that "these were thoughts that one day it would be possible to start something new, and there was a belief that everything would get better, although it was scary from the unknown."

After Italy, a new opportunity presented itself: Eduard received an offer from the country's largest bank to head its project office. This role really captured my client, and he enthusiastically began to study and master a new subject. Two years later he left for another company, which didn't turn out as expected, but nevertheless he significantly expanded his various business connections and acquired unique knowledge, which subsequently led him to a senior position in the corporation itself. Trying to draw a parallel between the difficulties he faced upon leaving the German company and the pandemic restrictions, he noted that what at one moment felt to him as the most difficult emotional situation, was topped by what happened recently with regard to the pandemic. After all, at that time it was his experience, his decisions; during the pandemic, it was the external context that had a critical impact which affected both the industry in which the client works and himself. The organisation experienced a shock when the main funds abruptly ran out. This led to extreme stress, with employees on the verge of dismissal or a nervous breakdown.

Remembering the help of his Italian friend, in the course of our work, Eduard decided to provide more support for his people and thus increased the number of meetings with staff, especially with his team (ten direct subordinates). During one of the sessions, he described his condition as a sticky swamp in which you are afraid to make a move, as any movement can pull you to the bottom, meaning it is impossible to somehow influence the situation, you just have to wait. Waiting—which is key to negative capability—was not a problem for him. Gradually, throughout our sessions he began to think over new projects, and these thoughts allowed him over time to gain support for the future inside himself. After a while, the situation in the industry stabilised a little, and proudly saying that they had "learned to invent under new conditions", he demonstrated the excitement that he felt from the search for non-standard solutions. At the beginning of 2022, he noted that the team had finally returned to its usual functioning.

In the spring of 2022, during the sessions Eduard started to focus more on his emotional state. He believed that in any case he would somehow adapt to the new conditions. A lot of metaphors appeared in his speech, rather vivid descriptive definitions of his states. The most difficult experiences for Eduard were caused by the exodus of employees, because "I have been recruiting and nurturing them for a long time, teaching them, it is difficult to let them go." Eduard called these employee departures "losses". Despite this, he still sees certain advantages in the circumstances—he did manage to get rid of inefficient workers.

At this stage in the sessions, more time is devoted to describing the complex emotions associated with grief: the loss of employees, the unusual schedule, changing the context of work processes (now up to 80 per cent of working time is spent on helping and supporting employees). Eduard says that because the external context is changing very quickly, this causes him a certain internal irritation. And again, I notice a desire for reflecting instead of jumping into action too quickly. Eduard decided to free up two morning hours of his working time to analyse the situation and study new ideas, thus forming his vision of the future. It is not surprising that this very moment in our work saw the emergence of the figure of the client's father, who died many years ago. Eduard, as never before, is feeling an acute lack of communication with him: "I would like Dad to be alive." It seems to him that his father would be able to support him and give advice, as he had experience of living through such difficult periods during the Second World War. At this point, Eduard recognises a new feeling in himself—the feeling of being an adult. Maturity is actualised in interaction with employees: he places himself as a father who should provide support and a calming influence.

Analysing this case, the earliest memories that the participant actively presented from the first minutes of work should be noted. Obviously, we can see an example of the formation of mental stability—from unbearable frustration to calmness. After a negative experience due to the absence of his mother, Eduard wakes up and feels calm, because now she is close. I assume that these episodes played a significant role in the development of the client's personality; we may say that the described situations represent the first steps in learning how to manage emotions and thereby developing negative capabilities in later life.

Eduard noticed that he was angry and shouting, desperately searching for his mother, but then moved on to the work of grief—he processes the "loss" through sleep, and then regains his mother when he wakes up and sees her next to him. We see the ambivalent attitude of a little boy towards his mother—first he sees a "bad" mother who wanted to punish him and then abandoned him, and then the lost mother reappears, but is now kind and accepting. So, the child had to admit that the bad mother he hated and was afraid would leave him is also the same mother he loves. Similarly, in difficult life situations, Eduard knows how to find something that allows him to resist, something that will give support in the future. For example, at the age of thirty-four he simultaneously lost both his job and family (divorce). When, during this period of crisis and strong frustration from the loss of orientation, his friend and former boss invited him to Italy, Eduard again found himself with someone important to him (as if his former boss, now friend, took the place of his mother in the unconscious) providing him with a home, a shelter in which no one asks questions, acceptance, and unconditional support. Eduard found himself in a safe place, thanks to which he could survive the frustration of losing his job and an unsuccessful marriage. Being in a state of uncertainty, not understanding how to move on and how to live, he did not panic, and felt not anger, but regret that reality turned out to be completely different from what he had dreamed.

It was a period of burnout, a period of failures followed by very deep disappointment and a serious reassessment of his self. Eduard noted that, despite his condition at that time, he continued to think about his life and tried to find something that could interest him and motivate him to do something he had not done before; that is, as if unconsciously the coachee was striving for his temporary incapacity to feel emotions. He had no fear that things might not work out: despite his destroyed internal state, he remained confident that he would succeed. It was patience without regret that helped him to continue moving forward.

We can see the same thing in recent events when, due to the coronavirus, the company headed by Eduard was forced to practically suspend activities. Eduard had to abandon the usual ways of doing business, and at some point he had to admit that neither he nor his team could influence the situation in any way, so they had to just wait and watch. Then, with new insight, he doubled the number of meetings with the staff, because they were under great stress due to uncertainty and misunderstanding. Taking on the role of an "adult", Eduard consciously provides a space for containing the anxieties and fears of his subordinates. The team continues to function despite the difficulties caused by the external context.

The dynamics of changes in the client's self-perception in the process of work is interesting: despite the fact that during the pandemic there were periods of both idealisation and devaluation of events, in the process of work it was possible to observe some softening of the sense of self-righteousness and superiority. A more complex vision appeared, and the negative capabilities of the client provided him with patience in this state of transformation. In this sense, negative capability can be considered a leader's most finely tuned research tool, which implies the ability to learn and allow others (people, processes, the external environment, organisations) to change their minds. Studying the environment and its impact on the operational activities of the company helps Eduard to maintain stability and continue effective activities.

Negative capability, unfortunately, is not a common skill. However, by knowing and understanding this quality of tension retention in conflict situations, we can maintain it in our clients by managing the emotional impact of the incomprehensible and unknown. Being on the verge of knowledge and ignorance, confidence and uncertainty, negative capability allows something new to appear with the help of habitual positive abilities and skills; that is, it can be said that the presence of negative capability complements and strengthens positive leadership skills.

* * *

This case study describes and explores how a leader in the difficult emotional times of the pandemic used his negative capability which he had built up over the course of his working life. It is particularly interesting how failures and difficulties contributed to the development of this inner capacity—a process which was partly accompanied by an external consultant.

Managing paradox

This is the next big subject, a key capability of contemporary leaders which is connected to negative capability in such a way that you need negative capability to deal appropriately with organisational paradoxes.

In today's management literature, managing paradox, ambidexterity, and ambidextrous leadership are intensely discussed. This is probably the case because of our fast, connected and instantaneously changing world, where paradoxes, which were formerly spread over time, suddenly become more experienceable.

Classical organisational and strategic paradoxes are the choices between stability vs change, long-term vs short-term profit, cooperation vs competition, exploration vs exploitation, local vs global, etc. Paradoxical choices induce anxiety or fear because a paradox always entails a conflicting choice which cannot be resolved. This often not conscious anxiety leads to also unconscious reactions such as denial, overlooking, repressing, rationalising, and projections. On a more conscious level, a different reaction could be possible: paradoxical thinking—the ability to juxtapose, explore, and integrate contradictions by actively thinking of these opposites or antithetical ideas as equally true. On the emotional level, dealing with paradoxes asks for the emotional capacity to hold the tension of the two seemingly opposite poles and integrate them into a new perspective. We will look deeper into this capacity in Chapter 11.

Additional capabilities which are connected to containment and negative capability are creating hope and identity in and for the organisation.

Hope and identity

On the individual level, the development of hope should be initiated from earliest childhood. As we have seen with Erikson, he links the development of hope directly with the development of identity.

The very first phase of childhood, which he calls "the epigenetic of identity", culminates in the child's idea of "I am what hope I have and give."[47] It stems from the development of a basic sense of trust of others as well a sense of one's own trustworthiness. As attachment theory has already taught us, children need their caregivers for bonding, which then creates trust and gives security, safety, and protectedness—an emotional state also called *Geborgenheit.*[48] Hope is the basic trust—it is very difficult to live without it. Attachment disrupted by a prolonged separation from a caregiver, for example, demonstrates that the loss of hope, shown by the child's empty gaze and silent resignation, is the final and most severe casualty when crying and protesting has no effect.[49] The psychic mechanism which creates *Geborgenheit* is containment.

Why do I first talk about hope and then identity? From my understanding, I would say hope is based on identity. Without a feeling of inner and outer cohesion, hope seems to be impossible. However, in the very early stages of life, as an infant, you can only "hope" for care, feeding, nurturing, soothing, holding. Although infants have an impact on their parents in the way they communicate on multiple levels, they cannot "tell" the caretaker what they need. They can only appeal to the instincts of parenting, by crying, screaming, withdrawing, and so on, but they can never be sure what they get back. Thus, from an ontogenetic perspective it seems that hope comes before identity can develop. In later life, real hope can only be developed by an unfragmented coherent individual when the individual has a sense of self. For a healthy mind and soul, we need both, hope and identity. Both will not only develop within the individual, but also between individuals in groups, organisations, institutions, and society. Therefore, an understanding of how hope develops is important for leaders.

Hope is an optimistic trust that a desirous expectation will be satisfied by applying goal orientation, tenacity, and fortitude.[50] Hope is not only a way of feeling, but also a "way of thinking, behaving and relating to the self and others".[51] It is not determined or stable over time, it can develop, and one can lose it, depending on self and life circumstances. Hope helps us survive both physically and emotionally in times of severe crisis. Hope is, as the American philosopher Martha Nussbaum[52] puts it, "the flipside of fear"—which also plays an important role in moments of crisis. Both hope and fear involve evaluation of an outcome as very important, great uncertainty about this outcome, and some lack of control or even passivity. The major difference is the focus: fear focuses on the potential bad outcome and hope on the good—fear and hope are well connected.

Hope is fragile, and in times of crisis hope can be questioned, shaken, or even disappear. The effects of crisis on hope depend mainly on the quality of containment—may it happen on an individual or on an organisational level. Fear and anxiety rise during a crisis. When the level of fear is not too high it can be managed cognitively and emotionally. For this, self-management and managing others, first, self-containment is needed and then, containing the other. This is the reason why some individuals and groups can manage a crisis, whereas others really suffer when there is little or no containment. Basic biological reactions such as freeze/fight/flight reactions may then take place—on a physical as well as on a psychic level. What we often observe is a tunnel focus and no action, or the opposite, overreaction, panic, and other psychological reactions kick in.

When, due to a crisis, needs are continuously unmet, and the pain of fear and other unpleasant discomforting feelings such as helplessness and impotence continue, they will be warded off by psychic defence mechanisms (we will go into more detail in Chapter 9). A problematic and dangerous vicious circle starts—when fear is not acknowledged and worked with, it will continue to create more uncertainty, more helplessness, more unmet needs, more defences … and it will become impossible for people to work on their task. That is why hope needs to be cultivated by leaders, not only in moments of crisis, but also in moments of change and transformation—when uncertainty is high. In today's organisations and their speed of change, you as a leader need to continuously think about instilling hope.

Of similar importance to the organisation as to the individual is identity. It is the answer to the question of "Who am I?" which gives a sense of self. This entails the question of "Where do I belong?" Only with the important other does identity become alive. As already described, hope and identity formation are the core developmental tasks in early childhood, yet never cease. Identity develops via experience and insights and via the people one meets. Over time, the feeling of identity develops when linking and comparing the inner with the outer world (consisting of objects, phantasies, feelings, experiences) in striving for coherence, integrity, and continuity. The inner coherence, continuity, and experience can (basically) only be maintained when they are perceived by the other(s). The perception of the self, the sense of self, its uniqueness, and its esteem develop with being together with other(s) and how they behave towards us (see Figure 6).

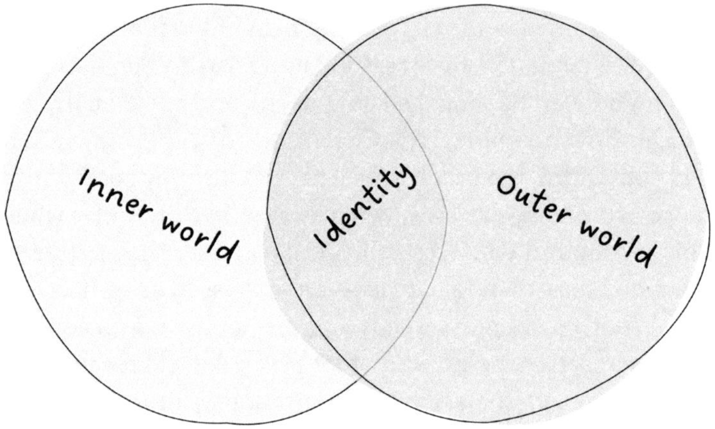

Figure 6: Personal identity (author's drawing)

Emotions are key in forming identity. The quality and content of emotional ties with the other shape identity formation by either identifying with or rejecting certain aspects, attributes, and properties of the other. For developing good relationships with others, good early attachment, containment, and basic trust are needed.

When relating with the other, identity is always threatened through "being different from the other", the conflict between the sense of own self and the perceived self of the other. As social beings we always compare ourselves, our capacities, capabilities, traits, behaviours, etc. So, we develop a fear of rejection which can amount to a fear of annihilation and death. This fear has to be continually overcome and lies at the heart of all social processes. The stronger attachment and containment are, the less easily the person feels threatened or rejected by an other.

In different life contexts different aspects of identity come alive, for example, being a mother or father, a leader, a caring friend, a golf player; identity is multifaceted and is also about aspects of ethnicity, gender, age, sexual orientation, physical attributes, political affiliations, and religious beliefs.

In our conversation here it makes sense to think about the identity of a leader. A leader's identity does not fall from heaven but can be created and crafted—this entails thinking about the gap between your felt identity today and your aspired leader's identity. These are some aspects you want to think about—how you perceive your identity, how others perceive it, and how you want it to be (see Figure 7).

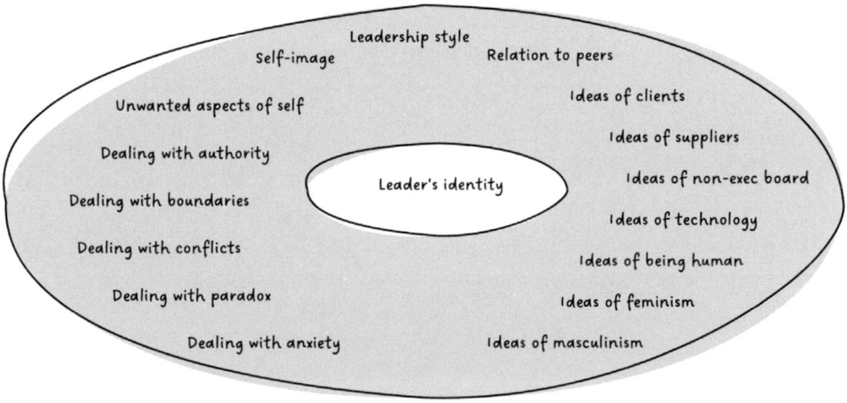

Figure 7: Factors influencing a leader's identity (author's drawing)

For this, it would be important to work on inconsistencies, conflicts, and contradictions.[53] Important to understand is which part of the identity is "real", which means that there is a possibility to enact it over time.[54] But sometimes the identity expectation an organisation has and the respective leader's identity do not fit—and it might take a while to find that out, because there are also unconscious aspects of identity as well as unwanted aspects which you want to keep out but not manage. So, either seeking help or leaving the organisation will be solutions for the leader.

KEY LEARNING

- Today's leaders must be able to hold the tension of opposites and exercise negative capability.
- For that, they have to have experienced holding to enable them to create containment and, by that, instil hope and create identity within the organisation.

CHAPTER 3

Effective and dysfunctional leaders

Everybody talks about effective leadership; it is all over the management literature. What we can state is that the more uncertainty we encounter in the world, the more we will read about recipes for how to get results and success, what to do, and how to behave to get there.

Yet we have already agreed at the beginning that leadership deals with people, and in this book we focus especially on the non-obvious, unconscious, hidden dynamics. When defining leadership "as a process by which an individual influences a group of individuals to achieve a common goal",[55] we have the key components: the leader and the team, the communication behaviour, and the shared goal.

When we are looking at you as leader, as the communicating individual being in relationship with others, then other interesting questions arise:

- What kind of communication is needed from you?
- What are people/followers looking for?
- How are leaders chosen? Who "makes" them? How do they emerge?
- What is an organisation looking for? And what does it not need?

In this chapter we will explore the first two questions. We will approach the questions in the third bullet point in Chapter 8 and those in the fourth point in the second part.

We have already looked at the biological/evolutionary hypothesis of what leaders are good for (coordination and protection) and that they are naturally chosen in natural environments. Effective leaders in today's complex environment have to fulfil a broad yet already standard array of expectations:

- They must be good with people
- They must have good technical skills and expertise
- They must be open and manage innovation on many different levels
- They must think strategically, have a vision, and convey it
- They must be good, authentic communicators (linked to the first expectation) on many different levels
- They must have a stable ego and self
- They must be able to be part of a team (at least temporarily).

You could write a separate book on each of these expectations; however, they themselves are more or less obvious, the art lies in the "how" you achieve this. When wanting to look behind the curtain or underneath the carpet for deep leadership, leaders need to have special capabilities, which we discussed briefly in the Introduction.

Cultivate your self

The most important features of a good leader are about being in contact with oneself—self-awareness, self-reflection, and self-regulation, which are not only connected which each other, but are also part of the overarching concept of "emotional intelligence". From long ago Socrates demands to "know thyself", and Peter Senge, not a philosopher but a management guru, calls this "the cultivated self" meaning "becoming a real human being", which is "the primary leadership issue".[56]

Self-awareness has two components—it is internally oriented, and externally oriented. With the internal part we look at our goals, beliefs, values, traits, competencies, strengths and weaknesses, motives (for being a leader)—in short, at our feeling, thinking, and behaviour in life; it is about perceiving, admitting, and knowing your own life story.

Part of what we can become aware of are our relationship patterns, which Kets de Vries[57] calls the internal theatre, filled on stage with people who have influenced our experiences in life, which we talked about in the first chapter. He claims that "All of us possess some kind of internal theatre and are motivated by a specific inner script," and asserts that people's "internal theatre" significantly influences their lives and castings as leaders.

Self-awareness is supported and achieved by self-reflection and self-exploration, which mean observing your thoughts, actions, and feelings, then also exploring and thinking about them. So, self-exploration and reflection are an integral part of creating self-awareness since the latter needs to be constantly adjusted. It sounds as if it is a cognitive rational process only, but in this exploration it is mainly emotions and intuition that should guide the process. The question of what have I been doing should be complemented by how did I feel and why might I have felt that way, what is behind the rational argument, what made me really do this?

The advantage and positive outcome of self-awareness is self-regulation which leads to an authentic and at the same time "cultivated" self, and not being authentic in the sense of doing what you want and saying what you feel in every moment—I would call the latter rather egotistic and self-absorbed. Cultivation means practice, exercise, and lifelong learning, and can be traced back not only to Socrates, but also to Chinese Confucianism and Buddhism.[58] Scharmer[59] has developed a model for this developmental process called the U-Curve. He explains what he means by cultivation—as he grew up on a farm, his father explained to him that every field has two parts: what is above the ground, and what is under it/in it. The harvest depends much on the quality of the earth below the ground, and it is especially this quality which needs to be cultivated. It is what we do not see which makes the difference—the analogy fits well here with the conscious aspect of our self and the unconscious aspect; it is there where exploration and cultivation need to take place. And that is why we spend so much time here—a full book—to explore what the unconscious means for leaders and how it can be explored and integrated into a larger, more whole self.

I guess this is also the difference between emotional intelligence and what C. G. Jung would describe as individuation. This is the lifelong process of an individual achieving his innate potential and, by that, experiencing the meaning of their life. The ultimate goal is wholeness—something which is probably, if ever, only achieved on the deathbed. It mainly means to integrate all the not-so-helpful, once-protective, now-destructive early behavioural patterns and other neurotic imbalances acquired over a lifetime into a balanced personality. By that, one can get to the core of the self, similar to the germ in the onion, out of which the real self can grow. The main aim of this individuation process is to gain more freedom to choose how you behave and act instead of reacting out of "outdated" emotional, reflective, and behavioural patterns. This freedom to act unpatterned, so to speak, allows you the possibility to also listen intensely to the other and their needs on an emotional as well as rational or technical level.

Self-regulation or self-management also plays a part. This entails emotional self-control, the capacity to adapt to other people, situations, and context. For a leader it also entails achievement of orientation together with hope or a positive outlook, as Goleman calls it. Goleman and Boyatzis (2017) summarise this as five aspects which are important for emotional intelligence from the side of the self. They also use an additional seven aspects to represent the outward oriented side of emotional intelligence—first, social awareness consisting of empathy and organisational awareness, and second, relationship management consisting of influencing, coaching, and mentoring, conflict management, teamwork and inspirational leadership (see Figure 8).

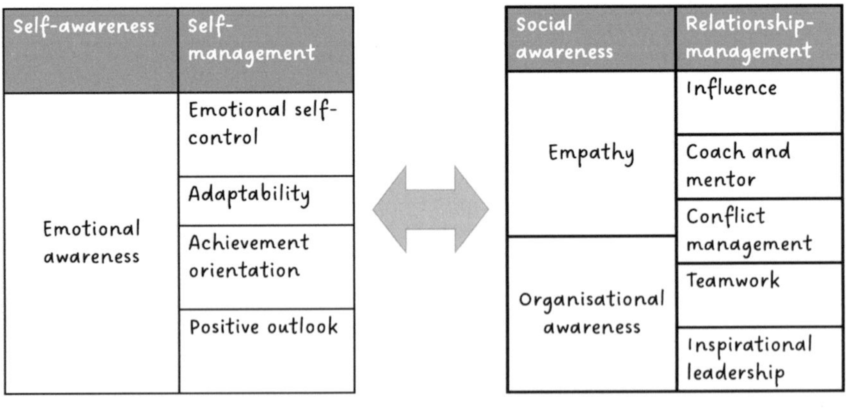

Figure 8: Emotional intelligence and its four domains[60]

There is nothing wrong with that: their model of emotional intelligence is rather instrumental and gives a good first orientation.

Social or external self-awareness is, however, more than empathy and organisational awareness. It is developing an understanding of the impact one has on others, of how one is perceived, seen, understood. It is already difficult to understand your inner world, but it is even more difficult to get an understanding of what others think about you. We talk about the gap between self-image and image of the other or, as written in the Bible, the difference between "the grain of dust in the brother's eye and the plank of wood in your eye" (Matthew 7.3). Asking others for feedback—especially in an organisational context, where hierarchy and politics play a huge role—does not lead to a full result. Both self-image and the image of the other are distorted, and the willingness for self-awareness needs a bit of theoretical and practical support to dive a bit deeper.

But let us first have a look at what you can do to achieve more self-awareness, reflection, exploration, and regulation:

- You can just take ten to fifteen minutes every day to sit down and reflect on these aspects. Observe what you did, what you felt, why you did what you did, and what for. Some people write journals, others do it in their mind or with their partner or friend. There are also workbooks out there.
- Meditation is another possibility. There is a whole school of mindfulness practices available.
- Asking colleagues and especially friends for feedback is also helpful.
- Working with a professional third person like a coach or therapist can provide some helpful insights as well as some structure or order for the exploration and reflection process. This can bring you some steps deeper.

But why is it so difficult to get to your true self? Three hindrances exist:

- Anxiety
- Unconscious patterns
- Neurotic or pathological developments.

Anxiety and fear

Let us have a look at anxiety first. Fear and anxiety protect us. They protect us from outer threats like wild animals in the jungle, from hot cooking plates, dark woods, high mountains, waterfalls, driving too fast, and so on—from all kinds of material dangers where we risk our lives. They also protect us from inner threats, by which I mean attacks on our ego, self-image, self-esteem, and identity. As Riemann[61] has found out, humans have four specific anxiety reactions. These four anxiety types can be differentiated as being afraid of the future and change (hysterical), or afraid of loss of control (obsessive)—which are both turned outwards towards external objects. They are mirrored to inward fear of attachment and of commitment (schizoid), and the fear of separation and loneliness (depressed).

The upper two types are more afraid of losing their autonomy, the lower two are more afraid of losing their attachment and dependence. These are the two basic paradoxes of life: attachment vs autonomy. The next figure gives an overview (see Figure 9).

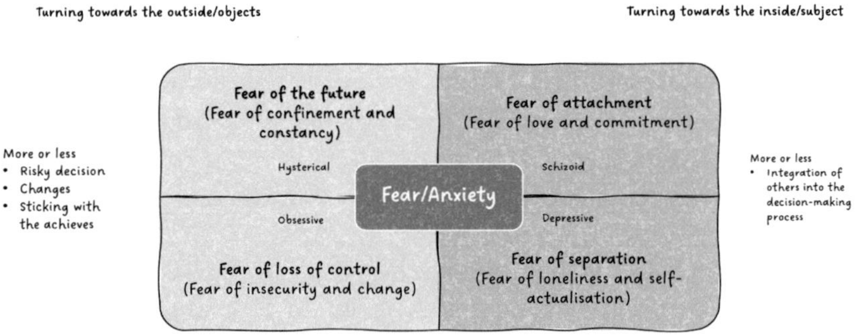

Figure 9: Four types of anxiety (author's drawing)

We all have all four basic anxieties in us but also have a tendency to react more often through one of them. These anxieties have quite a large influence on us and are built from basic genetic personality aspects together with early childhood experiences. For example, a mother who is afraid of every step the child takes when moving away from her might support a development for a depressed anxiety type. A caregiver who leaves the child unattended and alone might bring a schizoid basic anxiety type forward in the child. All these types, although they sound pathological because of the notions, are a normal part of us and not pathological. They are part of human life, and it is helpful to understand to which side you are inclined.

The anxiety styles influence the type of leadership one is most likely to exercise.[62] These styles are depicted here in a rather black and white manner for clarification. Yet there are also leaders out there who have developed pathological traits based on these anxieties.

Schizoid leaders are rather found in large hierarchical organisations. They seem to be isolated, distant, and unavailable, and have difficulty establishing and maintaining human interaction. They are (unconsciously) afraid of others because they could make a mistake through interaction and then lose the connection. The schizoid leader takes decisions on his or her own and does not integrate others' needs and opinions. These types produce excessive cautiousness and hypersensitivity in others and provide their followers with little emotional warmth or support.

Complementary in regard to the paradox of autonomy and attachment is the depressive character, which is rarely found in leadership positions. They can be described as overly adaptive, helpless, and dependent, but often with unconscious aggressive impulses. The decision-making style associated with this type would be to integrate the needs and viewpoints of too many, and consequently such a leader would face difficulty coming to any decision at all. Anxiety hinders the individuation process of the depressive character, because a commitment to seeing this process through would entail autonomy and independence, which could lead to fear of being alone, isolated, and separate from the other.

The obsessive character focuses on orderliness, precision, clarity, and control. These types can be found in statistical or number-oriented positions, such as finance or financial control. This leadership style fosters stable delegation of authority and clarity, and thus functions rather efficiently from an organisational viewpoint (in classic hierarchical organisations). The decision-making style of the obsessive character can lead to choices which do not allow space for change and room for the new. The high need for order, precision and control, micromanagement, and the associated pedantic attitude and risk of excessive sadistic components foster irrational fear and destroy active participation and feedback from others. It can also reinforce bureaucratic structures, which inhibit creativity and autonomy.

The hysterical type can appear slightly naive; excited, and energised by new ideas, actively making risky decisions, experiential, not planning ahead, and appearing thus uncommitted, superficial, and without depth. The need for freedom *of* something instead of the freedom *for* something (e.g. one can be free of constraints or free for commitment) can make these types act in an anarchic way, where rules and regulations are dismissed and ideas quickly stray from a recently chosen path. Furthermore, these types tend to not adapt well to reality, but rather adapt reality to their own perspective and needs.[63]

Another important leadership type, which does not fit into the above four fields due to its complexity, is the narcissistic personality. This style can be very detrimental for organisations and when pathological we call such types dysfunctional leaders. A growing number of leaders are being diagnosed as narcissistic—Kets de Vries and Miller claimed, "If there is one personality constellation to which leaders tend to gravitate, it is the narcissistic one"[64] Narcissism seems to be the driving force behind the desire to obtain a leadership position[65] and is arguably a prerequisite for anyone who hopes to rise to the top of an organisation.[66] The narcissistic type's intense need for power and prestige drives them to take up leadership roles, yet their leadership is driven by an egotistical desire for power and admiration[67] that does not take into account the needs of the organisation or other individuals.

A trait associated with narcissism is the ability to employ charm and create a good impression, hence narcissists are very good at attaining leadership roles, but they do not necessarily perform well once in the position. Narcissists do, however, have particular strengths; they can be highly visionary and as such inspire a great number of people.[68] This fosters loyalty and group identity through strong conviction of the righteousness of their cause, that their group, organisation, or country has a special mission. After a while others feel as if they are suffering an overdose of this person.[69]

Narcissists have a large number of weaknesses: they are hypersensitive to criticism due to their (well-hidden) feelings of inferiority, which also leads to an insatiable need for recognition and superiority; they are poor listeners, lack empathy, and can thus be exploitative and depreciatory; they can be highly irrational, angry, and inflexible, are unwilling or unable to mentor or be mentored, and are intensely competitive.[70]

Excessive self-reference and self-centredness, grandiosity, and over-evaluation hide the fact that narcissists are overly dependent on external admiration and desire to be loved by their followers. Under severe frustration or without the external admiration they crave, they may develop paranoid trends; they can then become suspicious, sadistically controlling, or enraged when interpreting minor opposition as a dangerous rebellion or hidden attack.[71] Dealing so poorly with criticism, narcissists rarely consult with colleagues, preferring to make decisions on their own. Other risks of derailment are: isolation from reality, conflict avoidance, abrasive behaviour, micromanagement, feeling like an impostor, and hypomanic behaviour.[72]

Narcissistic types tend to surround themselves with yes-men and are shrewd manipulators,[73] and thus are bound to leave damaged systems and relationships in their wake.[74] Furthermore, followers might collude unconsciously with their grandiosity, either through the mechanism of identifying with the aggressor or by creating a *folie à deux*, a system of shared madness and delusion.[75] Narcissistic types are "of high intelligence, hardworking, eminently talented or capable, but their narcissistic needs dramatically neutralise or destroy their creative potential for organisations".[76]

Case study

A narcissistic leader—a star or a showman?

Manfred F. R. Kets de Vries

Ronald, a senior executive at the XYZ company was the kind of person who would not go unnoticed. As one of the star performers in the company, he was often at the centre of attention. At industry events, he always stole the limelight with his lively presentations.

Ronald strived for recognition. Because of his networking prowess and activities in mergers and acquisitions (M&A), he managed to be listed in a publication as one of the more promising younger executives in the industry and the person most likely to reshape it. Without saying it explicitly, many people thought that Ronald could turn the company into one of the world's largest players in the industry. Also, what enhanced his reputation and ego was his role as an occasional columnist in a financial newspaper, even though he was paying someone else to ghost-write the articles for him.

Despite these accolades, some members of the board of XYZ company were rather ambivalent about Ronald. Did he really have the qualities to take the company solidly to the next level? Some felt that he was very good in impression management, "all mouth and no trousers". But since the current CEO was reaching the company's mandatory retirement age, many of the board members wondered whether Ronald would be the right person to become her successor.

The reason a number of the board members were sceptical about Ronald's potential to succeed the present CEO was a string of rash decisions he had made. Some thought that he had been pushing too hard on a dramatic expansion plan despite other people's cautionary observations. And in the case of one of his acquisitions, an industry publication commented that the company had paid far too much money for the acquired firm. In addition, what also troubled board members was Ronald's decision to relocate the divisional office to a new, more upmarket location. Of course, moving might have been the right decision given the cramped conditions his people had been working in. It might also have been a better location to attract talent. But Ronald had completely discounted the costs of the move. Moving to the other location turned out to be much more expensive than he had suggested.

The board members were also aware of the results of a recent 360 leadership feedback process Ronald had participated in. Some of the observations on his behaviours were cause for concern. For example, comments were made about a number of actions that Ronald had taken which raised the question on whether he possessed the sensitivity to understand the organisation's corporate culture, an important factor that had made the company so successful. According to the survey, Ronald often tended to ignore the "shoulds" and the "shouldn'ts" of the company's culture. A prime example of a "shouldn't" was a recent decision to charter a private plane to be able to make it to a meeting on time; not exactly standard company policy. The survey also contained veiled suggestions of Roland's behaviour during social events: making unwanted sexual advances to staff members when inebriated.

Also, if the observations of the survey were to be believed, working closely with Ronald seemed to be a challenge. A number of respondents viewed him as a "user" who was always taking advantage of them. Others commented about his "air of superiority" and his dismissiveness of the opinions of others. They noted that he had a tendency to claim all the credit for whatever work had been done, never acknowledging other people's contributions. Respondents to the survey also stated that Ronald was inclined to blame others when mistakes were made and that he always managed never to be wrong. Comments were also made about Ronald's sense of entitlement and his proneness to outbursts of rage if he didn't get what he wanted. Some of them went even so far as stating that he could be cruel and act like a "bully", making his subordinates afraid to disagree with him. One of the board members had overheard a friend saying that visitors to his office were often struck by the subdued and subservient attitude of the staff. They also noted, when dealing with him, that flattery would go a long way.

What made putting a finger on Ronald's capabilities difficult was that he seemed to be very talented in managing upwards. Longer-term board members recalled that many of his previous superiors seemed to only have pure admiration and praise for him. He really knew how to charm them.

Given all these "ifs" and "buts" found in the survey, some of the board members were conflicted on how effective Ronald truly was. Was he really a wunderkind able to transform the company and industry? Or, as others suggested, were many of his accomplishments just showmanship? Was he one of those people who had a knack for getting out of the way before the shit hit the fan? Was he the kind of person who knew how to convince others when things went wrong that he really had nothing to do with it? Many of these comments made a number of the board members uneasy, wondering whether Ronald was really the golden boy as he had been labelled by many of them. At the same time, they recognised that he was a fountain of great ideas and a great driver of change.

Given the observations from Ronald's 360 leadership development exercise combined with the commentary of others, the question raised at a recent board meeting was whether Ronald should be listed as the prime candidate to succeed the outgoing CEO. Would he be the right person to bring the company to the next level?

* * *

So, what is your take on that question? Would you want Ronald to be your CEO?

In his case, all the narcissistic traits come together—the feeling of superiority, the upwards charm, the collusion of board members believing in him as the star performer, his reputation and impression management, difficulties dealing with him as an ordinary human being, his ill-considered decisions, putting himself and his reputation ahead of the company. I guess you would abstain from further promoting Ronald.

KEY LEARNING

Based on the above description we can summarise in the following table:

Effective Leader	Dysfunctional Leader
Designs, creates, builds	Destroys, harms
Grows people, makes them flourish	Uses, abuses, manipulates people for his personal purpose
Delivers results	Pretends to deliver
Thinks about his impact	Good impression management
Authentic	Neurotic
Leads sidewards and downwards	Leads upwards
Listens first attentively and tells later	Tells first and listens partially later

Figure 10: What does it mean to be effective as a leader? (author's compilation)

CHAPTER 4

We are all mammals

This book is about how emotions and relationships influence leadership and work performance. Understanding what emotions are, where they are located, and how they intervene in our lives are some of the crucial parts of this book. However, there is no one-and-only theory about the development of emotions, nor is there even agreement on what emotions are. It all depends on the school of thought you are coming from.

Modern "affective" neuroscience was introduced in the 1990s by authors such as Joseph Ledoux, Antonio Damasio, and Jaap Panksepp. It is thus a rather new field in which the idea of the emotional brain was developed—that there is no thinking without feeling.[77] It combines cognitive neuroscience with the psychological study of affective experience, such as feeling, emotion, and mood, to investigate how these constructs are linked to behaviour, personality, and disorder.[78]

Panksepp[79] played an important role in that development. He was also known as "the rat-tickler", as his research led to the discovery that rats can "laugh" when tickled. In his work with animals, Panksepp was particularly interested in understanding their emotional life. Contrary to many other researchers, he believed that humans are not the only species to experience emotions. His research was important as it questioned the idea that emotions come from the cerebral cortex, the large thinking area of the brain involved in complex operations. Instead, via electrical stimulation of different brain areas, he found that deeper brain regions such as the amygdala and hypothalamus are involved in the generation of emotions. He and his colleague Lucy Biven[80] developed a system of seven basic emotions which follow a developmental path through life: SEEK, RAGE, FEAR, LUST, CARE, PANIC/GRIEF, PLAY. He uses capital letters to underline their very fundamental and innate role. They are "instinctual emotional responses that generate raw affective feelings that Mother Nature built into our brains" and are also referred to as "primary process psychological experiences".[81]

These base feelings create an energetic form of consciousness full of affective intensity, which Panksepp refers to as "affective consciousness". They allow us to instinctively deal with the world and learn about its potential from birth onwards. These primary emotional processes are "foundational pillars for the brain's mental apparatus",[82] as they are neural circuits in our brain. It seems as if all mammals have this type of subcortical structure—primal emotional systems—which are based on neuroanatomies and neurochemistries that share similarities across all mammalian species. They developed a long time ago and show that, on a basic emotional and motivational level, mammals share more similarities than differences. Before we explore the content of the emotional systems, I would like to briefly describe how they function and what they are good for on a very general level.

Our whole brain–mind–body system is based on homeostasis and works towards achieving and maintaining a physiological balance. Every imbalance (from a certain point onwards) endangers our survival and must be addressed and balance re-established. The body and the mind signal an imbalance with a need for something: when we feel hungry, we want and need to eat; when we feel thirsty, we want and need to drink. Being hungry and thirsty are unpleasant feelings and motivate us, drive us to do something about it. When we are not yet consciously aware of these feelings, then they are called affects.

Affects are processes which consist of three features: (1) an evaluation of the valence, which means good or bad, pleasant or unpleasant,

(2) a motivation, which is an action tendency on the spectrum between approaching or avoidance, and (3) an arousal, which is the physiological reaction of the autonomous nervous system—mainly a tendency to action. When there is an aberrance from the comfort zone of the organism, this action is needed to reduce the (destruction) risk (see Figure 11).

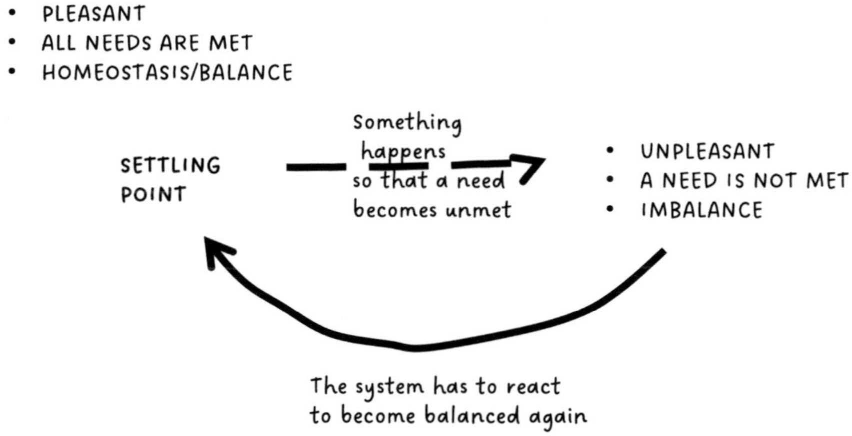

Figure 11. The reaction to unmet needs (author's drawing)

Although one is subject to these affective states, one does not necessarily recognise that one is having them, meaning that they may be unconscious—an unreflective, unthinking primary process form of consciousness that precedes the cognitive understanding of the world and is experienced in an affective form.

Affects, feelings, emotions, and moods

Whereas an affect is unconscious, a feeling is a conscious mental representation of a physiological bodily state, central neural activation, and environmental circumstances. For example, when I feel hungry or angry, this is conscious—something is happening in the brain and there is also an external situation involved (no food, another person). Feeling is a conscious affect and is concerned with homeostasis and allostasis for survival.

Emotions and moods are special types of feelings. Non-emotional feelings are about sensory states (sights, sounds, tastes, touch) (see Figure 12). Emotions are episodes, they don't last for ever, whereas mood is a prolonged felt experience and does not pertain to any object in particular. Emotions are rooted in evolution, implemented in physiological and neural circuits, are driven by external or internal stimuli, and inferred based on biological and/or psychological significance. They serve survival needs via allostatic regulation.

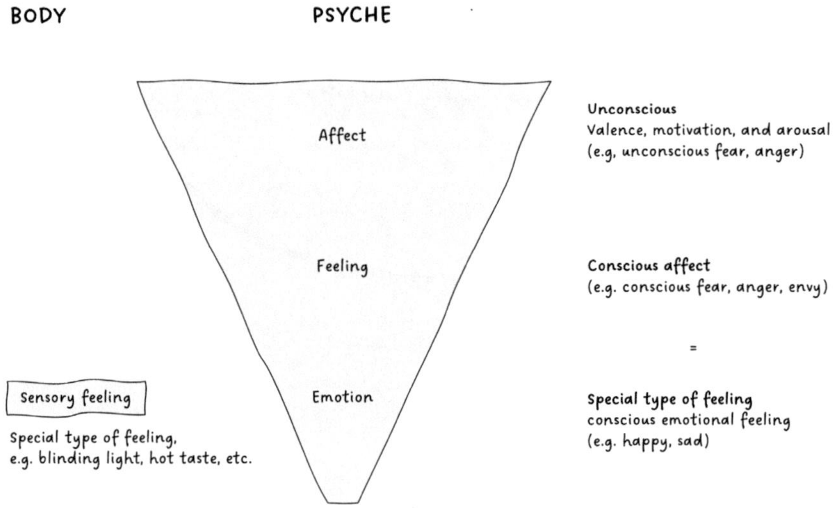

Figure 12: From unconscious affect to emotions (author's drawing)

Both the allostasis and homeostasis mechanisms of living systems arise from autopoiesis—it means that an organism as a system must self-organise and self-generate. Homeostasis corrects errors when deviating from the balance, whereas allostasis is an error-predicting process and meets predicted needs. Allostasis is a rather recent term, a somewhat diffuse concept which stands for "stability through change". It subsumes homeostasis and, by that, organises the system's regulation and behaviour to make sure that homeostasis can continue its main task of protecting the basic elements of the living system required to navigate the world in order to sustain life. Both are thus there to regulate physiological and psychological states.[83]

This explanation, I think, gives reason for emotions, how they have come to be, and how they provide an evolutionary advantage—else why would they exist? It is also helpful for understanding that psychological disorders and neurotic personality aspects are a result of severe emotional and motivational defects in generating and regulating feelings.[84]

The conscious and unconsciousness in neuroscience

What I described at the beginning of the book was a fascination for the unconscious and what it might look like. For neuroscientists and neuropsychoanalysts this is less interesting, since even an unconscious mind can fully perform all cognitive operations of perception and control.[85] An unconscious mind is more efficient since it uses automated responses to manage human interaction. Consciousness, by contrast, is much slower, takes more time and arises only when needed—as when something unexpected occurs, something requires attention or focus, or some kind of (re)action is necessary. Consciousness is always linked with feelings towards events (threat/benefit to survival, pleasurable/unpleasurable),[86] a link which enables the human being to assess and orient itself as to what action should be taken in a given situation (see Figure 13).

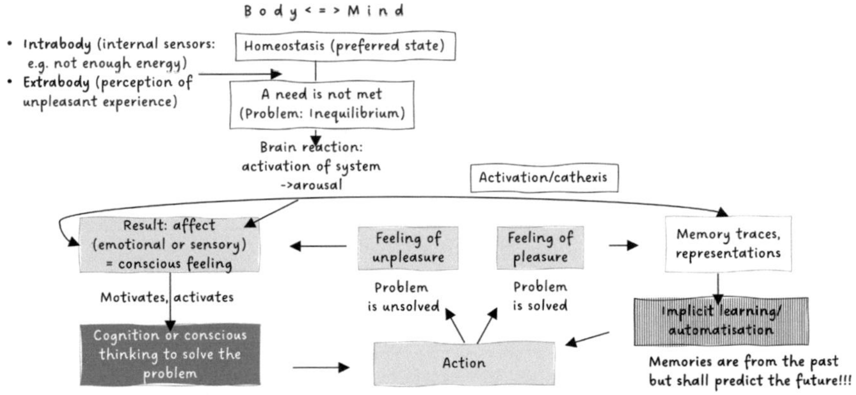

Figure 13: Rebalancing the system while learning for automatisation (author's drawing)

Cognitive sciences understand mental processes to be conscious and unconscious, the latter implying that both perceptions and cognitions may occur without awareness. Earlier cognitive psychology understood the unconscious as a waste bin (unattended or unrehearsed events), as a filing cabinet (passively storing memories which need to be actively retrieved), as pre-attentive processing (feature detection and pattern recognition as the basis for conscious attention and automaticity), or as where cognitive and motoric skills become automatised through extensive practice. Historically, the study of cognitive neuroscience has excluded emotional factors; however, emotional and cognitive processes and contents can no longer be so clearly distinguished, with both now considered mental processes.[87] Hence, affective neuroscience has become an aspect of cognitive neuroscience.[88] Cognitions can be understood as the mental representation of reality, whereas emotions are the subjective experience of reality, and motivation the guiding activation towards a goal.[89]

In summary, we can say that unconscious automated processes such as affects are always present; they are constantly regulating body and mind processes beyond our awareness. They manifest in two different ways:

> First, some processes are unconscious in the strict sense that they are executed automatically, in response to certain stimulus conditions. At least in principle, automatic processes are unavailable to conscious introspection and are independent of conscious control. Second, some mental contents—percepts, memories, and the like—are unconscious in the sense that they are inaccessible to phenomenal awareness but nonetheless affect the person's ongoing experience, thought, and action.[90]

Only special affects become emotions and get our conscious attention.

In neuroscience, Solms[91] defines three core claims about the mind:

- The human infant is not a blank slate; like all other species, we are born with a set of innate needs which are felt as emotions.
- The main task of mental development is to learn how to meet these needs, which implies that mental disorder arises from failure to achieve this task.

- Most of our ways of meeting our needs are executed unconsciously, which requires us to bring them to consciousness once more in order to change them.

Here we are now focusing on *emotional* needs—which are felt as separation distress, rage, etc.—not *bodily* drives—which are felt as hunger, thirst, etc.—nor *sensory* affects—which are felt as pain, disgust, etc. We can only meet our emotional needs by engaging with others—this is why relationships are crucial. You cannot attach to yourself, and you cannot successfully have sex with yourself.

Basic affective systems

The basic (hard-wired) emotions release instinctual behaviours, which are innate *action plans* we perform in order to meet our needs (e.g. cry, search, freeze, flee, attack). No universal agreement on the number of innate needs in the human brain has yet been achieved, but most mainstream taxonomies[92] include the following:

- We need to engage with the world—since all our biological appetites (including bodily needs like hunger and thirst) can only be met this way. This is a *foraging*, seeking or "wanting" instinct. It is felt as interest, curiosity, and the like—SEEKING resources in Panksepp's terms.
- We need to find sexual partners. This is felt as *lust*. This instinct is sexually dimorphic (on average), but male and female inclinations exist in both genders—LUST is controlling sexuality (a social response, strongly connected to seeking).
- We need to escape dangerous situations. We therefore need *fear*—FEAR is a defence.
- We need to destroy frustrating objects (things that get between us and satisfaction of our needs). This is *rage*—RAGE is to protect resources.
- We need to attach to caregivers. Separation from attachment figures is felt not as fear but as *panic*, and losing them is felt as *despair*—PANIC is due to separation distress.
- We need to care for and *nurture* others, especially our offspring. This is the so-called "maternal instinct", but it exists (to varying degrees)

in both genders—CARE is an often maternal and nurturing behaviour (and is positive as reward).

- We need to *play*. This is not useless. Play is the medium through which social hierarchies are formed ("pecking order") and in-group and out-group boundaries are maintained—PLAY is social engagement (and is positive as reward).

These affective systems form the emotional basis of every human being and serve to make the individual aware of his and her needs and take corresponding action to meet them.

Let us now first form an overview and then look at the details of each of the basic emotion systems and what they imply for leadership and organisations (see Figure 14).

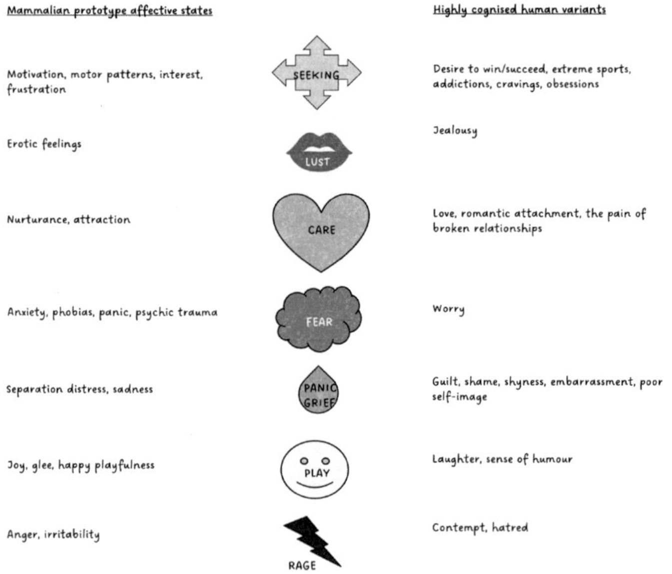

Figure 14: Overview of affective states in mammals and humans (author's drawing)[93]

The SEEKING system

The SEEKING network is a general-purpose appetitive system that many of the other emotions and affects utilise; it is the most basic of all affects, the others are more specific. It is the only one, if damaged severely, that compromises life itself, for it depletes foraging/enthusiasm resources (see Figure 15).

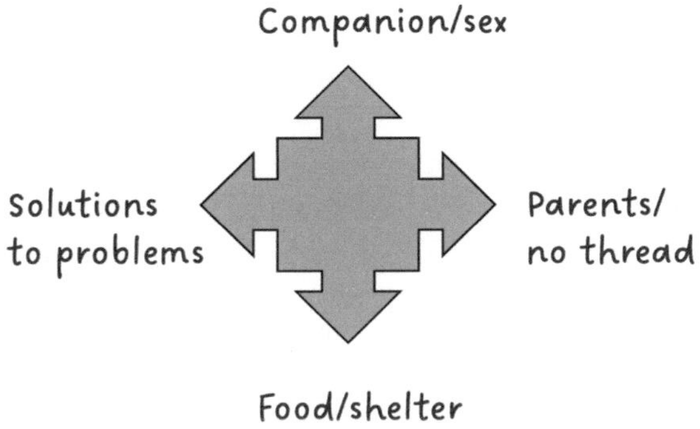

Figure 15: SEEKING behaviour (author's drawing)

Seeking behaviour involves screening the environment, foraging, and also looking for food and sex. It provides an urge to explore, investigate, and pursue all types of pleasurable rewards and avoid various negative affects that index fundamental survival issues. The SEEKING system motivates us to interact with our environment and harvest the resources needed for survival. Formerly it was understood as the brain-reward system—today we know this to be but one reward system of many.

SEEKING is felt as excitement, curiosity, and enthusiasm, which makes you get what you want. It can be triggered by new events, and stops being triggered when the event is not new anymore. It has an upstream effect that activates other needs/drives and a downstream effect insofar as, if other needs are not met, it will activate SEEKING.

SEEKING is a dopamine-dominated circuit—which means it is in itself rewarding—that goes through the midbrain, limbic system, and into the frontal cortex, which is the strategy-developing area of the brain. It can therefore trigger cognitive activity (and overactivation can also lead to delusions). It produces dopamine when the seeking is successful and that then influences the experience of time—we know how time seems to fly when we enjoy doing things. It includes appetite learning and is also connected to centres in the brain associated with addiction; for example, cocaine affects the SEEKING system.

In decision-making, SEEKING motivates us to explore options of choices and assists in learning, so choices can improve over time. It is also linked to the FEAR system, and via classic conditioning can protect us from danger. Thus, without this SEEKING urge, we as decision makers would be repeating our same mistakes over and over again.

Since SEEKING is the basic explorative system which is—although to different degrees—part of all of us, it is important in your leadership role to create opportunities for yourself and your team for exploration, curiosity, and the building of relationships. It is an important system for decision-making and, being responsible for innovation creation and guiding entrepreneurial efforts, it is the system which brings the new into the world.

The LUST system

LUST is a primary motive in all mammals, and although sexual feelings do not help our individual survival, they make the survival of our family genes possible.

Desire and want trigger the SEEKING and dopamine systems, whereas negative moods, stress, and starvation have the opposite effect.

Male and female LUST systems are as different as their bodies. Their development begins during the foetal stage. Men are defined when in puberty the testicles start to produce abundant testosterone, whereas female bodies produce progesterone and oestrogen. Men have their larger sexual glands in the middle of their brains, while women's systems are more distributed and complex. Testosterone fuels circuits that promote male sexuality and the urge for male dominance/aggression, which play a role in both sexual and social dominance. It can also sensitise RAGE receptors. Women react the same way if they are given testosterone. Oestrogen stimulates production of oxytocin, which encourages "female-typical" behaviour summarised as a drive to tend and befriend[94] and also to be understood as caring and nurturing. This is an aspect which men also have, since they also produce oxytocin, although less so. Testosterone triggers vasopressin, which in women makes them shift towards more male-typical attitudes such as being pushy and dominant.

From a leadership perspective, it is important to understand that although Eros is a part of all relationships and friendships with mutual attraction, it does not mean sexual desire. It is problematic when sexual relationships develop within hierarchical situations, worse even if (mostly) women through their dependence are forced into relationships. If this kind of dominance appears, you as a leader must protect the more vulnerable and dependent person, independent of gender questions. And even if the relationship is wanted from both sides, in many organisations the lower-ranked person—mostly women—must leave the organisation. I wonder what kind of unconscious power and social connection game plays a role here and how it could be rethought and looked at differently.

Leaders are called upon to take care of their colleagues and followers. We will look at this in the next part.

The CARE system

We are biologically wired to nurture, and the CARE system is the giving of nurture, of enabling and protecting. It is dominated by oxytocin and is a non-sexual love drive leading to SEEKING in a healthy individual. CARE is also experienced as rewarding, but it is differently perceived by individuals. A complex process, during pregnancy it prepares the mother for CARE. In our species it is very strong due to the long-term immaturity and helplessness of the baby. It induces the early attachment of the mother and other caregivers with the infant. CARE and PANIC-GRIEF together are the "attachment primary processes".

In animals, parental CARE can be facilitated during the care they receive themselves. It can be felt across species and, as Panksepp suggests, this is the primary process of empathy. CARE/oxytocin together with touch triggering opioids reduce grief. Stress reduces the capacity to CARE.

The CARE system is an important system for leaders who, from an evolutionary/social and psychological perspective are expected to take care of their followers, weaker members, and all stakeholders of the organisation. It is also mirrored in hierarchical and organisational structures, where the board takes care of the organisation and units take care of sub-units.

The PLAY system

The PLAY system is probably the most astonishing of all, since it exists in every mammal, and every young mammal enjoys playing. At an early age, roughhousing—rough and tumble play—brings the most fun and has nothing to do with other types of aggression. PLAY can only begin when SEEKING for survival is finished.

PLAY is a spontaneous activity done for its own sake and for fun; it is not like real life, more an "as if", and exhibits many repetitive and exaggerated activities that train for later adult activities. It is preparation for social life and its hierarchy—dominance and submission, winning and losing are both part of it. To experience both sides, turn-taking is key. If one always wins and never lets the other win, nobody will play with the winner anymore. PLAY is thus also important for social bonding. It is the only general drive which makes us seek out social groups, because groups are about play.

In adult life, PLAY is expressed as, for example, friendly teasing, which can also go back and forth and, if it matches, friendship can develop. Also, younger mammals prefer to be with those older ones who are still having fun and enjoy a game.

The PLAY urge is innate and very robust, since it can always take place when everything is good, but it is also very fragile, because all events that entail negative emotions such as anger, fear, and separation distress can reduce PLAY; hunger also inhibits PLAY. Interestingly, predatory animals enjoy object play; prey species enjoy running play with turns and twists—preparing for adulthood.

Going along with it is laughter. Mammals can laugh, especially when the young are tickled. Laughter is not learnt, it is an unconditional instinct response.

PLAY has multiple functions:

- It enables the young to learn physical skills like hunting, foraging, physical fitness, cognitive functions, skilful use of tools, and innovation in the face of unexpected events.
- It teaches social capabilities, especially dealing with nascent aggression, courting, sexual and competitive and even parenting skills.
- It teaches with whom to cooperate and whom to avoid.

- It teaches when to dominate and when to gracefully disengage, submit, or defeat.
- It establishes social bonding, social cooperation, social rank, and leadership.

We can summarise that PLAY prepares you to become a member of a social network within which you will remain for life.

PLAY is very important in leadership and organisations, since it is the only social drive. PLAY prepares for competition and it indicates the necessity of hierarchy, in the sense of winning—often the leader—and losing—often the follower. But if you as a leader never let the others win, they will not enjoy working with you. Winning here means being right, knowing better, having the solution to a problem. A turn-taking ration of 70/30 or even 60/40 would be needed. This contributes to a good working ambience—if one always loses, then disappointment and later rage and revenge can come up. PLAY is also active in creating communities and networks of people connecting and cooperating with each other. It is the root drive for organisational culture. Narcissistically injured and depressive people have difficulties with PLAY, as it is difficult to play in an ambience of fear and anxiety.

The FEAR system

Physiologically, the FEAR system stems from and is still connected with SEEKING. FEAR is the evolutionary protection system and makes us aware and keeps us away from dangerous situations while SEEKING is responsible for learning to avoid specific objects and functions already after a one-time exposure. Yet, like every other emotional system it is born objectless, that is why learning through experience is so crucial; it is there to anticipate and avoid bad things. We therefore have unconditional fear circuits in the primitive parts of the brain (a lion attacking you is no time to rely on the neocortex) which make you take flight or freeze. Only when the danger is manageable does one attack and fight. When the danger, the lion, is a bit further away, the higher regions of the brain can be involved and instead of running away one can look for a hideaway.

As with the muscles in our body, the more the FEAR system is used, the stronger it becomes—that is why untreated post-traumatic stress disorder (PTSD) becomes worse with time.

FEAR starts the startle effect, which, if already alert or wary, becomes even stronger. An overactivation by accumulated stimuli of the FEAR system leads first to free-floating anxiety; and if animals are exposed to a stressful fear-provoking situation for too long, they become depressive. Stress in general can increase FEAR response. Pain can lead to FEAR, yet FEAR does not necessarily lead to pain; FEAR can rather inhibit pain, because it can release opioids that will reduce the experience of pain, which is its evolutionary function. Of course, animals try to escape as a reaction to FEAR; it is an unpleasant feeling which they dislike—it initiates defensive reactions. Humans do the same and—when they cannot react by running away—use psychic mechanisms as defensive functions.

It is extremely important that leaders understand the FEAR system, with its fight/flight/freeze response and psychic defence mechanisms. Some people, maybe even many people, including leaders, are afraid of other people; they cannot reasonably judge whether to avoid them or not because of bad past experiences. Also, in a social system such as an organisation, one cannot easily avoid those people who frighten us. These people are more vulnerable because they are more easily frightened, and it would be helpful if the leader were able to take care of these sensitive people.

When FEAR and the fight/flight/freeze/defence reaction sets in, there is little energy left to perform one's job. In addition, this FEAR system—like all other emotional systems—works underneath our awareness level; people might not even know that they are fearful—of a situation, of a person. This can cause quite problematic situations in organisations. New processes, new technologies, and change, as such, could activate the FEAR system when work role and identity are threatened. It is neither helpful to lead with pressure and anxiety, nor is it helpful to ignore the effects of FEAR. Even McKinsey has started to talk about fear, which is a sign that this emotion has become a mainstream theme—probably prompted by the mental health problems stemming from the coronavirus pandemic and its uncertainty and anxiety-creating effects. In the section on self-awareness (Chapter 3) I talked about self-reflection and how it is particularly important for leaders to recognise their own fears and anxieties—only then are you able to detect them in others and create strategies and situations to overcome them.

The PANIC/GRIEF system

Mammals have a great need to feel safe. The loss of this feeling of being safe will lead to PANIC/GRIEF. At birth and in the early life stages this feeling of safety depends on the caregiver, and later in life to our close social bonds and, of course, on the (hopefully) early developed feeling of basic trust.

When the needed attachment person disappears, separation distress happens—then PANIC/GRIEF starts to kick in. First the child begins manically looking for the lost person via the activated SEEKING system—this is the PANIC part. It triggers the parasympathetic system that leads to crying, a tight chest, and reduced activity. When the missing person or object (for example, an important toy) does not come back, GRIEF develops and makes you feel bereft and miserable—GRIEF triggers the stress hormone cortisol. This then affects the hippocampus, and therefore episodic and biographical memory. It can under pro longed stress injure and kill neurons in the hippocampus. When GRIEF is alleviated, a deep sense of comfort and feeling safe and secure develops via the distribution of endogenous opioids and oxytocin occurs.

PANIC/GRIEF reflects the importance of social bonds and the problems caused by their disappearance—when love and friends disappear the separation distress causes grief. When one is in the grip of the PANIC/GRIEF system, it can be so strong that other systems like PLAY, LUST, and CARE shut down.

As we have already seen, when the earliest social bonds are firmly and securely nourished, psychological health is provided for the whole lifetime, therefore secure and warm caregiver relationships are the primary key for a happy life. If not, several emotional disorders (panic attacks, autism, depression, some social phobias, personality disorders) can develop and are rooted in the incapacity to enjoy the security of warm interpersonal attachments. And since this system's dominant chemistry are opioids, we can easily imagine that heroin and other similar drugs feed into this system and the resulting feelings of safety. If one does not feel loved, the drug withdrawal—the drug allowing for feeling loved—is especially hard.

In turbulent times, times of change and disruption, people have to deal with abandonment and loss of something (tasks, products) or someone (individuals or networks) which have become dear to them. Leaders therefore need to understand why sometimes the resistance to change is so high. People need time to grieve—grieving is not a sign of refusal to change, it is simply part of the process. Also, as a leader, you must not underestimate your own need to grieve when things change. The psychic pain of unresolved grief can lead almost anybody to depression.

RAGE The RAGE system

When mammals compete for resources as means for survival, they feel rage and anger. RAGE is triggered when one is obstructed from seeking or satisfying a need. This need could stem from PLAY, from LUST, from CARE, and from SEEKING—when the goal or the reward are withheld. Social desires are threatened by RAGE as well, so that, for example, rivalry between siblings results.

RAGE itself is an aggressive irritability, like raw anger. It makes people reach out to strike someone or something, physically or verbally. Nobody is immune to it, yet on a secondary level anger can be learnt to be expressed in ways other than physical violence. It can also be expressed as jealousy, revenge, or even hatred. Childhood maltreatment or neglect can engender anger that lasts a lifetime.

In difficult times, when resources such as jobs, love, or food are scarce, RAGE increases as it does when one is hungry. Indeed, research has found that judges convict with harder punishments shortly before lunchtime than after their lunch break.

Interesting, also, is that monkeys tend to direct their rage towards lower-ranked, submissive animals, while confrontation with more dominant higher-ranked animals is avoided. I guess we have all seen similar behaviour from ourselves or our colleagues.

The affective feeling of RAGE is very unpleasant, and most people try to avoid succumbing to it—except if there are some secondary gains within reach. RAGE is normally suppressed by thinking about the social consequences; that is why we say "choose your battles". RAGE can be very destructive and is an affect that cannot be effectively controlled by medication; none has been found so far, so society will remain vulnerable to dangerous individuals full of rage.

The main message for leaders and organisations is that RAGE needs to be avoided because of its destructiveness, and that it is much less likely to occur when all other needs are well met. So, the creation of a framework which makes people flourish, feel taken care of (CARE), with possibilities for exploration, innovation (SEEKING), social connection (PLAY), and time for making change happen (PANIC/GRIEF), creates a fertile ground in which fear and anxiety (FEAR) and anger (RAGE) are less likely to impinge on the task at hand and thus endanger work performance. What we also see is how much our brain is evolutionarily hard-wired and prepared from early childhood on to live in a social fabric where mutual care, protection, cooperation, and also mutual joy and fun create advantages when compared to disparate, disconnected groupings of individuals.

Case study

Affective states—firefighters in protection mode

Fiona Martin and Claudia Nagel

Introduction

This is a case about leadership development in the emergency sector.[95] Australian emergency services organisations respond to a range of emergencies including fire, flood, wind storm, air hazards, biohazards, terrorism, and accidents. Here we are looking at firefighters, who protect some of the most fire-prone landscape on the planet. The services we are looking at have both paid workers and volunteers. The origin of Australian fire services was farmers protecting their community, their property, and their families from fire. Many of the current volunteers do live in the countryside and are involved in agriculture but there are now many who live in urban areas. In the past forty years emergency organisations began employing paid firefighters to work alongside the volunteer workers. Since the mid-twentieth century, as populations have grown, government has taken an increased role in the management of emergency services.

In the existing system, there is a culture of the local community with regard to volunteer firefighters, and then there are paid firefighters as well as corporate roles for organisational development, finances, research, communications and other functional capacities. Many administrative and corporate workers also hold a firefighter role. It is a male-dominated environment where women are predominantly found in the corporate and administrative roles. The system is focused on managing bush-fire events and has a hierarchical command-and-control culture that is highly mobilised and has been very effective in responding to incidents.

Last century events such as fires, floods, and other hazards were relatively predictable in scale and behaviour and agencies felt equipped to manage these emergencies. However, in the twenty-first century climate change has brought catastrophic emergency events at an unprecedented level in Australia and the hierarchical command-and-control approach has been found to present some difficulties. This new set of conditions demands a paradigm shift in thinking to new ways of leading that enable and integrate collaborative thinking and shared responsibility.

Emergency services personnel do their work in the midst of powerful community and political expectations. Political and community expectations of being protected and saved continue to be projected onto these services. The command-and-control culture serves also the need of demonstrating to the communities that specialist services are in control of whatever kind of incident will happen, yet the reality of this expectation is less real than at any other time.

Presenting issues

This case study seeks to offer an understanding of what happens in this system and why, by exploring the effects of the human drives (instincts) on individual behaviour.

There are a range of presenting issues in this case study. Climate change and the environmental crisis has led to more and unprecedented weather conditions for which no incident management protocol exists. The rate and scale of them will most likely escalate with the increasing likelihood of multiple events occurring simultaneously.[96] This new set of conditions demands a paradigm shift; new ways of thinking, learning, and leading are now required of the emergency services, including expanding from the past micro-level responses to introduce macro-level thinking that will require collaboration on a broad level.

In the past, people in senior roles have worked from their knowledge and experience of how events have happened and how they have dealt with them. This does not work any longer for complex emergency events, but a command-and-control pattern of behaviour continues. It has been found that in a command-and-control environment people who see a problem or new piece of information may find it difficult to speak up. The culture needed under these changed conditions would be more dynamic and flexible, including being able to admit that you do not exactly know what to do but still feel that it is OK to do your best.

There are aspects of a command-and-control approach to leadership that have implications for the day-to-day work of these organisations; in addition, there is an unofficial network that functions in the background. It is a relational system of people knowing each other well. This can lead to bypassing the official hierarchy, and instead addressing the relational system.

Additionally, there are significant numbers of cases of bullying and harassment in the sector.

Furthermore, there are low levels of research utilisation and application of new knowledge. Organisational learning from mistakes has been found to be challenging.

The necessary shift in the work culture to meet the new challenges of climate change seems to be especially difficult to achieve—this is the main presenting issue we are looking at here in this case.

Reflection

The frontline work of firefighters is strongly connected with the hero archetype. Firefighters are a bit like supermen, in that they save people's and animals' lives, and receive admiration and praise for their courage and bravery. The hero archetype can form a part of their identity and can be an attraction for choosing the role. Yet the shadow side of the hero is to deny fear and vulnerability, which can lead to failure to note the reality of dangers or breakdown in the face of extreme danger.

Applying Panksepp's work on human emotional systems, the emotional drive behind that willingness to take on the dangerous work of firefighting is CARE. As mammals, we have in each of us a need for CARE and to CARE. Life starts with being cared for: parental CARE is about nurturing, feeding, and protecting offspring for their survival. This then continues later in life as taking care of the people you love and the community you are living in. CARE can have two expressions, which can be associated with being more male or female, although we carry both sides in us. In this case it is a male presentation of caring through protection.

When the firefighters' ability to perform the caring role in the way they could in the past is not possible any longer because of the changing circumstances, they are not fulfilling their deeply rooted need to care for and protect others. This gives rise to a bad feeling, just as it would be giving a good feeling when one is able to fulfil the need for caring. Wanting, but failing, to take care of others, the community, the people and animals in danger, is very difficult to bear and becomes a source of distress. The CARE which is part of the role of a firefighter is also part of his professional and personal identity and self-image: "I am a protector," "I am a provider," and "I am admired for my bravery." The community in which he is working is adding to this feeling by expecting to be protected from a hero-like person, saving them in cases of emergency. When this need is frustrated, explicitly or implicitly, RAGE is most likely to appear.

Within emergency services there are a variety of identities held by paid firefighting workers and volunteers. Paid firefighters' work identity is solely the firefighter, whereas the volunteers' work identity derives also from their main profession or occupation. Some of them may shift to the firefighter identity only during incidents; others hold most strongly to their identity as firefighter and hero most of the time.

RAGE is expressed as aggression. We differentiate between cold aggression—a predator looking for his lunch—and hot aggression, coming from another drive or need being frustrated. It may result in aggressive dominating behaviour. For example, it may lead firefighters in the command-and-control culture to manage their territory as "theirs", as their area, where only they have the right to fight. This aggression stemming from the unmet need for caring may then be acted out in bullying more vulnerable colleagues in the system. The RAGE and the hot aggression behind it may also be an explanation for the very rigid hierarchical command-and-control system.

It may also be the case that in a rigid hierarchical command-and-control system there is no space for PLAY, the drive that underpins social problem solving, creativity, and innovation. Within Panksepp's ideas about the PLAY drive is the 60/40 or 70/30 rule. This rule is about how to establish a hierarchy in a way that will be acceptable for followers as well. The leader, who can win in 60 per cent of the cases (being right, telling others what to do) needs to allow the other group members to win some of the time—in 40 per cent or at least 30 per cent of the time. If not, it will be experienced as an unfair "game" which the group members will either leave or oppose.

In a command-and-control culture, one letting the other have good ideas and, by that, win and contribute, may not be allowed enough of the time. By playing, we are talking about a more permeable leadership system in which not only the top dogs are allowed to speak, but also others who may have observed important aspects or changes of the fire situation.

The stuckness of not moving and learning between the incidents may be explained by a non-working SEEKING system. Normally, SEEKING is the default mode, when no other drive demands immediate attention or action. In SEEKING mode, curiosity and interest prevail and some optimistic attitude of expectancy exists. You would then normally update your ideas about how the world functions, your predictive model.

Yet, here in this case we can observe excessive seeking that has omnipotent aspects to it. Firefighters and the fire agencies look for new risks and new ways to satisfy the CARE drive through protecting. During times when there is little or no likelihood of incidents in their local area, firefighters get into a hyper-alert readiness state and the agencies join response teams for incidents in other areas of Australia and overseas. There is not much quiet time in the cycle of a year.

The observed behaviour is an acting out of the SEEKING system. It may even lead to a kind of crisis addiction, but it also hurts the individual FEAR system. When the firefighters are not able to listen to their FEAR system, it can also lead to traumatisation as a consequence of fighting an emergency in an unknown field. And as we know, FEAR is biologically an extremely important feeling, helping us or even making us survive.

Conclusion

The useful response in today's emergency incidents is to be open to the new, and to feel your way through a problem you have never faced before. Feeling through entails more interaction with each other across hierarchical boundaries. It will be necessary in the future, when facing unusual incidents, to actively share new and different observations, to listen to each other more attentively, and to allow and encourage thinking together. Although an emergency needs fast reactions, the wrong conclusions based on past experience which do not fit in the actual situation will not be helpful or could even be fatally detrimental. To move to a new way of working organisations will need to think about how to shift their identity and the resulting organisational culture. The shadow side of the hero, denying risk and reality, has to be taken into the equation as well. In the long run, a different way of taking up the role of firefighter is required and needs to be integrated into the system, which will be a major cultural shift.

With regard to leadership one would assume that hierarchical leadership and clear authority are best in the context of an emergency, yet research in safety-critical domains (aviation, military operations, nuclear or other chemical plants, emergency health, and emergency services) has shown that successful performance relies on team members sharing what they know, speculating about what they don't, and combining different perspectives to reach a collective understanding of changing conditions.[97] Understanding the unconscious dynamics of what we have just explored may be helpful for developing that culture.

* * *

This case connects several emotional systems and shows very well the interplay between CARE, RAGE, PLAY, and SEEKING.

The following figure gives an overview of the interconnectedness of all seven systems. It summarises the links between the different emotional systems and identifies whether they are reinforcing or inhibiting each other (see Figure 16).

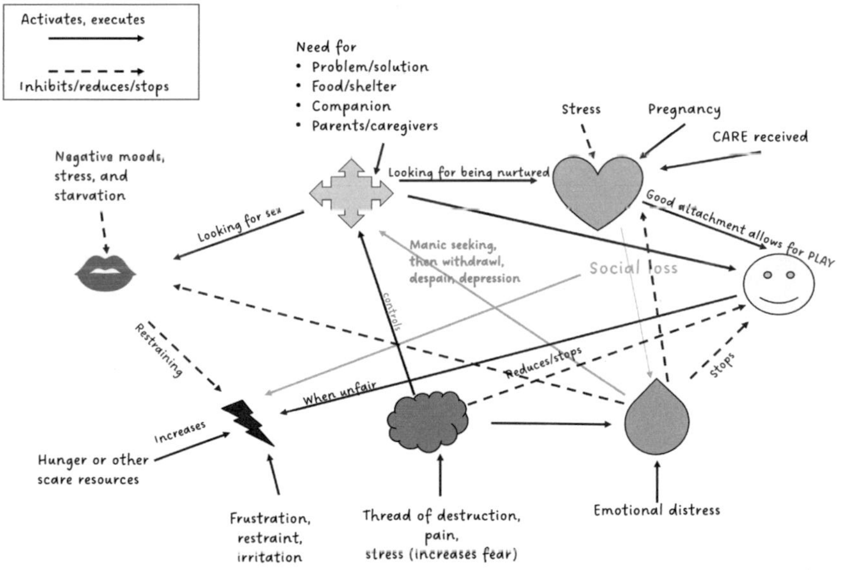

Figure 16: The interconnectedness of all seven emotional systems (author's drawing)

KEY LEARNING

You can find an overview of what leaders can do from the basic emotional system perspective to stabilise and enhance work performance in the following table.

Emotional System	Create/Avoid	Harvest/Result
SEEKING	Provide space for exploration	Innovation, new ideas, incremental change
CARE	Attitude of care towards employees and stakeholders	Safety and security, pleasure in working together
PLAY	Let others also win, turn-taking in problem-solving Create space for as-if and for cooperation	Social glue and social network which is good for collaboration
FEAR	Don't lead via pressure and anxiety to fail	Fear makes thinking and working difficult, people will try to avoid it with defences
PANIC/GRIEF	Think about the losses when things change and allow time for grieving	No grieving time means inertia and getting stuck
RAGE	Avoid giving reasons for rage by not frustrating others without need/explanation	Passive or open aggressiveness is destructive, no energy left for working
LUST	Acting out desire in a hierarchical situation should be a taboo – work on equality	Should be transformed into Eros as part of every good relationship

Figure 17: Leadership with the seven emotional systems in mind (author's compilation)

CHAPTER 5

Repeating experiences

The earliest social experiences in relating to other people are made in the family. As Ed Shapiro[98] puts it well: "Early family experience provides an initial emotional and cognitive map from which we all start in navigating our experiences in groups and organisations." This map will be enriched later with experiences with other important people like teachers, and, later, student and work colleagues, partners, etc. This is part of our human development—to enrich the map and not just stay on the familiar main roads.

These main roads design our life, and on a conscious or unconscious level we repeat family role experience in all kinds of relationships, especially with partners and in the work environment. Often, we try to solve unresolved family dynamics without realising. One of my clients has experienced a home where the general tone was always aggressive and accusatory, where one was shouted at for everything. She had two choices in her childhood: be nice and not too visible, or (verbally) fight back. This is an impossible choice, so she became emotionally ambivalent in private and organisational relationships.

Yet she is always alerted to fight back or—even better—to attack before the fight starts. This way, she continually recreates the tone and ambience of home. Learning that not everybody was prone to attack or criticise took her many years.

The Freudian oedipal triangle reflects on the relationship between the son, the father, and the mother. (It does not apply to the daughter, who, in intensely debated Freudian theory, is said to develop penis envy.) In the mythological story, Oedipus kills his father (without knowing—unconsciously), marries his mother, and has children with her. Translated into psychological life, it means the son desires the mother, envies and wants to overcome the father, yet the father remains also an authority figure—creating a dilemma for the son, not to mention the fact that the father would possibly castrate the son if he were to come too close to the mother.[99] Many Freudian analysts continue to work with this schema, whereas I would prefer to think in role archetypes, exploring their connotations and the expectations going with them.

An archetype is an image such as a holistic structure which contains good and bad aspects. Imagine the mother archetype: mothers can be warm, caring, nurturing, containing, whispering, tender, comforting, supporting, forgiving, generous … yet mothers can also be demanding, punishing, cold, yelling, screaming, unforgiving … You may list your own associations and experiences you have with your mother. These experiences, the dominant ones, are relevant to your life. The aim is to see the other aspects which you could not see or which were not there in your mother—either in your mother or in the person you are projecting motherly associations onto. The father archetype could comprise: teaching, showing, holding, generosity, or authority, telling-off, choleric, shouting, punishing. Whichever experiences you have, they will somehow be replicated in your working with and in a group. These experiences are always remembered together with an emotion, be it positive or negative.

If you look at a classical family model, a multitude of feelings is possible. Here are the most important ones in an overview of a "traditional family" structure (see Figure 18).

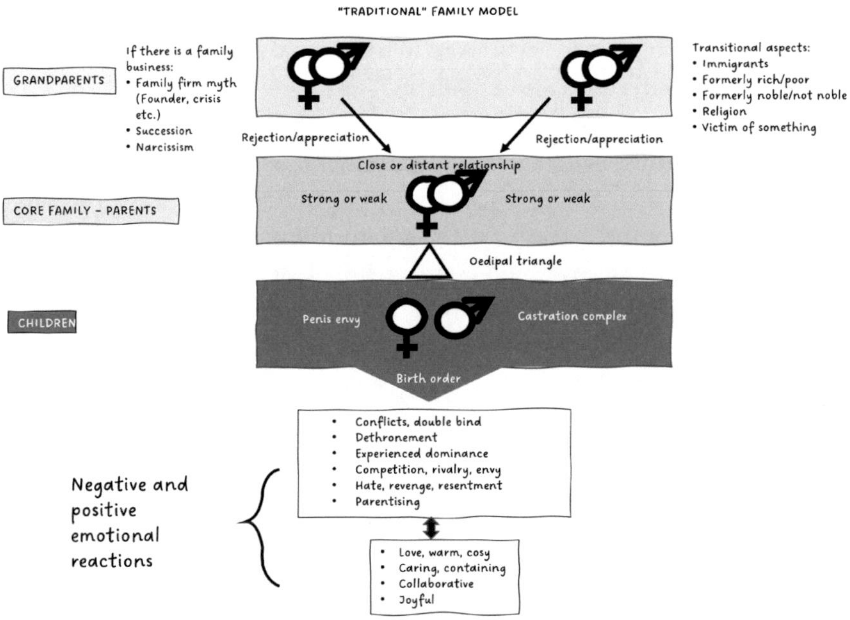

Figure 18: "Traditional" family model (author's drawing)

The emotions in the two lower boxes are crucial. They can come up on all levels. The parental pair in the middle set the tone but are influenced by their own parents and will, of course, influence their children.

The emotional relational experiences with parents will also impact how we deal with our leaders, with hierarchy, and with authority. This looking upwards is shaped by our experiences with our father and mother. The look to the side is closer to what we have experienced with siblings—the horizontal perspective. They are more likely to be found when interacting with a group as a member. Both ways, up and down, and aside, will shape your leadership style.

The relationship we have with our siblings in the family system creates the ground for our experiences with groups. Sibling relationships are extremely complex and ambiguous and not as well researched as one would expect. Siblings can be allies—extremely supportive and mutually caring—as siblings stand together against parents and the world. When these bonds between siblings get too close, sometimes no independence in adulthood is possible. The unresolved conflict between autonomy and dependence can lead to unconscious aggression, which is twisted into idealisation and altruism.[100]

On the other hand, the sibling relationship within the family is the first encounter with competition—siblings as rivals. When you have grown up in a family where the children had to fight for the love, attention, and appreciation of their parents, rivalry and envy may develop, resulting in love-hate relationships where revenge and resentment occur. In-group vs out-group dynamics can also be traced back to early and powerful sibling hate-love dynamics.[101]

> So finally, my answer to the question, how do we deal with sibling rivalry at work, is to invite you to remember that sibling relationships are passionate, volatile and intransigent, but at their best, they can teach us all the steps that are needed to co-operate creatively so that the game can go on. Infant sibling relationships contain intense love and equally violent hatred which is moderated and mediated through the help of the adults. So, in adult sibling conflict within an institution, there may be a need for an outside moderator, like a parent, to sort out the quarrel, for when sibling passions are revived at work or in the consulting room, they can knock one sideways with the unmediated quality of the encounter. For instance, when you sense your knees wobble and feel slightly sick in the pit of your stomach as you argue a point with a colleague, or when you long for an outsider to help you think through whether a critic of you is just, that is the moment when, like the uninvited guest, there may be stirring inside you some unremembered sibling conflict.[102]

Case study

Family dynamics—the hidden brothers

Claudia Nagel

Introduction

Thomas is the son of a man who owned one of the larger family businesses in the country. This family business produces technical products and the respective services to maintain and repair them. When Thomas was thirty-three years old, his father—at that time seventy-five—handed over the business to him and withdrew from the operational management of the business to the non-executive board. Before that, they had for some time been co-chairing the company.

Thomas's formative years

Thomas has a slightly younger twin brother, Michael. From early childhood on it became obvious that his brother's talent is in creative arts, in painting, drawing, writing—yet not so much in numbers, analytical thinking, and planning. He also enjoys nature and likes outdoor sports. Because of this obvious talent, which their mother had supported—initially against the will of the father, yet the mother knew how to appeal to his business instinct—it was also decided by the father that Thomas would therefore have to run the company one day. So, his father prepared him to take over the business. He was told to study business administration, did an MBA and later also a PhD, as was expected from him by his father, who has a PhD as well.

Fortunately, Thomas is a highly analytic thinker, with a brilliant mind, so he enjoyed his studies. At twenty-six, he was still very young when he finished his PhD, so it was again decided for him, before entering the family business, that he had to work in another company at an international level—not a family business, but one of the big auditing companies whose clients are international, large-scale family businesses—where he worked in the consulting branch.

He did this for almost four years and was—as to be expected—highly successful. When almost thirty years old, he entered the family business—first as CFO (the father being the CEO at the time), and three years later he became the CEO—the father was suffering poor health and had to reduce his workload—so it was time for Thomas to take over. A new CFO was also taken on.

The father

The father left big shoes to fill. He had built up the business from a small local family enterprise into a large, international, globally present firm. Although time and the economic situation helped him, he was also a highly successful entrepreneur, developing new products and services and expanding globally. At the same time he was a good manager. This is a rather unusual combination, but the father seems to have inherited his business acumen from his own father and, since he is very intelligent, was also good in building up and managing structures and processes. He reigned with an authoritative leadership style and his ability to delegate got better with the years. The family, but he in particular, also made big philanthropic donations in their region. Employees were supported and taken care of in a patron-like style. Whole families worked in the company—the company is highly reputable, the name stands for job security and fair payment. At the dinner table, when business friends were invited, which happened often, the major topic of conversation was the business and the economic situation.

Thomas as CEO

We are now in year three of Thomas's CEO-ship and I will describe what has been happening over these last three years, with Thomas and with his CFO.

Thomas feels the burden of his father's legacy. He wants to be as successful as his father, but also thinks that the company now has to be run differently, as times have changed and the authoritative leadership style no longer works. Furthermore, the economic environment is changing, and the product range, once so successful, is losing market share; the cash-cow product is not as sought after as it once was. The market wants new products which are not yet fully developed. So, you can imagine, Thomas's anxiety is rather high—he does not want to disappoint his father and he cannot bear to imagine an outcome where his company is not the biggest employer in the region and disappoint all the families dependent on the well-being of the company.

His way of coping with his anxiety is to micromanage the management team, especially Robert, the CFO. He often intervenes in the operational management of the finances, bypassing him in doing so. He criticises Robert in front of the whole management team, questions his decisions, and starts to talk directly with the department leaders. He also asks them additional questions to analyse this and that and go into more detail here and there—everything at extremely short notice, which adds to the workload of everybody working in the finance department. The staff start to feel at unease and controlled, their anxiety level also rises, and the mood in the formerly contented finance department starts to deteriorate. The information the CFO needs from his people is becoming less accurate under the additional pressure and the CEO accuses the CFO of not running his department properly. The CFO himself is becoming insecure and wonders whether he is the right person in the right company—he is starting to think about leaving the company.

At the same time, Thomas has set up a big cultural change programme to move towards more agile management methods. For that purpose, he has hired an experienced HR manager in the HR board position, a very creative and unconventional woman, with good ideas. But it seems that this cultural change is stuck as well. Thomas has intervened in her change plan, has questioned major steps she had planned, and—although she had asked for more support staff—has left her with a very small team, which is effectively too small to facilitate the intended changes within the whole company. Thomas is becoming dissatisfied and is starting to look for a new HR board member.

Analysis

What we can observe here is a typical case where the relationships with the parents and the sibling influence the well-being and the success of the company.

Thomas compensates for his own anxiety of failure and the fear of disappointing his strong and strict father by himself becoming overly strict and micromanaging. He is not only afraid of disappointing his father but also of losing the company, and by that the family fortune (although their family fortune had been diversified and is not only invested in their own company). Micromanagement gives him the feeling of being in control. This is what he needs, since his father is having regular meetings and still has an office next to Thomas's. Thomas's working hours are getting longer and longer and he has the expectation of his board colleagues to put in the same time and energy as he does. Yet, some of his colleagues are older than him and no longer have the physical ability to concentrate and work the sixteen-hour days demanded of them.

In parallel, Thomas is acting out his anxiety in setting up a large-scale change programme—at a time when the external environment is shifting, and one would question from an economic perspective whether this is the right moment to make such change.

The CFO is normally a relaxed and flexible person. His people like him because he sets the frame for their work but lets them make decisions and expects only that they report their results—his leadership style is the opposite of Thomas's, he is far from micromanaging his team.

Thomas's criticism is affecting Robert. He who has always managed to give his people a good feeling is now making devaluing remarks and shows an arrogance and distance which has not been present in his leadership before. Like Thomas, he had a father who criticised him often, so he never felt good enough. And like Thomas he has a brother who is very successful at what he does; the brother is more charming than he is, convinces people more easily, and is an excellent salesperson. Robert had come to terms with this relationship and developed beyond it, he thought. Yet under time pressure and criticism from Thomas this old anxiety has re-emerged and he has become aggressive, cynical, and angry.

What helps him—and that is part of the intervention—is to understand the level of anxiety which Thomas is hiding from himself and his management team. When understanding that he could adapt to Thomas's reactions without overreacting himself, the relationship between the two changes significantly, they start to have more open conversations, and the empathy Robert can now bring to Thomas and his leadership also helps Thomas.

The HR director was dismissed. She did not get the chance to show how her way of initiating change could have brought the needed agility to the company. Thomas treated her as he would have wanted to treat his brother when he was younger—just get rid of him. He had always felt a strong rivalry with his brother who got the motherly attention, the attention he thought he was himself deprived of. The motherly love went to his brother because of his artistic side, and he received only the love of the strong and authoritative father. This love was well hidden and only showed itself in little moments of pride when Thomas did something extremely well. The constant anxiety his father instilled in him makes him a hard-working, demanding, and controlling CEO. So, in refusing to give the support needed by the HR director, with her unconventional ideas and her creativity—a bit like his brother, Thomas ensured she was not allowed to be successful and became the unwanted representation and projection surface for his brother. This relationship could not be saved; the intervention came too late for that. Yet, in hindsight, Thomas starts to understand more about the hidden dynamics of his family life.

* * *

In this case the family dynamics play out between the son Thomas and his father, and between Thomas and his brother—an unspoken competition around the love of the mother. Robert also has a sibling issue, which he knows of and has been talking about in his coaching in the past; however, it is still reactivated under high pressure and stress.

Birth order

Birth order—the real or the experienced—is said to influence personality traits as well. Alfred Adler was the first to research this subject.[103] Any place in the birth order can develop into a strength or a weakness.

Firstborn children often have to take care of their younger sibling and thus develop a sense of responsibility. Yet they often fear dethronement when the first sibling arrives. This is a painful process and might create a narcissistic vulnerability.[104] This explains why they often develop into competitive high achievers and perfectionists and end up in leadership positions.

The second-born child strives to dethrone the first, and enters into competition with the older sibling, often looking for a different niche—when the firstborn is doing well academically the second might become a sports champion, often in a team sports, since they tend to be more socially competent. Finding a niche for developing an individual identity and role in the family is important for all siblings and helps to reduce competition.

Middle children feel sandwiched in a position where they are squeezed from both sides. They are interested in fairness and social justice and thus might follow a career in negotiations. Yet they can have difficulty developing a sense of belonging to the family.

The youngest child, the baby or the little princess/prince is often pampered by the rest of the family, especially when there is a significant age gap between the youngest and the next-older sibling. They can be charming and outgoing and develop their social skills from continuous observation of their elder siblings.

An only child without siblings is more used to dealing with adults, since he or she is constantly surrounded by them. This helps in the development of verbal and other skills and maturity. They have and gain attention, and later expect the attention to come to them when they want it.

Every firstborn was once an only child and has had to adapt to the new position, just as the second can become a middle child. Much younger last-borns can also perceive themselves as an only child.

Transference and countertransference

As Kets de Vries (2004)[105] puts it, "No relationship [in life] is a new relationship, each relationship is colored by previous relationships." All our encounters with others are informed and imprinted by our early and earliest relationships. When arguing about budgets with colleagues or about strategy with your board colleagues, you are unknowingly dealing with your siblings and parents over power and unresolved conflicts. This process is called "transference", which means that one confuses time and space, and instead of reacting to the person in front of us we are reacting to what this person reminds us of and thus reactivates in us—such as our dominant elder brother, our devaluing father: we reproduce the same feelings which we had with them in early childhood.

This process never stops and continues throughout our whole lives; the only way to deal with it is to acknowledge it—first as a possibility that may occur, then, with a bit of training, we can recognise the pattern of action, and then in a later stage we are able to change the behaviour and devise a new way of reacting in these kinds of situations.

Countertransference goes one step further in our mind, as here we experience feelings of the other which do not belong to us. For example, we may feel a sudden anxiety when talking with someone who is about to make a risky decision and is unconsciously pushing aside his or her own anxiety.

Two types of transference patterns are most often found in organisations—mirroring and idealisation.[106] Followers want to be mirrored—they want to be seen by their leaders as they once wanted to be seen by their parental figures (we discussed this in Chapter 1); they want to be appreciated and valued for their contribution. For followers, mirroring is a way of transferring the mirroring caregiver relationship to the leader. In doing so, they use their leaders as mirrors of what they want to see, and the leader, who enjoys this positive reaction to him, is flattered and cannot easily resist this admiration.

Admiration goes hand-in-hand with the second transference mechanism, known as idealisation. This process is a defence mechanism and protects our psyche and our self-image, particularly when we are feeling helpless—this can be compared to the early helplessness of an infant, and we "see" some powerful and ideal aspects of the caregiver become embodied in the leader. For the leader, this can be quite seductive, and as a leader you may tend to attribute to yourself more ideal qualities then you might have in real life. So, please check your openness and readiness for such kind of seduction.

In performing this idealisation-transference we shield ourselves against the unpleasant feeling of not being able to cope on our own and take in some of the power of the leader. Shielding and protecting ourselves from unpleasant feelings is an important task of three other important basic defence mechanisms: projection, splitting, and introjection. These protect us against inner or outer threats (a conflict, an unpleasant colleague, a difficult leader) and against anxiety, stress, and pain. They are very powerful psychic tools which work underneath the level of consciousness—that is why self-awareness and self-reflection are so important for leaders. I find them descriptive in themselves, but we will explore them together. Here I cannot spare you these technical terms: they are important for a deeper understanding of the conscious and especially unconscious mechanisms at work.

When projecting, or externalising something internal, one "throws" (*jacere* is Latin for throwing) unpleasant, unwanted aspects of oneself onto another person, to find them in the other person and react to them with irritation, failing to admit or recognise them as one's own. Projection can take different forms:

- You transmit and thus "see" aspects of an inner figure such as a parent in an outer person (e.g. the male boss in his behaviour is perceived as and confused with the father, and the individual reacts to these aspects as if they were real).
- You see yourself as if you were the other (e.g. when identifying yourself with a character in a book).
- You see and seize the world from a very individual perspective which shapes your whole perception (e.g. professional deformation—as a psychologist you only see psychic problems in other people, as a painter you look for gaps in paintwork).
- You attribute denied aspects of yourself to another person and deal with them as a "straw man" instead of acknowledging them as components of your own self.[107]

These different forms of projection share both the externalising of an inner aspect and its identification in another person, a construct, or a real thing. By inner aspect, I refer to any representation of inner life—an experience, a feeling, an attitude, a trait, a dream, a wish, a relationship, etc. Projections have a role in normal psychic reactions but can also emerge as a defensive reaction. A simple way of recognising that one is in "projection mode" is noticing when one becomes very irritated and angry with another person. One can then assume that one is projecting an unpleasant and unwanted aspect of oneself onto the other. Traits or behaviours of this other person may also invite this projection. Jung refers to this as a "hook" for the projection onto the other.[108]

A subcategory of projections that plays a crucial role in management is projective identification. This term was coined by Melanie Klein[109] to describe a process by which the separated content projected onto another person is unconsciously accepted by this person, who then identifies with this inner aspect that did not originate from themselves. We've talked about it already—when you identify with an idealising projection, for example. This may sound peculiar, yet it is a common occurrence (it can also be actively affected with subtle or even explicit manipulation). For example, a feeling of grandiosity or the opposite feeling of guilt that an individual cannot perceive or recognise in themselves is separated and projected onto someone else. This target of projection then makes it their own, and as a consequence acquires this feeling of omnipotence or guilt.

Splitting uses mechanisms such as denial and suppression to cut off inner or outer reality and relocate it elsewhere. One separates within oneself into good and bad, and the bad part is split off so one stays with the good part only—this feels much better than trying to admit that these bad parts are part of one's self.

Denial and suppression work as defences as well. Denial is the refusal to accept reality or an aspect of reality, whereas suppression is understood as holding off or pushing away unpleasant aspects.

The concept of introjection, first developed by Sándor Ferenzci[110] and later used by Freud, can be understood as complementary to projection. In simple terms, "good" things (feeling competent or wanting to be kind) are (mostly) introjected, which means they are assimilated as an aspect of the self, and "bad" things (e.g. anger, aggression) are projected to the outside world.

The emotional relational experiences you have in your life also determine which kind of defences you use. Our psychic system is well equipped to help us not to have too many negative feelings since this would endanger our self-image. It protects us against inner (i.e. self-image) or outer threats resulting often in fear, anxiety, and other pains. Yet these feelings are there, in our mind and in our body, so we would be better off knowing about them than having them warded off. Such warding off may have helped during the helplessness and powerlessness felt as a child, but in the adult world it can be dysfunctional and even destructive.

KEY LEARNING

- The quality of our early childhood relations with parental figures and siblings determines how we relate later in life with other people in a social context, in organisations as well as in private life.
- The psychic mechanisms which are there to protect our inner well-being and our identity stem from these early relational patterns.
- Self-awareness and self-consciousness help us to develop a broader repertoire of reactions in order to overcome the first patterns and not be stuck in unhelpful initial and later reactive patterns.

CHAPTER 6

Do women lead differently, and do they want to lead?

What is your expectation when you read this question? And does the answer depend on whether you as a reader are a man or a woman?

Although the same question could be asked of men, it is not asked that often, and there are reasons for this. From both groups, male and female, some would say yes, others no, and others would say it depends. Yet the size of the male group differs from the female group, and we all know which one will be larger—isn't that so? Many people still believe that women are "opting out" for family reasons—yet this is not true. Only around 10 per cent of women take leave to stay at home to take care of children. The rest stay in part-time or full-time work but must suffer many compromises in the job and often cannot find their way back to the intellectual, financial, and emotional fulfilment and advancement which they had been aiming for before having children. This often happens in indirect ways: the fact that women, for example, are not considered "key players" is communicated in various, sometimes subtle ways. They may have been stigmatised for taking advantage of flexible or reduced schedules, passed over for high-profile assignments, or removed from projects they once led.[111]

In 2021, 26 per cent of all CEOs and managing directors (not only of listed companies) were women, compared to only 15 per cent in 2019.[112] And thanks to nine new entries, the *Fortune* Global 500 reported twenty-three women CEOs in 2021, including six women of colour.[113] Although this is celebrated as an all-time high, the numbers are rather sad. Among the largest publicly listed companies in the twenty-seven countries of the European Union in 2021, only 20.2 per cent of executives and 7.8 per cent of CEOs were women.[114] A 2020 analysis by Mercer of over 1,100 organisations across the world found a leaky pipeline for women in leadership:[115]

- Executives: 23%
- Senior managers: 29%
- Managers: 37%
- Professionals: 42%
- Support staff: 47%.[116]

Why is that so? Over the last twenty years much has been written about this and not much has changed.

I would like to give a short overview of reasons for the gender leadership gap in its complexity and then explore what we as female and male leaders can contribute from our leading with depth perspective. Figure 19 gives an overview of the factors influencing and maintaining the gap.

We have three main players in the field: first the self, representing the female (potential) leader who has to choose, and next to it, in brackets, the male leader influencing her choice of wanting to become a leader; second, we have the other, which is any other person or group of people, such as men, other women, mothers, fathers, employers, company owners etc.; and as the third player we have society as a larger system to which the other(s) belong and which constitutes a larger body.

These three entities are mutually influencing each other—the boundaries are blurred and not as clear-cut as they appear here in the drawing. In addition, we can assume two levels for each player: a conscious level on which people think they make their decisions, and an unconscious level. For our work here, the unconscious level is more compelling. In addition, we often find rationalisations on the conscious level which are covering up an unconscious motivation for rejecting or not admitting women to the top of organisations (see Figure 19).

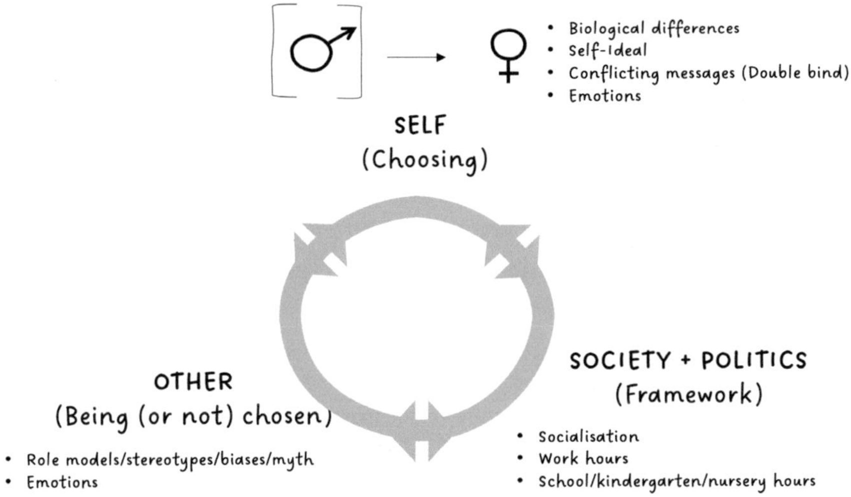

Figure 19: Factors for the gender leadership gap (author's drawing)

"Society and politics" provide the framework in which organisations employ people. This system is of course influenced by the perceptions of politicians and government and the people that vote for them. The point which I will be making concerning the others is that they are influencing societal choices; for example, stereotypes about women being responsible for care work because of their nurturing quality, therefore they must care for children while men (in politics) create the conceptual framework for nurseries, kindergarten, and the school system—which depending on the opening hours could allow for both parents to work, or not. And due to this system, which is not equally well-developed in all countries, either parents can both freely choose, or one parent must adapt more to the opening hours than the other—which then, due to the role stereotype, is still often the mother.

The alternative for some women is to not have children so as to become free and flexible in their career choices. Socialisation, which stands for all social aspects of influencing the upbringing of children, is also important. For example, school systems which allow a choice between boys-only and girls-only schools have proven that women educated in an all-girls' school often show more independence from societal ideas when choosing their profession. All-girls' schools often aim to overcome social and cultural gender biases, which helps women to find their place and develop their full potential instead of adhering to stereotypical norms. In the absence of boys, they develop more self-confidence, self-esteem, and show greater determination.

An important aspect of separate school education is the factor of competition. In all-girls' schools, girls are naturally allowed to compete against each other and to learn that failure and standing up again are part of the game. In mixed schools, girls are often still not allowed to compete, but have to behave nicely and in a socially acceptable manner and leave the sphere of open competition to the boys. Instead of open competition, hidden competition can be observed between the girls: competition to be the most attractive, most beautiful, most wanted for friendship. Open competition is certainly a healthier way to learn that winning or failing are just part of life and not the only aspect of being a lovable and valuable person.

Socialisation is not only influenced by school education but also by implicit public education through all kinds of consumer marketing and sales activities using gender stereotypes. So even if parents are open-minded and the ambience at home allows for intellectual freedom and choice for the girl, the societal environmental factors are still creating a strong imprint which would need to be continually reflected on in order to overcome its powerful grip and influence.

The "other" here stands for the person who is judging whether a woman is allowed or even wants to become a leader in an organisation. The other is acting out and applying role models, gender stereotypes, biases, and myth, all of which are accompanied by emotions—consciously and unconsciously.

One typical explanation for not seeing enough women at the top is saying that there are not enough female role models—which seems to be a "nice try" to excuse the gap and to abstain from taking any action to change it. These people using the role-model argument are giving evolutionary justifications (hunters vs gatherers), yet "forgetting" the active role women played in hunting in many foraging societies and also in matriarchal societies.

Stereotypes

Multiple gender stereotypes exist which make it difficult for women to be chosen for or to stay in leadership positions. One very basic and persistent stereotype is male agency vs female communion. When referring male agency to relationships, for men, competition is permitted and seen as fun, verbal aggression is allowed and up to a certain degree OK, and listening is of secondary importance to being assertive. For women, we hear the opposite: competition is unwomanly, and aggression is unwomanly or hysterical, and social communication and empathy are expected. In couple relationships, men (often have to) take care of the finances, create security, take care of technical aspects, computers, cars, soccer, whereas women (often have to) provide emotional security and mother men and children, and take care of the household, children, and social relationships.[117]

The problem with stereotypes is that they are so schematic that most would say "no, these convictions are far from my own". That will also occur to you when reading the stereotypes—and I am also convinced that you are different, but many are not. In addition, the Implicit Association Test (IAT)[118] shows that there is a gap between what you say you think and your more implicit thoughts. When openly asked whether women or men are more effective leaders, only 20 per cent said that men were better leaders, 60 per cent stayed neutral, and 11 per cent claimed women to be more effective; the implicit associations revealed that 50 per cent implicitly believed men to be more effective leaders, 25 per cent were neutral, and 25 per cent held that women are more effective leaders. It seems that unconscious biases as well as social desirability have influenced these answers.[119,120] In another study using the IAT, women are associated with followers, whereas men are associated with leadership.[121]

Looking at more general role expectations and staying within the dichotomy of agency vs community, men can claim that career is important, power/money/success makes them sexy, and being successful means standing in the front row of organisations. For women, power/money and success are said to make them lonely, career is less important than sense and purpose, and women should stand in the second row or behind (a successful man).

Men are allowed to overestimate their own capabilities when applying for a new job; they are hired for potential, whereas women are hired for what they have achieved.[122] Unfortunately, potential is rated higher as a predictor of future success. Men need to be assertive: it is acceptable behaviour and they are allowed to use their elbows to get ahead. They (still) think that there is no space for emotion in business and are often successful when applying an authoritarian, performance and task-oriented leadership style.

Women are told to be modest, humble, undemanding, and not pushy (which is a translation for unwanted female assertiveness). And because women can communicate better, they must deal with soft (less important) factors. Women also pay too much heed to emotions (and not to the task) and their leadership style has to be participative and integrating.

Some of these attitudes seem to be challenged by Generation Z, who are asking for a better work–life balance and more focus on purpose than on money—this works well as long as they are still studying or when they have their first child. Later, when the second child is born, the more traditional role model comes into being—demonstrated also during Covid-19 times—where working women again took over more of the care, cooking, teaching, and so on at home.

Myths about women's difficulties

Several myths and metaphors are also standing in the way of women's rise to the top: the glass ceiling, the glass slipper, the sticky floor, and the labyrinth. The glass ceiling represents the invisible obstacle women collide with when aiming for executive positions. The glass slipper stands for the ascribed lower interest in personal power when women are associating male partners with heroism and chivalry.[123] The sticky floor is a metaphor for obstacles women face at the beginning of their leadership career, whereas the labyrinth is a complex and ambivalent metaphor for the difficulties in reaching the top.

Since the use of metaphors can transform how people perceive, think, and act, it is very important to find the right one for prevailing in a specific organisation. This could then be helpful for becoming aware and changing the organisation. Yet, metaphors supporting stereotypical judgements are adding additional negativity to the hurdles to be overcome.

The associations of all the metaphors mentioned above are primarily negative:

- Glass can be associated with fragility (women are too fragile) but also with destruction and wounds. These wounds can impair and deface the women breaking through the glass ceiling.
- The sticky floor metaphor sounds similar to "stinking floor"—very unpleasant and thus full of mud where you rather get drained and drown.
- The glass slipper is a fairy tale reference reminding us of Cinderella and a princess, which have nothing to do with the hard work of leadership.
- The metaphor of a labyrinth which a woman may conquer unfortunately alludes to helping the male leader, just like Theseus was helped by Ariadne's red thread to kill the Minotaur. This is not a pleasant image either, because after Ariadne was supportive as women have to be, she is abandoned on an island by Theseus, despite his promises to marry her.

Although these metaphors were intended to create awareness of women's difficulties in getting to the top, they also created mythical evidence for a hostile environment which in a way can only be overcome by a fairy-tale miracle and not hard work and performance.

Other myths are disguised as rational arguments. For example: women have no experience in leading a complex organisation, leadership does not function part-time, women do not want to become leaders, there aren't enough qualified women, the quota reduced the quality even more, and so on. Some have lost their impact, but many of these arguments are still used today.

In addition to these stereotypes and myths we can also see some biases at work when hiring for leadership positions. The most important in this field are central tendency, the halo effect, the logical error, and the mirror-image error:

- *Central tendency*: the tendency to choose the mean value over the extremes (for which you would need more explanation)
- *Logical error*: the tendency to link two unconnected aspects in judgement as if they were logically connected (appearance and performance, rhetoric and abstract thinking)

- *Halo effect*: the tendency to assume that a person who performs well (or poorly) in one area, also performs well (or poorly) in other areas
- *Mirror-image error*: the tendency to use oneself as starting point: "I am good so the other has to be like me" (recruiting in one's own image).

Biases can reduce complexity and be helpful heuristics, but they can also hinder good decision-making. We will investigate them a bit further in the next chapter. We also saw that biases have a psychological protective function against pain and anxiety. So, we are now approaching one of the more interesting questions: which emotions stand behind all the judgements?

We can assume that men and women have different, often unconscious reasons for not correcting their stereotypical judgements and behaviours. The strongest and most unconscious emotion for men is their multifaceted anxiety, and this presents itself in many different ways, some more obvious than others:

- Men are afraid of losing their power, their position, status, and identity.
- Men are afraid of being confronted by their own (punishing) mother figure because of their projected experiences with their mothers, grandmothers, and sisters.[124]
- Men are afraid of being seduced by female Eros.
- Men are afraid of losing their specific club atmosphere with a specific Eros which only takes place between men and their "brothers" in a "*Männerbund*", a specific secret society only for men and bound by an oath.
- Men are afraid of women as the other—one who thinks and behaves differently and is therefore not easy to understand.

I have also observed women expressing opposition to there being more female leaders in the world of business and politics. Some are also sabotaging themselves, which we will shortly explore a bit further. Such unconscious anxieties include the following:

- Women want to be mothers only and think of female executives as "*Rabenmütter*"

- Women are afraid of power and the respective loneliness at the top
- Women are afraid of not being loved anymore
- Women are afraid of not surviving in a man's world
- Women are afraid of their father's ego.

Further emotions may arise, such as:

- Failing is perceived as an existential threat
- Guilt and shame when letting others take care of their children.

These anxieties on both sides are very powerful hurdle creators for women in top positions. Facing them can be a shameful and unpleasant process—yet it needs to be done.

The front against women in leadership positions built up by "the other" and by society is, as you can see, very strong and has a huge impact on the individual woman and her individual self.

The fact that there is a biological difference between men and women cannot be denied—women give birth to children after nine months of pregnancy and can breastfeed them. Over this pregnancy and feeding, a special bond develops between the infant and the mother, yet the caregiving function, which is important for attachment, cannot solely be executed by the mother—fathers, grandparents, uncles and aunts, and professionals can all take over or at least take part. Many studies have demonstrated that children do not suffer when they are well taken care of by others—so there is no need for her 24/7 attendance. However, the self-ideal cannot stay uninfluenced by the surrounding context we have just analysed. This may lead to women wanting to be both the perfect mother and the perfect leader—an impossible demand on themselves; "good enough" in both would be largely OK. I have always thought that we will only reach equality when we have as many incapable women in top leadership positions as there are incapable men—yet this seems to be an unrealistic goal for the near future. Often, we can observe women self-sabotaging to avoid the claimed choice.

In addition, women seem to be in multiple double-bind situations. By "double bind" I refer to the impasse faced by most women: when they take agency they are easily seen as being too tough, too assertive, too aggressive or strident, whereas when they focus on communal behaviour they are seen as being too nice or too soft, not tough enough.[125] This is complemented by the expectation of men, who are allowed and supposed to be both (authoritarian and participative). Women shall not be authoritarian, because then they are perceived as being pushy and aggressive.

The fear of not being liked and loved as a strong leader and the myth that only men are born leaders add to a specific amalgam of emotions. It spans anger, frustration, and disappointment of the other and also of oneself, completed by feelings of shame and guilt, fear of failure and rejection—both consciously and unconsciously. How can anyone perform on task if the context and the others provoke this complex set of feelings?

The following case will showcase some of the issues women encounter when aiming for leadership.

Case study

A woman in leadership—facing up to family socialisation and stereotypes

Rob Ryan

This case study reflects the complex dynamics present in this and other work systems, and the challenges in understanding them to enable productive interventions via the medium of coaching and organisational role analysis. The experiences of a female leader and the possible implications for the influence of gender on female leadership are both important dimensions of this case study.

As is often the case, the initial presenting problem is a manifestation of previously unrecognised deeper challenges. I am also describing the ways in which an initial coaching task can evolve with the emergence of underlying complexities, including role and systemic issues, during the course of the coaching programme.

Introduction—the who, what, and why?

I worked with Sarah as her coach for a period of about eighteen months. She was a very skilled and experienced middle-aged senior manager, and we met monthly for a total of twenty sessions. We met only on Zoom, primarily because she was based in another part of the country.

I have been working as a psychoanalytic consultant and coach for the past twenty-one years. Sarah initially contacted me via my website, and we agreed to work together, initially for six sessions.

She was working in a large debt collection agency which focused on retrieving unpaid employee pension entitlements—the primary purpose of the organisation was to collect these payments from large, non-compliant employer organisations.

In the initial contracting conversation she described the issue to be explored as one which involved her leading a project of organisational transformation in the agency—and that she had emerging ambivalent and conflicted feelings about it.

She said that she was looking for a "safe harbour" to reflect, debrief, and learn about her experiences of the work transformation project.

The how?

It was with this background context that we met on Zoom for ninety-minute sessions. The first three sessions were held two weeks apart, then monthly. After the end of the six sessions, we continued to meet monthly.

Our earlier meetings were characterised by Sarah giving long descriptions of her various working experiences with the project. Usually, she was very polite and engaging, while also appearing very "flat", with little expression of emotions. I could see that these detailed, transactionally focused descriptions were important for her to provide, because she described them as lightening her burden.

It seems to me that the Zoom context was ideal for her to mask difficult emotions which were out of her awareness at the time. It also meant that I had no other source of data about the organisation—I was limited to her verbal descriptions of her experiences in it, without any other visual data.

I also struggled in my role to stay fully present to her in the face of copious detailed descriptions. I would say such things as: "I notice you are giving a detailed description here again, but let's just pause and reflect on the fact that I asked you to describe your feelings. It seems to be difficult for you."

In hearing her stories, I found myself feeling outraged at the described injustices in her experiences—I was occasionally emotionally "drawn in" to judgement of the organisation rather than continuing to remain curious about it. I occasionally used uncharacteristically strong language in response to her stories—I surprised myself. My hunch is that

I was unconsciously being mobilised to express strong emotion because it was too difficult for her to do so on her own behalf.

Overall, my working hypothesis was that she had some very strongly repressed emotions which were being held down so tightly that they were difficult for her to feel, acknowledge, and explore.

Eventually, she agreed with this hypothesis as an accurate reflection of her experience.

Her experience of leadership

Sense of purpose

In our first few sessions, we clearly established that Sarah's primary sense of meaning and purpose at work was to contribute to the long-term well-being of all employees in the not-for-profit sector which her agency serviced. In particular, a focus was on supporting those groups of employees who had little individual power, for them to gain rightful access to their withheld employer-paid, pension benefits. Addressing ongoing worker inequality was also evident in her previous senior roles in other organisations.

She was concerned about the well-being of her own agency staff group, whom she described as having previously been poorly supported in their professional development.

She concluded that a dependence culture had developed whereby staff felt disempowered—collaboration, creativity, and professional growth had been largely absent. She wanted to change this, but also felt conflicted because she also knew that some staff would be made redundant, without an opportunity for her to redress the perceived wrongs that they had experienced.

Paradoxes emerge

Sarah's emotional pain was heightened as she contemplated one sure outcome of the project's change process—the forced redundancy of about ten people from a total workforce of forty.

However, she had great difficulty acknowledging and naming her pain. She often seemed flooded by her anxiety and was caught up in detailed, transactionally focused descriptions of events. I experienced these as a distraction from difficult feelings, and that therefore she struggled to process them and develop useful insights into their deeper meaning and significance.

Sarah seemed torn between working with the destabilising impacts of the project on staff morale and her feeling empathy for staff, while simultaneously describing them as too well-paid to be motivated to change their ways of working. It was as if she needed to correct the negative aspects of the change process on staff by being a more compassionate presence in the role. However, she was internally conflicted because she was also blaming the staff even though they were victims of an inadequate work system and performance.

There seemed to be a debilitating impact on staff caused by their previous manager's behaviour, and presumably other contributing, but less well-acknowledged systemic forces also. He was described as "command-and-control" in style, not addressing the shortcomings in the workplace, and being complicit in preventing development of the individual staff, as well as the staff group as a whole. No staff performance challenges were addressed—including his own.

So, we had a situation where an experienced woman leader was hired to lead a change process—part of which was to rectify the impact of the previous poor performance of a male leader. This poor performance was never formally recognised, acknowledged, or acted on within the agency.

Perhaps here we have an example of characteristically nurturing and humanistic behaviours, often attributed to women leaders, being in conflict with more mechanistic, urgent task imperatives of the organisation. However, it is unwise to make the assumption that females and males have inherently different leadership characteristics. There are many complex dimensions to how leadership is taken up by different people and different gender identities. Gender stereotyping and socialisation have a powerful impact on the perceptions and practice of leadership.

This case study illustrates that gender analysis of leadership styles is useful but complex, and simplistic stereotypes cannot adequately account for the way different women take on leadership roles.

There is strong evidence that Sarah brought a particular quality to her work, as many staff (including those in other agency teams) sought her counsel regularly because of her empathic approach. These supportive behaviours were previously lacking for this work group. This role of being the "behind the scenes" support person seems to have been present in her previous work roles in other organisations too.

As commented earlier, this supportive behaviour is often associated with women in leadership roles in the workplace and aligns with the general caring role women are socialised to take on. I sensed that Sarah had readily taken on this role, and this was appreciated by staff.

At the same time, it was also evident that she struggled to be self-empathic, and also seemed to be absorbing the high anxiety which was present in the organisation. This reflected a level of perfectionism as well as a reluctance to trust her staff via appropriate delegation. She worked long hours—every night and weekends—often eighty-plus hours each week with little respite. My question to her would be, could she ever be just "good enough"?

As we discussed these difficult feelings, it suddenly emerged that Sarah was morbidly fearful of being sacked for inadequate performance. It is ironic that she was being asked to terminate others who failed to satisfy the agency's performance metrics but who had also been betrayed by the agency. This theme illustrates another important dimension of her experience—that of her relationship with her supervisor—Ruth, the CEO.

Role tensions and holding

Exploration of this relationship with Ruth seemed to illustrate many aspects of the work system and Sarah's experiences of it.

Our early sessions were centred on Sarah's anxiety about the project, but it slowly became clear that a key challenge was her relationship with Ruth. I see that the dynamics of this relationship were systemic. They were also indicative of Sarah's underlying personal and role challenges, and the different ways each took up her leadership roles.

Sarah experienced Ruth as lacking empathy, sometimes micro-managing, and difficult to predict. In her interactions with Ruth, Sarah frequently lost her sense of personal and role authority—exemplified by her incapacity to respond to Ruth's sniping questions and acerbic judgementalism in their meetings. Sarah lost her voice, metaphorically speaking.

Examples cited from statements by Ruth were:

> "Get on with it ..."
> "I'm accountable to the board and I'm under pressure."

For Sarah, this reflected Ruth's unwillingness and/or incapacity to support her in the difficult project leadership role. Ruth seemingly had little interest in understanding the nuances and challenges presented by the project, which, arguably, reflected years of neglect by the organisation. This heightened Sarah's anxiety and her need to get everything done perfectly. She felt unsupported and feared that her role would be terminated.

Ruth exemplified the emotionally distanced characteristics of the work system and showed some behaviours of a "command-and-control" manager. I think she was now more strongly representing this style in the work system, which already had a well-established work culture embracing "command and control". This was also illustrated by the previous male manager's approach to the role. Once again, this is indicative of how gender stereotypes may have been contributing to a range of complex organisational dynamics.

My hypothesis is that Ruth also experienced her own role tension and anxiety, as evidenced by her micromanagement and incapacity to empathise with Sarah's vulnerability. In our coaching sessions we spent a lot of time reflecting on Ruth's behaviour, her emotional distancing and its implications, and developing Sarah's strategies to work more productively with it.

The two women leaders behaved and managed their anxieties very differently, with Ruth's behaviour amplifying Sarah's vulnerability and effectively denying her needs.

The system selects ...

Earlier, I described Sarah's recognised capacity to support and empathise with staff's emotions, while simultaneously distancing herself from her own emotional experience. Through using a role biography exploration, we established that Sarah's family of origin had a strong culture of denying vulnerability, with an emphasis on task completion ("getting on with the job"), even in the face of significant illness or incapacity. Sarah had chronic, serious health issues.

So, individual physical and emotional needs were denied and a sense of duty to others was highly valued. My working hypothesis was that the work system unconsciously selected her for the project management role, given that the work culture seemed to be one where the sentient needs of staff were not met—there was a systemic emotional deficit. A female leader with a capacity to support staff, who works ridiculous hours and does not directly challenge the systemic shortcomings, was an "ideal" candidate. In addition, it may well be that Sarah "selected" a role which, perversely, replicated her family of origin dynamics.

Significant moments and inferences

Sarah's anxiety about the project and making people redundant was the presenting challenge initially in our early coaching sessions, but it gradually became clearer that the relationship with Ruth, and Sarah losing her voice, reflected a more profound challenge. A key underlying question for Sarah was: "Am I good enough here?" It seemed that her previous career successes at being the self-described "problem fixer" could not sustain her in this agency. She observed: "I'm terrified that I will become irrelevant and be made redundant."

This fear replicated the experiences of her staff who were judged to be unnecessary or inadequate, and hence were to be made redundant.

She described a lot of mechanistic analysis of people's work performance—linked mainly to the agency's focus on revenue returns to the organisation. There was high reliance on the service's performance metrics, without any evidence of exploration of systemic influences. In a sense it was a case of staff being blamed, with the systemic impediments to performance never having been allowed for or addressed.

Sarah also blamed herself for any mistakes. We discussed the perversity of her overcompensating to prove she wasn't physically inadequate—it represented a denial of her own vulnerability in the extreme, and no doubt contributed to her extended suffering. She often felt outraged that the system (via Ruth) didn't look after her physical and emotional needs.

Throughout our sessions, she saw herself as consistently failing to achieve a work–life balance and underrating her own competence and capacity. She reported a similar experience in one of her previous roles, where she was the deputy leader who behaved in ways which made her male CEO look more effective and powerful. She did this by denying her own needs for acknowledgement and focusing on "cleaning up" his mess after him. Although arguably her achievements were notable in that role, she felt that it was hidden from view and, when that CEO retired, she was not considered for the CEO role.

This role of supporting more senior male leaders to be seen as successful, and "fixing up" things behind the scenes, has been described as a common experience of women leaders and other female staff. There are indications that women may be more likely to focus on loyalty and collaboration in an organisation rather than recognition for individual success. It is ironic that collaboration and commitment to collective achievements are highly desirable leadership behaviours, yet they are not always valued in traditional assumptions about what it takes to be a strong and effective leader.

Sarah was angry about lack of recognition for her skills and abilities in this and several previous leadership roles. She saw male leaders being rewarded and she knew that she had made a significant contribution to their status, while her achievements were relatively unrecognised and therefore not rewarded with promotion.

While this gendered perspective resonates for Sarah's situation, it is one which calls for further exploration about how it can be a factor in many organisations. My view is that it is often reflected in unconscious bias in leadership selection and recognition processes.

This is a challenge that we kept returning to in many of our sessions.

Finally, Sarah found some personal agency and freed herself from being trapped by what she experienced as a sniping and unpredictable CEO. She said: "I have to let them [i.e. the staff] mess it up." In observing this, she recognised that "mistakes" were necessary for learning to occur and that she needed to model a more supportive work culture.

So, eventually, from our work together she was able to recognise her fantasy of controlling everything, her fear of punishment, and this enabled her to sit with managing ambiguity more effectively. Ironically, she could also enable the staff to grow in their roles by delegating and trusting them more. In doing so she was more trusting of herself and found some inner strengths. She could also acknowledge the underlying factors which had previously been unconscious drivers for her.

Her unproductive, long-term work habits were addressed and started to change. Seeing and acting on the impact of her family of origin experiences and influences of always being the dutiful daughter were an important part of this shift. The impact of gender on her experience of leadership was also better understood.

As a result, she found more of her personal power and could articulate this more clearly with me, and also at work. She became much more connected with her own feelings and their importance in her being able to make better informed work choices.

However, being able to act on her insights and achieve her desired balance was still difficult for her while she worked in that agency. She left the organisation a few months after our programme of coaching sessions concluded and went to work in a business training college.

* * *

This case reflects some of the problems women have in a leadership position. It shows how socialisation and stereotypes frame a leader's role, how she works in second place to clean up a male superior's mistakes by being supportive, nurturing, and caring. It also shows how the coachee repeats the roles and patterns of her family of origin. The case also demonstrates nicely how a coaching relationship develops over time.

The role the second woman, the CEO, plays is also interesting—she behaves rather in a stereotypical male fashion. The case thus shows that some women fall to the other extreme when confronted with the double-bind situation and choose (unconsciously) to belong to the male organisational hierarchy and system. The double-bind situation is sometimes solved in the "female" way, yet other women choose to act as a male stereotype in order to avoid the "female problems". It is rare to find someone who is able to manage the double bind in its ambiguity. The coachee does, however, seem to be getting there through the self-awareness created in the coaching.

Your task as a leader, whether you are male or female, is to understand your own position in this confusing field of hurdles and obstacles and also the actual position of your organisation (not the claimed one).

What is needed is awareness, support, and commitment from the top, the CEO and the board, more transparency and tracking of what is really going on in recruiting and retention, integrating women in the approach, and collective enablers like infrastructure, etc.—McKinsey calls this a "new ecosystem".[126]

KEY LEARNING

- Guidance for both women and men seems to be crucial—either from you as a leader or from professional coaches—to ensure that women are allowed to find their own way of managing these expectations, biases, and male-dominated organisational cultures in order to achieve and fulfil their own job ideals and needs.
- Women must be enabled to develop self-awareness of their own competencies and capabilities, to connect them with their wishes and hopes, and align them with the outer reality and real situation of the organisation.

Several rules can help women find a path through the jungle:

- Question your own role prejudices which might stand in the way of a more fulfilling job.
- Get some distance on the situation from a play perspective—different actors having different goals and aims.
- Don't take devaluing or aggressive behaviour from men as a personal attack. Develop the capacity to split off emotional attacks instead of taking them to heart.
- Remember the basic rule that everything comes at a price, and everybody must make choices, regardless of gender.
- There is always the possibility of leaving the organisation for a more suitable job environment.

CHAPTER 7

Making leaders

Evolution and emergence of leadership in autonomous teams

In most organisations, leadership is still designated—someone gets declared the leader of a team, division, board, or the organisation as a whole. How this process works and how it can be influenced should be of interest to every leader. To better understand what is important about leaders, it helps to look at situations where at first there is a leaderless group of people who have understood that some degree of cooperation is needed to achieve more than they could do on their own, and to achieve this it would be helpful to have a leader.

The pre-stage of this group formation is best depicted by the stag hunt game developed by Rousseau, which is analysed in game theory to understand how social cooperation develops.[127] The situation is as follows: a group of hunters have heard from one of their peers that there is a large stag in the area and decide that if they all work together they could kill and share it. They prepare their traps and wait for a while, a day, several days, until the hunters spot a hare. A hare is much easier to hunt down, and this can be done by a lone man. But if the hunter who saw the hare first leaves the group to chase the hare, he jeopardises the group effort to capture the stag, by revealing their whereabouts, and all will starve except him. If he does not do it, however, another hunter might take their chance at the hare, and then he and the group will starve. There is also the additional risk that the stag does not show up at all.

For the individual hunter it is thus a double dilemma, hence his personal choice to give up some autonomy in order to achieve the larger goal. This is the basic choice people must make when wanting to adhere to social groups. Deciding whether you stay in the group depends on the trust you have in the abilities of the leader and in the other members to themselves stay in the group. As we know, trust is one of the most important ingredients of social cooperation—the difficulty lies in developing and maintaining it.

In unstructured social systems it is very likely that leadership will naturally emerge after some time—for the purpose of coordination efforts. This most likely happens when there is a lot of uncertainty, chaos, entropy, and pressure to produce something new and different. In these moments of rupture in a leaderless group, a whole social structure emerges. "When the levels of interaction reach a critical mass, patterns begin to emerge, and the group self-organises into a social structure,"[128] which consists of primary and secondary leaders and non-leaders. How the leader differentiates from the non-leader has, of course, also to do with the primary task of the team, for instance, production, coordination of intense activities, or creative problem-solving. But one can say that primary leaders have a broader repertoire of social skills, whereas secondary leaders are more limited and seem to play more specific roles.[129] These kinds of situations resemble what autonomous or self-managing teams experience in "agile organisations". They come together under the pressure of creating something new and different and within a situation characterised by change and uncertainty about the future of the organisation.

Although it is sold to us as a completely new approach, you should know that, since the 1940s, theorists have suggested alternatives to the rigidity of bureaucracy. Max Weber[130] warned us of being trapped in the unchangeable "iron cage" of bureaucracy; despite its usefulness for control, we become so fixated on following rules and regulations around decision-making that no flexibility is left to address changing circumstances or for the people involved. Also, in the 1950s the British psychologist Eric Trist,[131] a founder of the Tavistock social research centre, analysed self-regulating coal miners in his now famous article, "Some social and psychological consequences of the longwall method of coal-getting".[132]

In the 1980s and '90s the call for de-bureaucratisation and flat hierarchies was intensified by integrating the notion of organisational culture. Leadership consulting gurus such as Peter Drucker and Tom Peters together with Robert H. Waterman claimed this as a necessary change, yet forty years later we have not yet solved the problem. Anyway, self-autonomous teams are anything but new, and research shows us that these teams, for example, function best when both the emerging leader and the team have high leadership capabilities, which are associated here with conscientiousness, extraversion, and emotional stability.[133]

Behind the concept of autonomous teams stands "concertive" control, which means that the locus of control shifts away from management to the workers themselves, who collaborate to develop the means of their own control. Barker observed how in a small manufacturing company that introduced this way of cooperation, the system "matured from a loosely held consensus about abstract values to a tightly bound system of rational rules and powerful self-control". He concluded thirty years ago that "concertive control, as it becomes manifest in organisational interaction, is more powerful and has a greater ability to control than the bureaucratic system it replaces".[134] These insights also apply to agile or lateral team leadership.

Choice—traits and other ingredients

Even when leaders seem to emerge, groups have (often unconscious) good reasons for choosing their leader. Over the years, the idea of what leadership is and why people are thus chosen as leaders has changed a lot.

In the first twenty to thirty years of the last century, the overall theme in leadership was domination, control, and centralisation of power. Respect and loyalty were expected from the followers. The 1930s saw a gradual shift away from dominating and impressing ideals and towards influencing, and the personality traits of the leader gained some importance. In the 1940s, leadership of groups became more important than leadership of individuals—probably because of WWII and the influence of military psychology. In the 1950s, group dynamics and group theory, as well as leadership effectiveness and leadership behaviour, came into focus. In the 1960s the focus was clearly on a leader's behaviour, and in the 1970s organisational behaviour entered the discussion.

In the 1980s, leadership became more and more important in academia and research. At that time it ranged from influencing people, leadership as excellence and a personality trait, to transformational leadership. All of these have stayed with us and in the twenty-first century further aspects such as authentic, spiritual, servant, and adaptive leadership have seen light.[135] Looking at this, we can state that former details or features of leadership have now developed into a leadership style on their own. Whether this is useful for practitioners can be questioned. In the end, we understand leadership as a combination of individual personality traits, a basic attitude towards leadership of the organisation and the leader (authentic, servant, spiritual), and a specific, sometimes situational need in the organisation (agile, lateral, hybrid, ambidextrous). These are the fundamentals that existing and future leaders will be measured against and chosen by.

Leadership traits

We know quite well and can also easily imagine what followers look for in their leaders: guidance into a shared (and agreed) direction, active protection against threats (e.g. competition), and judicious dispute settlement (conflict resolution, dilemma management).[136] Organisations have similar demands, albeit more detailed and specific. What we also know is that leaders in complex environments require a certain intelligence; they need the will to lead and thus the will to dominate. We have already discussed why they also need social and emotional skills.[137]

> Theoretical accounts of the relationship between leader trait, positive affect and leadership criteria have typically proposed a positive relationship that is driven by (a) mood contagion

> processes (i.e., leader displays of positive affect imbue follower displays of positive affect that subsequently result in high leadership ratings), (b) the relationship-building qualities of positive affect (i.e., positive affect strengthens the bond between leader and follower, resulting in higher leadership ratings), and (c) the notion of affect as information provided by the leader (i.e., positive affect serves as functional information provided by the leader to the follower and this information is a component of effective leadership).[138]

The effect of positive mood and affect on leadership effectiveness is connected to personality traits such as the Big 5. It shows that high extraversion and low neuroticism are positively correlated with positive affect and effective leadership.

The Big 5 model is common, well-known, and well-researched with several reliable and valid test-instruments. Following the OCEAN acronym, they are the following:

- Openness to experience (inventive/curious vs consistent/cautious)
- Conscientiousness (efficient/organised vs extravagant/careless)
- Extraversion (outgoing/energetic vs solitary/reserved)
- Agreeableness (friendly/compassionate vs critical/rational)
- Neuroticism (sensitive/nervous vs resilient/confident).

You can certainly imagine that the director of a nuclear power plant and the director of a design and advertising agency need to have very different profiles. Following the Big 5, the ideal leader is rather open to experience, conscientious (yet not rigid), extraverted (but not too much), rather agreeable, and not emotionally oversensitive. Not only does the organisational context play an important role in choosing the right person, the role context does also.

Another way of looking at traits and character is through leadership archetypes. Kets de Vries has found eight leadership archetypes. These are basic roles that leaders take on depending on what is needed from the organisation and the followers, as well as what they bring through their personal predisposition:

- The strategist: leadership as a game of chess. These people are good at dealing with developments in the organisation's environment. They provide vision, strategic direction and outside-the-box thinking to create new organisational forms and generate future growth.
- The change-catalyst: leadership as a turnaround activity. These executives love messy situations. They are masters at re-engineering and creating new organisational "blueprints".
- The transactor: leadership as deal-making. These executives are great dealmakers. Skilled at identifying and tackling new opportunities, they thrive on negotiations.
- The builder: leadership as an entrepreneurial activity. These executives dream of creating something and have the talent and determination to make their dream come true.
- The innovator: leadership as creative idea generation. These people are focused on the new. They possess a great capacity to solve extremely difficult problems.
- The processor: leadership as an exercise in efficiency. These executives like organisations to be smooth-running, well-oiled machines. They are very effective at setting up the structures and systems needed to support an organisation's objectives.
- The coach: leadership as a form of people development. These executives know how to get the best out of people, thus creating high performance cultures.
- The communicator: leadership as stage management. These executives are great influencers and have a considerable impact on their surroundings.[139]

Of course, nobody represents only a single archetype—we are all a blend of different aspects; which in the end reflect a composition of the aforementioned personality traits and individual life experiences.

Choosing

So how do you choose your successor, or how are you going to be chosen?

First, I would like to share a case study on how leaders are chosen with the support of a specially trained consultant.

Case study

Leadership choice—talent is not everything

Olya Khaleelee

The tasks involved in talent recruitment and management involve far more than ensuring that the executive hired for a role is the correct choice.

Initially, there is the issue of recruitment and the basis of thinking about the job description and job specification. There are also issues of induction, especially when an executive is changing sector. A further aspect is the question of development, ensuring that the executive continues to be effective in his/her roles and can see a career progression within the new firm. Finally, crises sometimes arise because an executive is not just a person at work but someone who has a life, perhaps a family, possibly ageing parents or fractious teenage children, and this other "family" organisation with its own dynamic is always present in the background during working time.

Psychological assessment can help with thinking about the executive in all these different ways. The goal is to maximise the possibility of making good selection, developmental, and career decisions by increasing the information available to them and to those who are recruiting them. The focus of the assessment is in exploring how the executive's personality has developed over time. This includes underlying factors such as cultural elements and life events, which have contributed to personality formation and how these might impact on the fit between the executive and the role under discussion. It is the fit which is the key factor in ensuring successful talent recruitment and management.

The assessment methodology involves:

- Tempering a subjective method—the interview process—with techniques which bring some objectivity to bear, and which help in the formation of hypotheses about underlying factors which affect behaviour.
- These include the Defence Mechanisms Test developed by Kragh,[140] which generates a profile of emotional development over time together with when specific defence mechanisms were mobilised to

protect the self from stress at different points in the life cycle. The test indicates whether the executive was an early or late developer, or whether he/she regresses under stress. The test also shows how sensitive or thick-skinned the individual is, and which defences are mobilised to protect him/her from stress. It also gives an indication of maturity and resilience.

- Use of the concept of "time span of discretion" in the measurement of capacity, which enables predictions to be made about the individual's future capacity to work effectively at senior levels where strategic thinking takes precedence over operational decisions.[141] The time span of discretion is the target completion time of the longest task, project, or programme assigned to that role. For a middle manager this might be six months, but for a chief executive it might be up to ten years or more, depending on the task. Emotional resilience is a key factor because the executive has to bear the uncertainty of not knowing whether his/her decision was correct. It underpins the ability to contain anxiety and to remain steady while working in stressful conditions of ambiguity. Hypotheses are drawn from test results and are checked and elaborated through discussion before offering the executive extensive feedback.

Here are some examples of how assessment which provides both an understanding of conscious and unconscious aspects of the executive's personality can impact on recruitment, induction, development, and crisis intervention.

Recruitment

The subsidiary of a financial services group was recruiting an HR director to take over from the one who was retiring. The company had decided that it wanted someone who was able to contribute to the strategic development of the business, as well as being a human resources specialist able to work successfully at an operational level.

There were two candidates, Alan, an internal candidate aged fifty and Bob, an external candidate aged forty, both of whom met the company's needs. Bob was an energetic, pushy man who came from a family where his father had worked his way up through the company to his final role as marketing director, while his mother had provided traditional support. The father had encouraged his two sons to believe that ambition and hard work would produce results. Bob, the elder of the two, admired and emulated his father's success. His test results indicated that he was resilient, was neither thick- nor thin-skinned, and his potential time span of discretion was high. He had the capacity to work on a broad canvas matched with good problem-solving skills. His capacity was going to be far in excess of the role once a planned change in direction in the organisation had been implemented. It was clear that in order to sustain his motivation and level of performance, he would need to be promoted to a larger role within two or three years.

On the other hand, Alan's capacity was well matched to the role both now and in the future. He was already in the group and had been made redundant from his previous role in another part of the company. Alan was the middle of three children with a successful older brother who worked in IT and a younger lawyer sister, currently on maternity leave. His parents were divorced acrimoniously when he was six, leaving him with little contact with his father, a middle manager in a large corporation. His mother was left with the responsibility for bringing up the children while simultaneously continuing to work freelance as a hairdresser. The divorce had shocked Alan and for a while it affected his self-esteem. He presented himself as a reflective, slightly introverted man, keen to please those in authority. He worked in a determined and conscientious way, consistent with his test results, which suggested that he had an "old head on young shoulders" and a tendency to withdraw under pressure in order to protect a vulnerable inner self. His test results also suggested that while he was intelligent and operationally very competent, he had little long-term strategic vision.

Discussions with senior management enabled the group to become clearer about their policies on recruitment in two areas: first, under what circumstances should priority be given to good internal candidates compared to outstanding external candidates? And second, was it in their best interests and in the candidate's best interests to offer him a job which was below his capacities, without being clear about a plan for his next move?

After careful thought, the group decided to appoint Bob because the current role required his additional strategic ability and because they could see a possible role to match his abilities within two or three years. The assessment provided the opportunity to reflect on the important issues of matching capacity to the role, both as it was at that time and to how it would develop, and to consider the ethical issues involved in favouring an external candidate over an internal candidate.

During their discussions on the ethical issues it was acknowledged that the decision to appoint Bob conflicted with their view that at a time of recession, priority should be given to an internal candidate who would otherwise be made redundant. As a result, a policy was developed which made them relocate Alan, and they were able to find him an equivalent HR role in another part of the group.

Induction

Jennifer was being recruited by a large multinational company. This company's policy was to have all senior managers assessed before they joined the company. The aim was primarily to give the manager the opportunity to consider their strengths and weaknesses, and reflect on their developmental needs and how they were likely to spend the early months in their new role. From the company's point of view, it provided additional information about the candidate, and in some cases this caused them to make a different decision.

Jennifer was in her early thirties and had already been working as a financial consultant to the company in a review of the business. The role for which she was now being recruited was head of planning for one of the major companies within the group. As we talked, it emerged that while Jennifer had been successful both academically and professionally, early formative experiences had led her to feel under-confident and to have difficulties with authority. She was the youngest of four sisters, with quite a long age gap between her and her next older sister. It seems she was an unexpected albeit much-loved addition to the family. All the children had doctorates, with parents who were both university professors.

In such a high-powered environment it was hard to feel confident and competent. Her relationship with her father was particularly difficult. Jennifer felt he had difficulty changing roles at home and being a father rather than a demanding teacher. She felt she could never please him and that because her mother, to whom she felt closer, supported her father, this had led to a sense of inner isolation which fitted with the defence of heavy "isolation" in her test profile. As a result, she had difficulty making close, trusting relationships with others, and was wary of authority figures onto whom she projected the high demands emanating from her formative experiences.

The assessment raised questions about how she would make the transition from her present consultant position to working as a member of a large team, with resonances of sibling rivalry, and to the difficulties she might experience when working with a particular kind of superior.

Jennifer was helped in making the transition by having external coaching support during the early weeks in her new role. This gave her the opportunity to explore the difficulties she was having and to frame strategies to overcome them. The work allowed Jennifer to establish a supportive relationship with her new superior which enabled her to contribute to her full capacity more quickly than would otherwise have been possible.

Crisis intervention

The person being assessed was Roy, a forty-one-year-old finance director of a subsidiary of a large financial services group. The assessors were informed that, after a period of high performance, over the previous two years his work had deteriorated, and he had been performing unsatisfactorily. Just prior to the assessment Roy was moved to another role, which was seen by his superiors as his last opportunity to regain his former high standards. Failure to do so would lead to him being dismissed.

During the assessment and our discussions with him it became clear, both from his test results and from the way we experienced him, that Roy was a man of considerable capacity who for underlying reasons was trying to fail. Roy was an only child who, with the support of his parents, had performed exceptionally well at school, especially in mathematics. Exploration of his formative experiences brought to light that the significant event of his childhood was the sudden redundancy of his father from a finance company at the age of forty. This blow caused his father to have a breakdown, which meant that for a significant period he was unable to work. As a result, there was immense pressure on his mother to support the family. Roy had to leave his high-ranking, fee-paying school and transfer to a state school in order to complete his secondary education. Despite this setback he managed to get a scholarship to a top university and seemed set for a successful career in finance following in his father's footsteps.

The hypothesis formulated was that Roy, now the same age as his father was when his redundancy occurred, felt guilty about surpassing his father's achievements and therefore was unconsciously trying to fail. This hypothesis was presented to Roy, who acknowledged the guilt and could then see how his identification with his father was impacting on his present performance. The resulting insight made him face the reality of his situation and make a choice between using his capacities fully or failing. We were told a few months after the assessment that his performance in the new role was outstanding and that thought was being given to promoting him to managing director of the subsidiary from which he had moved.

Career development

David was an intelligent, capable, fifty-five-year-old divisional managing director in a large multinational PLC. Until about eighteen months previously, when there was a change in the group's chairman, he had thoroughly enjoyed his work. He subsequently became increasingly uncomfortable at the different, more authoritarian style that the new chairman was introducing to the group.

Indeed, this was in sharp contrast to his own authority relations, both from his formative experiences and during his career up to this point. David was the younger of two children with a much older sister who had already retired from a career in banking. She had been like a second mother to him during his formative years. He was the cosseted younger child and, as a son, was an important addition to the family, especially for his father for whom he became a best friend. David had grown up in an unusually protective environment, and was a "late developer", with benign experiences of authority figures. This had generated for him the expectation that working life would be similar, and he had been lucky that, for the most part, his expectations had been met in that his superiors had been consultative and therefore a good fit for his personality. In discussing his discomfort with the chairman, he was given the opportunity to consider whether he would like to retire early from the group.

Talking it through during an assessment, he was better able to understand his mixed feelings about leaving an organisation and "work family" where he had spent much of his working life, and he began to take a more balanced view of his opportunities. Coming from a culture where careers were generally in one organisation, David had felt that he wanted either a single academic role or, as a less preferred option, another major industrial challenge. The assessment process was able to introduce David to the idea that he had the capacity, experience, and flexibility to develop a portfolio of roles, which might include working in an academic environment, and in consultancy, and also offered the possibility of being a non-executive chairman of one or more companies.

Within a few weeks of the assessment and our talks, David made a reasoned decision to leave and seek a range of roles. He began to work to an agreed date to retire and for a smooth transition for himself and the group.

Conclusions

It can be seen from some of these examples how the executive takes his "family in the mind" to work, how his effectiveness relies not just on a good fit in terms of his time span of discretion and other factors in the job specification and company culture, but also on the more hidden emotional issues and, in particular, authority relations that lie out of sight in the past but which affect current performance.

* * *

We will now look at the emotional and relational perspective in more detail.

Biases and stereotypes

Most deterring are the kinds of biases which are grounded in the fact that we like and prefer to choose people who are similar to us. This includes the tendency to think that if we are successful and the other is a bit like us, they will also be successful ("recruiting in one's own image", "mirror-image error"). Connected to this is the "halo effect", which is the tendency to assume that a person who performs well (or poorly) in one area, also performs well (or poorly) in others. Yet it can be quite problematic, for example, to deduce from analytical skills that the person also has emotional intelligence. Neither is it appropriate to connect two very different aspects to deduce from one the other, for example, appearance and performance, or rhetoric and abstract thinking ("logical error"). Another tendency is to choose types who are not too far away from the mean, as extreme types are more difficult to explain to colleagues ("central tendency"). Although biases are thinking shortcuts and save time and energy, they are not at all helpful in personnel decisions since they reduce complex human beings to simple categories.

This leads us to the use of stereotypes for judgement—especially gender stereotypes (as seen in Chapter 6), but there are many more (weight, religion, skin colour). This is not only about outer stereotypes, however, but also inner "self-stereotypes". Imagine a man and a woman with identical credentials, who both lack experience of a higher-level position. They mostly come to different conclusions about what being prepared for the promotion means. The man is more inclined to assume that he can learn what he's missing while in the new job. He says to himself, "I am close enough". The woman is more inclined to be wary, and less willing to step up in that circumstance.[142]

Becoming aware of one's own tendencies is the only way to avoid their influence on the selection process. Using psychometric tests, projective tests, real on-the-job tasks, and role plays, together with external assessors like those shown in the case study, can give deeper insights, especially if they are accompanied by a specialist.

Leadership, power, and vulnerability

Power can be formal (designated) or informal (through people and relationships). It can be legitimate or based on rewards, coercion, expertise or by referent and charisma.[143]

We want (and need) to have power to influence other people to do what we want them to do, which means it entails control. Power always means control, and being in control means not feeling uncertain and helpless. Yet the feelings of invincibility and invulnerability are an illusion—power and vulnerability belong together, and you do better in a leadership position if you acknowledge this. Why and how are they connected?

Leaders of and in organisations are prone to fear and the flight into control because they continually experience strong triggers of fear. Any large-scale change in the social environment of relationships will trigger fear, and thinking about a future that cannot be planned, and the necessary decisions that accompany this, also lead to fear—the source of the fear being a threat to self-esteem and identity.

The social environment obviously changes constantly—either precipitated by the environment (markets, suppliers, competitors, customers) or as a result of the arrival and departure of people within the company and its structures. This type of fear seems to be manageable for most leaders, or at least they think it is. The fear of the future cannot be avoided—feelings of anxiety emerge in the same area of the brain where planning resides –the frontal lobe.[144] Strategic decision-making is about thinking into the future and is thus the main trigger for this mostly suppressed, ignored, and denied fear. Yet, humans need to think into the future: it is emotionally important to enjoy nice daydreams and also to imagine and prepare for difficult experiences. And it just feels good to control the future (see Chapter 10).

Unfortunately, our archaic biological reactions take over, often unconsciously, in stressful situations: fight or flight, attack or retreat. Strategic thinking in business is obviously grounded in military strategy (in Greek, *strategos* refers to the military commander; it is based on *stratos* (army/division) and *agein* (leading). In Latin, *strategia* refers to the areas that were under the control of a *strategus*). Whereas in the eighteenth and nineteenth centuries, mathematical models dominated in the development of strategies, one great military strategist, Carl von Clausewitz, asserted the importance of a trained individual, the power of dialectical thinking, good judgement, and the human factor, as these two citations demonstrate: "Under no circumstances may general thoughts overtake the role of the individual thought process,"[145] and

> The theory should also take the human aspect into consideration, also the courage, the daring as well as the audacity should be granted its place. The art of war is about the spirited and moral powers, which means that it can never achieve the absolute and the certain.[146]

In his time this view was very unusual and opened up the military world to philosophy and psychology.

In the Far East, this insight arrived around 500 AD, with Sun Tzu writing,

> If you know your enemy and yourself, then you do not have to worry about the outcome of 100 battles. If you know yourself, but not your enemy, then you will suffer a defeat for every victory you achieve. If you know neither your enemy nor yourself, you will lose every battle.[147]

These insights are still valid for leaders, and when choosing them, these capacities should be taken into account, with the core capacity to admit and experience fear so that it can be understood and lessons can be drawn. In avoiding confrontation with fear, the positive, action- and decision-guiding effects of fear are lost. Because fear functions like an alarm bell, a feeling of fear points to something to which one should pay attention. Dealing with fear is therefore decisive in personal development and personal maturity. Power and status can be used to hide repression and aggression. Even the opposite, cheerfulness, can be used as a mask for repressing fear.

How to prepare for leadership

How one becomes a leader depends on several different aspects: the most obvious are education (the right university, the right studies) and grades (better good or even excellent ones)—so hard work is needed. Nobody gets to the top without hard work. I guess that this is self-evident. Hard work on the job combined with passion and enthusiasm can make up for not having studied at an elite university or not having excellent grades.

The less obvious, although arguably more important aspects are: parental education and socialisation, having the right role models, the right attitude, and—always needed in life and not to be underestimated—luck, which means being in the right place at the right moment in time.

Looking at the first point, we can say that parental education level influences education and later professional success. This concerns several facts: children learn from observation and thus from role models; better-educated parents spend more time and more active time with their children, and they position children in more achievement-oriented environments i.e. after-school activities which can range from art or music to sports lessons, from libraries to museums.

If you haven't had the "right" parents, you can still learn by observation how to behave (table manners, small talk, and dress code) and how to build networks. Building relationships during studies and as a young professional will provide you with implicit and explicit advice. More important yet seems to be finding a successful mentor from whom you can learn the rules of the game. She or he can be your key to a new world, a sounding board and mirror of your ideas, a wise guide and teacher, as well as an opener of doors. But there needs to be some mutuality in such a relationship: you also have to bring something to the table so that the other person does not feel (ab)used.

The "right attitude" entails being willing to work hard and sacrifice your personal time; work–life balance is not something you put to the forefront of your work life. More important, though, is attitude towards people and the organisation. If you do not really enjoy being with people, if you are even afraid of them, their reactions, their criticisms, their talking behind your back—then you are not cut out to be a leader. You must be able to put your personal needs second and have the willingness to serve the organisation.

This leads to my next point—and it would be good to be honest with yourself here. The obvious motivations of wanting to have an impact, to contribute to a better world, work with great people, or wanting to improve things are probably not the (only) real ones. The hidden motives are more difficult to explore, and you need to be realistic with yourself. If you want to become a leader to acquire money, power, fame and/or prestige, these are probably not the best reasons. They will undermine your intentions and wear away your soul and your authenticity. They may make you corrupt, not only for money but for what you are seeking, that is the currency you want to be paid by. That, in turn, will make you very vulnerable, even more than the basic fear we talked about when thinking into the future.

Feeling, for example, a victim and seeking revenge for devaluing behaviour in early years, wanting to beat the odds, can be strong motives. But they will narrow your view since you will be under the permanent stress of not making any mistake revealed to the world, that you are better than you think they expect. Yet in reality you may be fighting against your negative self-image—this fight will not be won until you change your self-image. All the latter points might provide you with the energy you need to achieve top leadership positions, but whether you manage to keep up depends also on your physical strength and on the people you meet, how benevolent or malevolent they are.

How do you stay in a leadership position?

There is no single answer to this question, one would reply: it depends—on both the organisation and its market position as well as the leader's-life-stage one is in. Every phase needs a different focus and involves different risks. The next figure gives an overview of the dangers to their position that leaders face (see Figure 20).

Stage	Description	Advice	Risks
Infant Executive	On the brink of becoming a leader	• Seek your own mentor • Look for support	• Loneliness • Anxiety • Inexperienced and misreading
The schoolboy/girl with a shining face	Novice in leadership, first real position	• You are always on stage, and everything will be inspected • Low-key entry is best	• Projection surface • Overdoing it at the beginning
The lover with a woeful ballad	Having come up some ranks already	• Whom to listen to and whom to trust? • Don't focus on the most glamorous = most needy follower	• How to relate to former peers? • Envious peers • System will keep the status quo • Need to fire others is painful
The young soldier	Slowly becoming an experienced leader, comfortable with leading	• Nurture and make others shine • Be generous with other people	• Forgetting the impact of the words • Thinking you get what you need • Thwart competition
The general full of wise saws	At the height of their career	• Listen to unpleasant truth, be authentic and learn	• Arrogance and deafness • Hesitation to do the needed change • Failure to understand the context
The statesman/woman with spectacles on the nose	Preparing to pass on their insights and their work	• Look and build up followers	• Holding yourself irreplaceable
The sage, second childishness	Add value to next generation of leaders	• Being a good mentor and enjoy the learning • Build your adaptive capacity	• Detach yourself, because the other is not worth it (you think)

Figure 20: Dangers in the life of a leader (author's compilation)[148]

The leader's life stages develop over time in parallel with leadership experience. This is self-evident.

It is also evident that different organisational stages need different leaders and leadership styles. This will be depicted in the next figure and does not need much explanation (see Figure 21).

Stage	Situation	Business	Structure	Decision making	Strategy	Leadership
EMERGENCE	• Small • Young • Homogenous	• Develop product • Build relationships	• Informal • Simple • Owner dominated	• Centralised • Trial and error	• Prospector - First Mover	• Visionary • Innovator
EARLY GROWTH/ SURVIVAL	• Medium-sized • More competitive	• Drive sales • Launch different solutions • Build loyalty	• Functional • Some formality	• Some delegation • Begin formal information processing	• Analyser • Second mover • Differentiation	• Evangelist • Communicator
RAPID GROWTH/ SUCCESS	• Heterogenous • Larger size	• Set the market standard • Ward off competitors	• Formal • Bureaucratic • Management - team	• Reliance on internal information processing	• Defender • Segment • Control	• Builder • Conqueror • Strategist • Change catalyst • Coach • Transactor
MATURITY	• Very heterogenous • Very large	• Dominate the industry • Expand and add • Re-invent • Milk the cash cows	• Divisional and matrix	• Sophisticated controls • Formal analysis for decision-making	• Analyser • Combine low cost and differentiation	• Explorer • Processor
DECLINE/NO GROWTH OR RENEWAL	• Homogenous and competitive environment	• Redefine value proposition • Consolidate	• Formal, • (Over)-bureaucratic	• Less sophisticated	• Reactor • Low cost • Breath	• Defender • Bureaucrat

Figure 21: The connection between organisational life-cycle stage and leadership (author's compilation)[149]

KEY LEARNING

The interesting question is: why is leadership so difficult?

- It sounds pretty easy: create a vision, set a goal, choose the right people, listen and communicate well, make informed decisions whilst integrating the team, create a psychological safe space, and be positive and realistic. Yet, what is only said between the lines is that leaders must deal with real people who are not only very different from each other, but also live real lives by which they are shaped and influenced.
- Being with other people and leading them from within a team or from a superior hierarchical position is all about interacting with these very diverse people, having relationships with and influencing them—although they might not want to be influenced and want to do things their own way, not necessarily your way.
- This means that not everybody will like or love you, which can be difficult to bear. Furthermore, many people think they are as good, if not even better, than you are at your job—like how everybody at times is the best football trainer or the best driver or the best MP.
- But most important, and behind everything else, is that the otherness of the other is frightening. Depending on the stability of your own self, the other person, just by simply being there, might question or even threaten your identity. Everybody wants to be special in their own way and, in observing and being with other people, you realise what you are not capable of or not good at, which makes identity unstable; it evolves and changes over a lifetime.
- We are constantly measuring where we stand, whether we belong to this or that group, and how we are perceived. We want to belong as well as be different from the other—a dilemma most of us have already experienced. We all also know how hard it can be to change habits or attitudes which have become part of our identity.
- In a leadership position your identity and your behaviour are constantly under surveillance and under threat. This is emotionally and energetically demanding, and the surer you are of yourself—and I don't mean thinking that you are super(wo)man—the better you can navigate these questioning and anxiety-provoking waters.

CHAPTER 8

Do you need leadership coaching?

Coaching is only for the weak and failing

Why would you need a coach? After all, coaching is only necessary for those who lack competence or have psychological problems, right? So, *you* don't need a coach, do you?

Here are ten good reasons why you would not need a coach:

1. You do not need a coach when everything feels good and you are happy—with your life, your relationships inside and outside your work organisation, and you are only getting positive feedback.
2. You certainly do not need a coach when you know what you are doing—because you have studied hard and have lots of experience in it.
3. You do not need a coach when you are in a stable environment—for yourself and for your organisation; things are not changing and besides, you have seen it all already.
4. You do not need a coach when you know yourself and your strengths and weaknesses, and of course you also know the image you present to others.

5. You do not need a coach when you know the rules of the game and you know how to play it to achieve what you want.
6. You do not need a coach when everybody is happy with your leadership style and you do not hear any complaints.
7. You do not need a coach when you have reached the top of the organisation, since this is proof that you must have got things right.
8. You do not need a coach when you have achieved everything you wanted and could have possibly imagined.
9. You do not need a coach when you think you have become who you are today without the support and help of others.
10. You do not need a coach when you think that you are your own best sparring partner—or if your partner at home is.

If you can tick the boxes for the above points, congratulations, you really do not need anybody to talk to about your job, your professional role, or your leadership, so, you might want to skip this chapter ... But seriously, for all those who are at least hesitant to see themselves in that way, we'll continue to explore what leadership coaching is and how it can support you in your efforts.

Leadership coaching

Leadership coaching is, as it suggests, the process of providing support to a leader in their effort to become a better leader. By now most people know that the word "coaching" stems from the coach, in former times a carriage to transport people and other things from one place to another. Another meaning derives from sports coaching—a person who teaches skills, tactics, and techniques and for that she or he needs to be a role model, good in observing, analysing, and assessing the skills needed.

The way we see coaching today and from the perspective of this book is a bit different. The leadership coaching I am looking at will not give you advice or teach you skills and techniques—I would assume that you have already invested the time to develop the basic skills you need. In a nutshell, the focus is instead on developing your full personal potential as a human being to assume your roles and responsibilities in organisational life (and beyond) in a way which is good for you, for the people you lead, and for the organisation you work for.

So, two basic questions come up with this definition:

- What does "developing your full personal potential" mean, especially with the very broad notion of "as a human being"?
- What is meant by being good for you, others, and the organisation?

Let us start to explore the latter. "Being good for you and others" implies emotional, moral, performance, and success aspects.

When you feel good about what you are doing and how you are doing it, feelings of congruence and coherence develop, and you feel like you are in the right place at the right moment. You enjoy what you are doing and moments of flow may develop. This does not simply mean that everything is easy, since "The best moments in our lives are not the passive, receptive, relaxing times … The best moments usually occur if a person's body or mind is stretched to its limits in a voluntary effort to accomplish something difficult and worthwhile."[150] Creating containment and psychologically safe spaces where people can flourish and develop results is emotionally good for others and for the organisation.

Morally good is a leadership approach which takes not only the social context and the moral values of an organisation into account, but also entails thinking about the negative or destructive aspects of your work or the organisation's work, for example, impacts on climate or health. Not being corrupt or breaching the law obviously also comes under this imperative. Yet it is much more than that; it is about having an inner compass, about using continuous reflection and decision-making regarding how one reacts and behaves. We might also use the term "character". As Charles Read (1814–1884) put it: "We sow a thought and reap an act/ We sow an act and reap a habit/ We sow a habit and reap a character/ We sow a character and reap a destiny." One could then say that character develops from actions and the decision to act.

This perspective was held by the Ancient Greeks, for whom the word *character* was defined as "the engrained/the imprinted" and was initially used as a stamp in branding livestock. In Ancient Greece, the development of character was closely connected with the "doctrine of virtues" initiated by Plato, claiming wisdom, courage, temperance, and justice to be the main virtues. In contrast, Aristotle understood a good life based on *eudaimonia* or happiness, the highest human virtue, as a goal in itself. Every human being has a task or a function in life, hence happiness is excellence in this task or activity, where "excellent" means "in accordance with virtues". Virtues are achieved by practising good actions. Possessing and exercising virtue delivers the best life possible for a human being. Good actions mean reacting appropriately, not acting out of strong emotions, unconscious biases, or deviations which are inadequate and do not take reality into account. It also implies determination in what one does and how one reacts—making conscious and self-controlled decisions in accordance with one's individual way of being. Virtue is thus a state of character concerned with choice.[151]

That personal growth as an individual leads to personal and organisational performance and success is a rather recent assumption. Up until the 1980s it was mainly believed that setting clearer goals and improving motivation would contribute the most to success and performance. Yet by now it is acknowledged that hidden personal and institutional factors can stall and sabotage growth and advancement.[152] Behind this lies the idea that organisational success (which is a positive state or condition defined by, for example, financial parameters, client happiness, or any way the organisation defines success) depends on individual contributions achieved through a high level of personal performance based on personal behaviour.

Personal performance can be differentiated as either task performance related with participating in producing the goods and services the organisation is selling, or context performance maintaining the wider-ranging organisational, social, and psychological environment in which the task is executed.[153] The higher one ranks in an organisation, the greater the significance of contextual performance. Whereas task performance depends on (cognitive) capability, contextual performance is tied to the capacity to effectively relate within the organisation and its network of stakeholders and within the specific role the person is supposed to assume;[154] this could be summarised as, to become a more effective leader, the coach should "coach me, the leader, so that I can handle my emotions and (work) relationships."[155]

Developing your full personal potential as a human being is connected with personal growth that stems from self-knowledge, self-actualisation, and, in the context of leadership, a leader's identity. The individuation process is at the core of personal growth and stands for the full development of one's own innate potential. It is the process by which the individual develops uniqueness and differentiates his or her personality—"Man has to become what he is meant to be" or, as Erich Fromm puts it, "Man's main task in life is to give birth to himself, to become what he potentially is. The most important product of his effort is his own personality."[156] It is the unfolding and development of the Self.

> As an empirical term, the Self defines the totality of all psychic phenomena in human beings ... it comprises that which can be experienced, and that which cannot be experienced, or cannot yet be experienced ... In as far as wholeness, which consists of both conscious and unconscious contents, is a postulate, it is essentially transcendent ...[157]

Transcendent means bringing the opposites in the psychic reality together to create something new and different—it is best understood as overcoming one-sidedness, as in neurotic developments, ideologies, or psychic defences.

Developing your personality is a very broad and somewhat unhelpful notion. For me, it stands, on one hand, for what we have just discussed—developing innate potential—and, on the other, character development and nobleness of the heart. Up until the nineteenth century, achieving "nobleness of the heart" was considered an important educational endeavour. Closely connected with "good character", this was understood as a complement to intelligence and referred to the ability to react in an emotionally educated way. It can be partly translated as "emotional intelligence",[158] yet the old-fashioned wording more clearly represents a certain attitude of kindness, empathy, friendliness, moral education, dignity, elegance, and the capacity to open up to another human being—an attitude which is developed and refined over the course of a lifetime.

Individuation process

I am more concerned with the broader psychological concept of identity, which Jung would probably call *personality* or *personal identity*. It is the goal of the individuation process and comprises the conscious confrontation with one's own being, one's being-ness. The individuation process is about becoming who one really is, in essence: "Become who you are!" The lifelong goal of development is to realise the wholeness of the self. "Individuation is therefore a process of differentiation which has as its goal the development of the individual personality."[159] It is precisely this development of the individual personality that I am concerned with when I speak of the development of identity. Part of the individuation process is to question and give up one-sidedness and any identification that does not fit the personality. These non-fitting identifications can be with collective values, with the persona, or with archetypes. Jung himself writes, "The purpose of individuation is now no other than to free the self from the false shells of the persona on the one hand and the suggestive power of unconscious images on the other."[160]

Müller[161] describes the following aspects as belonging to the personal identity: vitality, emotionality, self-activity, autonomy and authenticity, relative stability, continuity, and self-esteem. Central to the development of an identity is the positive reflection of one's own being by our attachment figures (see Chapter 1).

The connection between persona and personality is important in that only when this connection is present does the person come across as authentic. This also applies to the professional aspect of the persona. If persona and personality or the self are not connected, identification with the persona can occur. The person then appears impersonal, inauthentic, and somehow empty. This happens quite often in relation to the professional persona: the person identifies completely with his professional role and the corresponding social requirements.

The conscious confrontation with and the shaping of the persona are important components of the individuation process. Above all because in it the shadow aspects and the instinct nature are also found. With the development of a well-functioning persona, however, the individuation process does not (yet) stop, but is further driven by the natural pressure for individuation.[162] This, Jung also refers to as the "drive toward self-realization".[163]

The concept of occupational identity is thus broader and includes the occupational persona, as well as the conscious, and unconscious, inner attitudes related to occupation and work. It is the occupational part of the personality, which is different and unique in every person.

Now, what and how can leadership coaching contribute to this complex individual process? The more complex something is the more difficult it is to understand it all by oneself, especially when we are ourselves at the core of this complexity.

Leadership coaching is about exploring and making sense of that complexity by connecting the inner world with the outer one. It is not about advising what to do and how to do things; a coach is not the expert or the role model for leadership behaviour as maybe a sports coach would be. I understand the role more as being a sparring partner for shared reflection, as a mirror, and, by that, also as an investigator or private eye.

The main aim of (leadership) coaching is to develop an inner freedom to act out of free will, and not being unconsciously guided by patterns or psychic defences, for the betterment of the organisation and its multiple stakeholders, and especially for the people one works with. This free will shall be informed by a realistic perspective of yourself, the context you and the organisation are in, as well as of the people you are working with and for; and by the growing possibility for choosing how to react (instead of automatically reacting out of a pattern) by making unconscious reactions conscious through developing awareness of what is taking place in one's own inner world. This process entails seeing, feeling, and understanding the inner governing factors which influence our daily thinking and feeling—affects, patterns, rules, hypotheses, conflicts—as well as seeing, feeling, and understanding how external events such as relationships with other people and social occasions provoke specific reactions which are solidified as patterns.

The coach should facilitate a shared reflective space to support the inner and outer developmental process by asking questions which engender a deeper self-reflection and foster insights into your own and others' unconscious processes and emotional influences.

In observing your behaviour and listening, the coach should provide you with carefully considered feedback on your present reactions as a means of exploring behavioural, emotional, and thought-pattern recognition—without imposing their own view.

It is important that the coach strikes a balance between maintaining a supportive attitude and asking challenging questions, without distressing you too much. You should only work with a coach you feel you can trust—since exploring the inner world is a rather intimate endeavour. It can therefore be difficult to use the same coach as your colleagues or your superiors—although a professional coach should be capable of maintaining confidentiality. Let us now take a look at a case study.

Case study

Coaching individuals—losing the ability to lead

Halina Brunning

Introduction

In this case study I shall describe how I worked as an executive coach with a director of a private care home within a metropolitan city in the United Kingdom at the start of the pandemic and during the first wave of the Covid-19 lockdown in the spring of 2020.

I shall locate the issues which the client brought within three theoretical frames:

1. The first one describes the world of work in which she operated at the time.
2. The second one places the coaching work within the Six Domains model.
3. The final one will name the steps we followed within the time frame, longitudinally, from the moment of entry to the ending of our work.

Attention will be focused on the overlapping zones between the various domains explaining the interconnectivity and interdependence between the individual, the organisation, and society, paying attention to the conscious and unconscious, contemporary and historical elements in the presented material. Lastly, there will be an attempt to integrate all issues and draw general conclusions.

The referral

Towards the end of April 2020 I received a call from the human resources department of a care home located on the outskirts of a big metropolis.[164]

The director of HR asked whether I could offer a few sessions of executive coaching to a female director of one of their care homes, who since the outbreak of Covid-19, appeared to "have lost her ability to lead".

I agreed to meet her online, initially, for the purpose of assessment, and subsequently, for a number of sessions. Working online was the only possible way one could meet in order to deliver any coaching programme at the time of the pandemic.

The client

I had never met Annabel Green[165] before.

During our first session, Annabel presented as a serious woman who appreciated her role within the industry of social care, and as experienced and committed to her clients, their families, and the staff within her domain of responsibility. At that time, she struck me as rather depressed and perhaps also "frozen" in her capacity to act, leading to a hypothesis that rage might be behind that frozen appearance. I was not sure whether this would be addressed during our coaching work.

I opened by quoting the last sentence of her HR referrer, who intimated that Annabel *"has lost her ability to lead"*. I knew we were in search of *an episode*. "Episode" could be described as the trigger which leads to a chain reaction in a line of work, or life events, which might connect a number of unconscious traumata. These emotion-filled events usually arrive suddenly and unexpectedly from the past. They might break out as purely work-related challenges, yet experience shows that this is seldom the case, as the deeper you search, the more likely you are to find some childhood or family related theme, usually untouched for years, and therefore unresolved, making a surprising reappearance on the work stage.

It was important within our first session to reveal slowly, safely, and calmly the trigger which led Annabel, a professional and experienced leader, to have suddenly *"lost her ability to lead"*.

The episode—entry via an episode

During the session Annabel seemed to have lost her hesitancy and proceeded to describe how she understood her apparent *"loss of ability to lead"*.

This coincided with two events within the national care system: the first one was a nationwide decision taken by the then health minister to send Covid-recovering (but not fully recovered) patients from NHS hospitals directly to care homes,[166] stating that he thus "put a caring embrace" over the entire care sector. The real reason for this ominous action was the blocking of beds within the National Health Service by Covid patients and strong pressure to have them discharged sooner, ready or not. Subsequently, it was described as a dangerous political mistake.[167]

The second reason why Annabel felt unable to lead became obvious at the point when the care staff were being forced by the company management not to leave work but to live in the care homes together with their clients, instead of being with their own families, so as to avoid taking the Covid infection out and spreading the virus in the community. Annabel was opposed to both decisions but was powerless to act against them.

Having a broad outline of the client's dilemma and her inner conflict, we agreed a contract for coaching.

Ecology and expectations

Annabel and I, in the role of her online coach, agreed to work together to help her feel more empowered within her organisation, while recognising that her scope for free will was currently limited by the new governmental decrees, which inevitably cascaded downwards from the politicians via her headquarters to her and the staff.

The atmosphere within the country was one of controlled, or better said, hidden panic, and despite daily and then weekly government-led public Covid briefings, the social anxiety was rising, as were the cases of Covid deaths. The country was gripped by real fear of death and annihilation.[168]

The hierarchy above Annabel was just as frightened as she was to put a foot wrong; subsequently, any scope for free will or any local initiative was forbidden. All changes to daily protocol must be reported and agreed by the top-level executives and the owners of the company.

Annabel's expectation of our work was somewhat limited, as by then she realised that her role was to keep a steady state, as opposed to exerting her own influence on those she was managing. There was a need to examine this theme within a psychodynamic coaching framework for her to understand its roots.

Engagement—exchange—exploration

At this stage I asked Annabel to describe her career trajectory and to tell me about her status and role within her own family. I worked on the assumption that her basic personality features, as well as her own biography, once seen psychodynamically, might help her to resolve her dilemma within the current work role.

To facilitate this process I used the Six Domains model of coaching (see Figure 22).[169]

Expressing—excavating—enacting

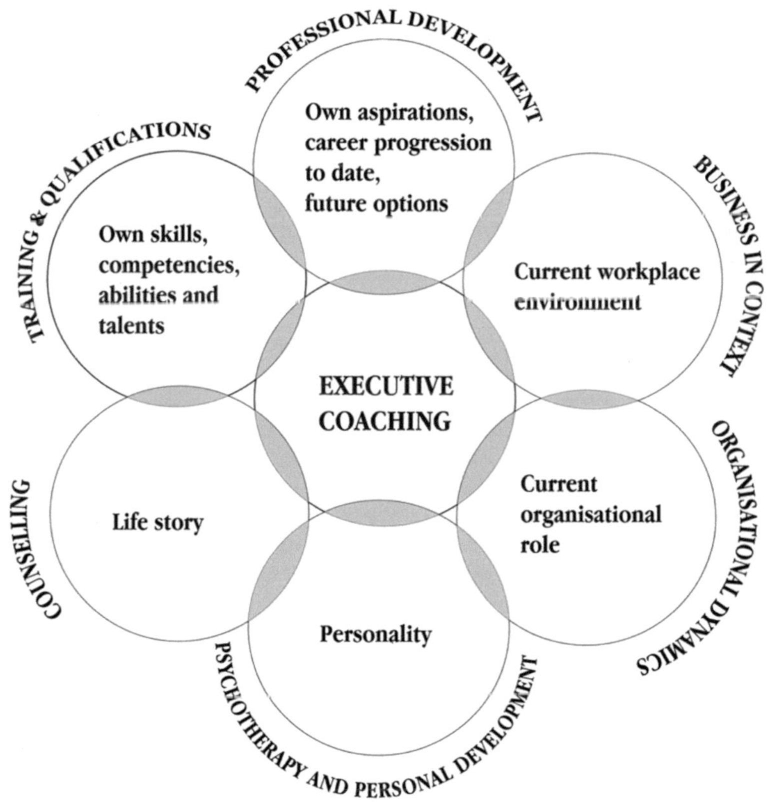

Figure 22: The Six Domains model of coaching © Brunning, 2001[170]

Presented with the picture of the Six Domains model, Annabel shared the following about her private life.

She was the oldest among three sisters. Her mother was a primary school teacher, her father a soldier in the British army. That meant he was often absent on manœuvres, perhaps even abroad, but the news of his whereabouts were often kept secret. When she was fifteen her father was killed fighting a war overseas, details of which were withheld from the children.

This tragic loss put pressure on her as the oldest daughter to share her mother's responsibility for the well-being of the family. Annabel was a keen scholar and was planning to study medicine, but the family's new status and limited finances would not allow such a brave move. Instead, she went to the local university, studied business management, and put all her ambition into developing her own career, which directly led her towards the care sector.

After a few years in different institutions, she became the director of the Green Acres Care Home and was known for her strong leadership as well as definitive and innovative solutions to most encountered problems. Top management appreciated her strength of character, professionalism, and resolve. She was allowed to work independently within her care home, and the good CQC[171] score was a measure of her and her team's success.

Some might say she was disappointed at not becoming a doctor, as working within the care sector created a yearning gap within her. The shadow of her father's lonely death on foreign soil and her choice of an alternative career in social care, which, essentially, focuses on end-of-life care and on death, makes sense in that context as an unconscious resolution of the loss, exposing her to ministering over and reworking his death. However, I knew that to open this theme would have led us into a psychotherapy domain, rather than coaching. Sometimes a coach needs to keep some ideas to oneself!

That said, Annabel saw herself as a strong independent professional able to lead a diverse team of staff while remaining caring and receptive to her clients and their families, proud of the good name of the care home she led.

I took all these overt elements from our second meeting and knew they would become important stepping stones in our immediate coaching work. The "excavating work" was, to a certain extent, completed, remembering this was coaching and not a psychotherapy engagement.

Emerging—establishing—embedding

What emerged from our previous session was that Annabel's job as the care home manager helped to recreate her own "family" setting that featured in her life story. This type of work both allowed her earlier need of "putting a caring arm around" those she cared about to be satisfied and got her closer to the medical environment, yet at the same time offered a constant disappointment about the fact she never became a doctor, just an administrator. However, she felt compensated by her relative freedom of decision-making and the fact she was held in high esteem by the top management at the company headquarters.

The death of her beloved father, who sacrificed his life for higher values—at least this was how the mother explained it to her daughters—caused Annabel deep pain, which stayed always in the shadows; seldom was it talked about within the family. However, his death often appeared in her nightmares. This led her to be extra sensitive to the theme of loss and perhaps even helped in dealing sympathetically and honestly with bereaved families, a regular and anticipated occurrence within any care home.

However, the Covid pandemic accelerated the death rate of the residents, making all staff uneasy and often disturbed by the sudden and dramatic losses that were occurring all around. She felt particularly anxious when she first heard the subsequently infamous statement made publicly by the health minister that said in effect: "we are putting a protective arm around the care home residents". This statement jarred her for two reasons: because it was exactly what her mother used to say to her daughters to calm them down, and also because she thought that this act of "embracing" was exactly what she was doing in her professional role! Suddenly, she felt worthless in all her work efforts as this strong value-driven statement was "stolen" from her and became just an empty political slogan. It also evoked the thought that her father was also sent to war and to his death by powerful politicians!

I tried to stay contemporary and *contrasted* the politician's dishonesty contained in that manipulative statement of "the protective arm" with her own honest and deeply felt attitudes towards her clients and her staff, but she wasn't pacified. Unexpectedly, the health minister lost his job in unrelated embarrassing circumstances, and this was her triumph. Then a different aspect of her problem emerged as she juxtaposed the overwhelming sense of death and loss in the country with her father's sacrifice and death, questioning whether he had any choice regarding fighting a foreign war. The sense that he was coerced to fight, she associated with having to coerce her own staff to fight Covid by sacrificing themselves, especially as there was no adequate PPE[172] to protect them. Not only that, "her" care home had suddenly become the "jail". Annabel feared that her current job made her uncaring about the staff and in effect "a jailer" not a manager. This felt very wrong and conflicting to her.

We reached a difficult moment in coaching as well as in our life in the UK. Covid was claiming high numbers of lives and, regardless of what we, citizens of the country or the world, did or did not do, nothing much offered any respite from our own fear and annihilation anxiety.[173] I sensed that sharing this made her feel less isolated and less exposed in her role.

Envisioning—empowering—enhancing

The next theme we tackled was that of being stuck and not able to lead. It was true that she could not take any initiative at that point as no initiatives were allowed to be taken, and those aspects she incorporated into her own image as a good caring professional were being ignored by the unappreciative and exploitative politicians in the UK.

At that point I brought to her attention a pairing of two concepts—*power* with *vulnerability*[174]—and asked her to identify where her power was located and where her vulnerability was.

I invited her to imagine that she was the new health minister and asked where she would see the power and vulnerability in that role. She started laughing when she realised that the health minister also had no freedom of movement as his role, suspended within the Cabinet of the Conservative government, had no freedom of movement to exercise.

This was an important integrative moment, as my client was able to see herself locked by the circumstances in a societal pyramid where all layers from the top downwards were struck by the same sense of powerlessness and were struggling with their own vulnerability. The health minister and her boss might have had a greater scope to use social manipulations and acting-out, yet they were just as vulnerable and powerless as she and her own staff had become during the pandemic.

The befalling of the prime minister to a severe case of Covid was a point in question!

Exiting and evaluating

We met again online a few weeks later.

Annabel was much better in herself and her sense of agency was stronger, yet there was no concealing how difficult her role had become at this time of Covid. She appreciated how much of herself had become revealed as a result of our brief coaching process. She felt deeply understood in her struggles. We ended our work then.

Ending

When the first wave of the pandemic subsided, Annabel spontaneously wrote to me describing what she did after we finished our coaching work.

She took the initiative and coordinated regular meetings with other directors of local care homes. During those meetings, which by then were face-to-face, she learned that she was never alone in her sense of being powerless, and her desire for taking control and initiative returned to her as a result of hosting and attending the meetings with people whose role she shared.

Postscript

This vignette illustrates how new links that can be made between the unconscious historical events at an individual level, placed within the concurrent events at a societal level, and if examined jointly and thematically, using a psychodynamic coaching as opposed to a psychotherapy frame, could bring surprising new insights and freedom for the client to act purposefully and wisely within the appointed role.

* * *

This case shows how family history and relationships sneak into our daily organisational leadership life. Coaching can help to unearth these hidden links to the past and create meaning out of unusual behaviours in the present.

Coaching can also be used to detect unconscious group patterns. It can be constructive to analyse the parallel process between the client and the coach. This concept stems from the use of supervision in psychotherapy.[175] Searles found that the process of reflection between patient and therapist is mirrored in the relationship between therapist and supervisor. Through this re-enactment, the supervisor can develop an understanding of and an insight into the psychological process of the patient. The parallel process is based on transference and countertransference, as well as projective identification (see Chapter 5). Applying this concept to the coaching relationship, a parallel process in the relationship between the client and the coach can mirror the defences enacted in the respective work group or organisation. This requires that the coach be capable of dual-listening, and entails the dilemma of whom the coach does the work for: the organisation or the client?

KEY LEARNING

- To summarise, psychodynamic coaching proves effective when you as senior leader wish to further develop a connection with your inner world and to grow personally and emotionally.
- It is also most helpful when strong emotional states are encountered, when intra- or interpersonal tensions and conflicts cannot be solved, when at the individual, team, or group level performance problems are prevalent, or when dysfunctional behaviour occurs.
- It also provides support when going through change processes in organisations which are emotionally charged and demanding. When entering into a new position it can help in making sense of the "funny behaviours" of others as well.

Part II

The systemic

In Part I we looked at the individual as the leader and at the influences you are exposed to when leading a team or organisation. This second part will focus on the systemic view—understanding how teams and organisations work and what hinders them from working well, and what happens to people and relationships when collaborating. As a leader you need to develop an understanding of these organisational aspects to be able to not only lead yourself or another person, but also a group of people. Groups can act as a psychological unit, and it may appear as if they speak with one voice. The reason for this is something we call "contagion", and which stems from the mechanisms we talked about previously—transference, projection, and identification with the projection. We will explore in detail the emotional and relational forces at work in groups, teams, and all kinds of organisations.

CHAPTER 9

Not staying on task: how we take care of our fear and avoid working

We all have experienced moments in organisations when the group or team is not working on task, not producing the product or the services or the internal services that keep the organisation up and running. Not working on task entails, for example, getting excited and angry with another team or another hierarchical level, complaining that one specific colleague is never doing the job the way she or he should, blaming others for our own failure, irrational hope that in difficult times the leader will do the right thing and save the company, forgetting parts of the task and duties, and so on—the list is long and you can certainly imagine similar situations when this is happening to you or in your organisation.

These moments mainly occur when there is a difficulty in the organisation around which unease, distress, fear, a wish for running away or for not wanting to see it might develop. This could be an upcoming project, a new strategy, a shift towards a different product line, a merger or an acquisition where the networks people are part of will undergo change. The negative emotions which may cause distraction from the task are manifold. However, very often we are not even aware of these negative feelings; they are not consciously felt although our body and brain experience them somewhere under our conscious radar screen.

We have already seen how they develop on an individual level—often caused and pre-designed by important early relationships with caregivers and the like. The individual defences can be understood as an immune system in the service of the individual's psyche. Freud coined the term "defences" because he was fond of military metaphors and enjoyed using them for educational purposes. What he observed as "first-line defences", such as repression and conversion, he understood as processes operating in protecting his clients from overwhelming and unpleasant feelings—at the cost of them not living a full life.

Today we assume that they prevent two different things: the pain one feels when experiencing unpleasant emotions such as fear and anxiety following a threat, and the pain one can feel when having an insight which is too unpleasant to be taken in. The latter is, in a way, also a result of threat and the accompanying fear, but more so a threat to identity.

Psychosocial or organisational defences

Taking individual defences to the next level of aggregation, we speak of psychosocial or organisational defences. These work in micro-systems (groups, departments, organisations) and can be best understood as "unconscious collusions or agreements to distort or deny those aspects of experience that in phantasy give rise to unwanted emotion".[176]

We are concerned about these social defences because they often do not have positive effects and are mainly detrimental. They divert thinking, acting, and feeling away from "the reality" and lead to more or less unproductive and even destructive detours from fulfilling the "primary task".[177] Since the reason for the existence of an organisation and the people the organisation is made up of is the work on the primary task, it may cause problems.

So, what are social defences and what are they there for?

One way of looking at these defences is to start from the idea that a group, a team, an organisation must maintain and enhance a shared self-esteem and conserve and protect organisational or group identity. To protect them, denial, rationalisation, idealisation, phantasy, and symbolisation[178] can occur. Although they have a protective function or, one could even say, *because* of their protective, shielding-off function, they may hinder organisational and group learning and are thus counterproductive to the necessary development and decision-making processes—as these are always based on processing and applying new information in the present context. Although for systematic reasons these defences are discussed separately in the literature, they tend to appear together and reinforce each other.

Denial could happen when a team (unconsciously) does not want to see that they need to change and adapt because the context has changed. Rationalising is finding good reasons for unpleasant insights in unpleasant organisational changes. When the actual leader or a new third person come from the outside of the organisation—it can be you or maybe also the hierarchy level above you—they may seem to be the saviour in a difficult situation.

Phantasy is a way of projecting something very special onto, for example, an object—we then speak about phantastic objects. A phantastic object is like Aladdin's miracle lamp—fulfilling the wishes or desires of your imagination and mind. In the financial market crisis of 2007/8 for example, collateralised debt obligations (CDOs) were phantastic objects. They gave the illusion that one could get rich quickly without any need for risk or risk analysis. "Tulip mania" in the 1630s saw tulip bulbs become objects of speculation. Diamonds today may also be considered phantastic objects. A phantasy in the context of this book is a process of imagination in which conscious or unconscious desires are fulfilled.

Symbols in organisations can be artefacts, myths, uniforms, titles, and hierarchies—they are used for their calming, soothing, and reassuring capacity,[179] yet they can also distort or conceal reality and restrict the capacity to perceive and process information.

When phantasy, rationalisation, and idealisation come together, "groupthink" can develop. Most people in leadership positions have heard about this concept—also popularised by the very famous film *12 Angry Men*. This 1957 film depicts how one person on a jury goes against the grain and questions the jury's guilty verdict on a young man who is accused of having killed his own father and liable to a death sentence. The other jurors came to their conclusion based on class and race prejudice and weak evidence. The juror that questions the group's conclusions manages, over the course of a day, to persuade the other eleven that the young man is in fact innocent of the accusation. This phenomenon, whereby the eleven men came to a premature conclusion, is called groupthink.

The concept of groupthink was introduced by Janis.[180] He depicts it as a "premature concurrence-seeking behavior" that results in defective information search-and-evaluation processes and is born of stress and anxiety.[181] Groupthink is a decision trap, which Janis observed taking place in political events. He found that in the decision-making situations leading to the invasion of Pearl Harbor, the Watergate affair, the Vietnam War, and the North Korean War, the decision-making group made poor, unrealistic decisions. Groupthink occurred because every member of the decision committee was subject to a supposed group opinion and hence held back their own viewpoint so as not to upset the ostensible harmony. Janis claims that in specific situations characterised by cohesion, isolation, high stress levels, and strong leadership, behavioural factors such as self-censorship, peer pressure, the illusion of invulnerability, and simplified reductions of reality result in possible alternatives being overlooked. The decisions made are then far removed from reality. In the case of groupthink a number of defences come together: rationalisation (simple reductions of reality), idealisation (of the group leader), and phantasy (this group is knowing it all) play a role.

Groupthink has become a widely, unfortunately often imprecisely, used term for negative group dynamics in decision-making situations involving managers and politicians.[182]

Basic assumption mode

These defences are also the basic ingredients of very powerful group-level mechanisms called "basic assumption modes". This is a quite technical term which is close to what Schein meant when he explains that organisational culture is: "a pattern of shared basic assumptions that the group learned as it solved its problems of external adaptation and internal integration".[183] Yet Schein speaks for a rather long-term, that is, cultural perspective. They are patterns of thinking and feeling and acting which the group have invented, developed, or discovered when adapting to external changes and internal integration and its problems. Having been shown to work well enough, such patterns are then taught to new members as the one and only way to perceive, think, and feel in relation to those kinds of problems. This "teaching" is not an active teaching, it is the implicit knowledge which groups develop over time when thinking about new solutions or new ideas. Then they return to the successful way they have done things before. It could be, for example, the basic assumption, "you have to dare to speak up, if you want something to change" or the opposite: that you have to "look for allies before you speak up".

When we talk about the basic assumption mode, a term introduced by Bion in the sixth decade of the last century,[184] we mean a shared mentality a group develops; an unconscious thinking and feeling—which develop out of a specific situation or problem. We can distinguish between two different types of mentality—one is the work group mentality: this is concerned with completing the primary task while at the same time consciously and effectively dealing with the emotions that arise within and from this process. Confronting factual and emotional reality is part of dealing with the primary task and is an important aspect of leadership.

However, when the leader and/or the structures, rules, and regulations do not contain the underlying anxieties (see Chapter 2), when there are no opportunities to discuss and work through sorrows or worries, unconscious group-level defences can set in to help transform and neutralise strong tensions and affects. By that, the negative emotions are dealt with, and the group continues to feel unthreatened—when the group is in the grip of these unconscious group-level defences we call it a "basic assumption group", being in a "basic assumption mentality". This only takes place on a shared mental level and not on the individual level.[185] Both mentalities, work group mentality and basic assumption group mentality, may coexist; however, one will prevail over the other.

When a group shifts away from the primary task and the work group mentality to a basic assumption mentality, group members may not recognise this as a shift and even think that the work atmosphere has improved—because the negative emotions have "disappeared". If a group member detects these patterns and shares this insight with other group members, that member will most likely be ignored or attacked, hence the basic assumption mentality will prevail.

This arising basic assumption mentality may be either short-lived or persist as the dominant mode. Although originally intended to mitigate emotional threats, basic assumption mentalities can over time become dysfunctional and bureaucratic, since they not only reduce anxiety, but also replace compassion, empathy, awareness, and meaning with control and impersonality.[186] Therefore, the perception of reality becomes distorted, and decision-making is impaired—which is the most important and thus problematic aspect. We know of six different basic assumption mentalities. Figure 23 provides an overview of known basic assumption mentalities.

Collective phantasy	Basic assumption mentality	Dominant defence mechanism	Dominant affect
Dependency	The leader should feed and protect	Idealisation of the leader or his "word"	First depression, jealousy, guilt, then worship and alignment
Pairing	Resulting from the pairing of two group members, something new, a new idea/person will rid the group of negative emotions	Phantasies via an utopian ideal	First despair, destruction, hate, hopelessness, then hope, trust, enthusiasm,
Fight/flight	The existence of an external enemy, who necessitates fight, defence, or flight	Projection and splitting	First fear, hopelessness, depression, then anger, suspicion, and relief or even hope
One-ness	Powerful connection with an almighty power, an oceanic feeling of unity	Denial of individual differences	First identity fears and conflicts, fragmentation, animosity, then shared identity and togetherness
Me-ness	The individual's inner world becomes a place of comfort. The group does not exist	Splitting and projection in society	First fear of destruction and loss of self, sadism, passive aggression, then individualism and independence
Group-formation	The group oscillates between one-ness and me-ness	Attacks on alliances and integrative attempts	First threat to the group identity and individual identity, then connection and individualism
Victimism/ Supremacism	Via feeling as a victim the group develops a feeling of supremacy	Attacks on minorities, devaluing them, narcissistic omnipotence	First threat to the future and to individual existence and identity, then feeling of control and security

Figure 23: An overview of basic assumption mentalities[187]

The table reads as follows: the group develops unconsciously a shared phantasy (first column); by that, the group members create an unconscious basic assumption mentality (second column). In this mentality, some defence mechanisms are combined (third column) to better deal with a set of difficult emotions. The result of this unconscious defence is that the group feels better by achieving a positive emotion (fourth column) which can then hinder or support the work on the primary task.

In dependency mode (Bion) the group invests the leader with omnipotence and avoids solving its problems itself. The leader ought to do that, it is the leader's responsibility. She or he is also expected to protect and nurture the group emotionally. The group has no belief in its own skills and abilities; the behaviour is rather passive and immature. For the leader, the projection of omnipotence is initially received as a confidence boost, being perceived as very competent and goal oriented; however—as she or he soon realises—this is an unrealistic expectation of the group. When this magic leader does not perform in line with these expectations, they will immediately be attacked and replaced. A cycle of leader-seeking, idealisation, and denigration occurs. No leader proves to be good enough; they are constantly replaced since they will fail to solve the problems of the group. An example of this dependency mode is a department in an organisation which is difficult to manage and change. The staff may resist and insist on their own way of doing things; they wear their leaders out: none of them is ever good enough. Group feelings of depression and guilt are avoided through this mentality.

The pairing group (Bion) is in hope of being rescued from a difficult situation. They refuse (unconsciously) to take up their own responsibility, so that a state of stasis and stuckness develops. The rescue should come through the collaboration of two separate people. As a leader, you might feel this through an (unusually strong) desire to collaborate with a certain person to think together how best to solve the problems of the group. This can also be a leader/consultant pair. When this successful coming together does occur, then the group is stuck in pairing. The reason for this is that hope is easier than taking action and showing responsibility. Yet when the pair tries to create a new solution, they are dethroned, so that the group can carry on being inactive and maintaining hope rather than taking responsibility and moving forwards. Then the consultant or leader is suddenly not good enough. The fear of failing and hopelessness with regard to the necessary changes must be high to develop such a mentality.

The fight-or-flight group (Bion) wants to preserve the group at all costs; they feel threatened and will resist the change so that they can survive via fight or flight. In both ways the focus shifts to an (imagined) enemy which will be seen as a scapegoat. For the leader this is a strong pull towards rejecting another group or organisation without the will to understand what is going on—the other is clearly the enemy. This mode gives the group a lot of energy and they feel motivated and powerful when dealing with the outside world. The behaviour of the group is outward-looking—it aims to place blame on another group and to avoid taking responsibility. In fight mode the group rejects responsibility and refuses to take part in the change.

The mode of one-ness (Turquet) occurs when the group feels threatened and wants to avoid the necessary change by giving up all sense of individual and group identity. The group turns into an undifferentiated stage of wholeness and feels as one. This happens via seeking a powerful connection with an almighty power, so that a feeling of oceanic unity develops. The individual group members give up their identity for the sake of well-being gained by a feeling of being part of something larger. It is committing itself to some kind of movement beyond itself to feel secure and able to survive. For you as a leader this entails becoming part of the movement—the movement sets the tone, not you. For the group members it feels like being in a very special union all together, mysterious and pleasurable—only this group knows about this secret.

The opposite of that mode is me-ness (Bain, Lawrence, and Gould)—here the members of the group act as if there is no group; each member is only an individual acting on their own behalf and not on behalf of the group. The inner world of the individual becomes a place of comfort. There is no relatedness or connection within the group as such. By this denial of the group, the group members defend themselves from the destructive aspects of group life. Since this mode is very close to modern Western values of individualism, nobody really wonders why and how such kind of behaviour sets in.

Victimism/supremacism (Nagel) is another mode which deals with the threat of annihilation because of one's own sense of failure and the resulting feeling of helplessness. People claim to be "victims" even though they are not real victims of oppression, but rather "victims-in-the-mind". Together with other "victims" of the seemingly same class of oppressed people, they create a sense of belonging as a group, which, however, later turns out to be illusory in terms of its psychological effect. This group of victims feels persecuted, humiliated, and oppressed by an imagined aggressor. The group of self-proclaimed victims surrenders its own capacity to act, its autonomy and responsibility, and thus projects the fear of a lack of power and its own failure onto a phantasised all-powerful leader (think Trump or Putin).

They promise a land of milk and honey which functions as a kind of container, yet it proves to be more of a "fake" container because the leader will not help to digest the fears and transform them into a positive energy of solution and departure, rather the contrary. Such a leader is eager to force a further devaluation of the others into "the bad guys", splitting and transforming fears into hatred and aggression. The differences between the victims and the others are emphasised—a false identity built on distorted differences is the result. The victims are now united in their victim mentality, sharing a mutual understanding against the rest of the world, here against the West, for example. The imagined morally necessary struggle against their own oppression gives rise to the feeling of moral superiority. One can also find this mentality in organisations when, for example, older members claim to be the victims of digitisation and, by that, look to devalue younger organisational members.

Whether and which kind of basic assumption mode the group develops depends on the situation and context, and the valency of the group members as well as of the leader. As you can see, all are in one way or the other connected to changes which seem to be difficult to bear and induce distress and fear.

KEY LEARNING

- Knowing that these social defences exist is helpful for you as a leader, especially when you are wondering about unusual feelings within yourself: reactions you observe which cause astonishment or even anger about your own fear. This knowledge can help you to better understand the emotional needs of the group, team, department, or organisation—whether they need to be inspired, protected, nurtured, developed, etc.
- Another reason to dig a bit deeper is when people do not recognise or do not feel invited to take up a role in a system.
- Also, as a leader you are part of this basic assumption mentality or of the social defences. As Ettin et al. (1997)[188] describe, groups have "an uncanny knack for finding leaders who manifest latent group dynamics and thereby find their niche and sources of power". With your way of being you fit into specific situations and group dynamics—so the major task for you is to really understand where your weak points are and what kind of (unconscious) hooks you might offer a specific group dynamic. Ultimately, it is the leader who is responsible for accomplishing the primary task.

CHAPTER 10

Facing difficult decisions: dealing with defences, moral choices, and paradoxes

Just think about which decisions in your life have been the most difficult. Most people find it very hard to decide to marry a partner and bind to someone else for a lifetime. It has implications for the rest of your life, hopefully, and may thus appear to be frightening—how do you know whether you will still love the other in ten, twenty, thirty years' time? And what if the person changes? And what if you change? Or the other person becomes seriously ill? Many imponderabilia which cannot be fully assessed today. Sometimes this decision becomes so frightening that you prefer not to decide—yet. According to Watzlawick, who said you cannot *not* communicate, not making a decision is also a decision. You might also think that you will lose your freedom and autonomy; however, you will hopefully gain connectedness, containment, love, and warmth—a very difficult choice to be made.

This guides us to another class of difficult decisions encompassing a conflict which has a moral aspect to one side of the decision space. It could be a decision that grants pleasure, but is at the same time doing harm to something or someone—like travelling for a holiday in times of climate change. You want to go on vacation far away, contribute to international understanding, as well as broaden your thinking—yet flying many miles is contributing to climate damage. Is there an effective method to come to a decision? How can you think about the decision space and integrate your feelings without hanging on to biases and old patterns?

Let us start with the first problem of decision-making which plays an important role for you as a leader: strategic decisions. Key features of strategic decisions are that they are highly uncertain: the probabilities of occurrence of the different possible events and scenarios for which one prepares with the decision are not known, neither are possible future scenarios—you have to decide today to prepare and deliver for a future you do not know and might not even be able to imagine. This causes some major issues because (1) the brain has a special way of thinking into the future to which (2) the emotion of fear is deeply connected, and which (3) has major consequences for strategic decision-making.

Fear and thinking about the future are closely related because our feelings of fear emerge from the same brain region as our ability to plan—the latter of course is part of strategic thinking. Both take place in the frontal lobe, the phylogenetically youngest part of the brain, which is located directly above the eyes. To it is attributed the ability to project oneself into the future, specifically so that we can reflect on upcoming actions and events while imagining ourselves as acting in these future situations. Corresponding experiments and the study of specific clinical situations of brain lesions have proven that the destruction of the frontal lobe reduces our ability to plan, but at the same time leads to a reduction in our feelings of anxiety. People with such deficits can no longer think about the past, present, and future. Without being able to imagine the future, they live only in the present and—this is really interesting—they show no fear.[189] Thinking about the future and fear of the future are thus inseparable and belong together.

The brain wants to control future experiences, and therefore thinking about the future helps us form a picture of it.

> We look to the future in order to make certain prognoses, and we make prognoses so that we can control the future.... The surprising reason for this is that humans enjoy wielding control—not to

> manipulate the future but simply for the sake of exercising control. Being busy—changing things, influencing things, allowing things to happen—is one of the most fundamental needs with which the human brain is biologically equipped, and from childhood on this inclination for control explains a large portion of our behaviour .... The fact is that humans are born with a passion for control and that they leave the world in the same manner. Research shows that you become unhappy, helpless and depressive when you, at some point during your life, lose the ability to control.[190]

Illusions of foresight

So, it just feels good to (think you) control the future. That is why we do it and that is why we cannot help it. We want to feel a sense of control and influence, and even the illusion of control has the same effect on us as real control does. Presumably, this desire for control also explains why management is always concerned with looking into and planning for the future, and thereby trying to exert influence, preparing, and steering the company in the desired direction.

The only problem is that we cannot imagine the future as it will be, because not only do things "always turn out differently than we think", but no matter how cleverly we proceed, we are subject to three systematic, psychologically conditioned types of illusion, which Gilbert has called "illusions of foresight".[191] These are realism, presentism, and rationalism. And to top it all off, the fear of deciding also plays an important role. We will discuss its function in more detail later. These three illusions, however, are strongly related to our cognitive biases (see Introduction and Chapter 8).

By realism, we mean the tendency to believe that things are as they appear to us, and deficiencies in memory, perception, and imagination are not perceived but overwritten or filled gaps (the blind spot is an example of this).

Presentism means that present experiences influence our view of things. Thus, although it is possible to put oneself emotionally into a future situation, which entails our having to feel ahead, present feelings are stronger and override this, unconsciously. This means that if someone is feeling bad today, it is hard for them to have positive feelings about the future.

Rationalism involves our ability to find many good reasons after the fact for decisions once they have been made. Our "psychic immune system" helps us maintain our positive self-image, because in hindsight everything looks different than it did before. For example, the failure of a major deal with an important new client is a terrible experience that leads to different evaluations depending on whether it is in front of you or behind you. If it is imminent, it is imagined as an "exceptionally bad, career- or company-destroying event". If it has already happened, the brain, with its psychological immune system, reshapes it in such a way that it is now regarded as the "most important experience in one's entire professional life". Through this changeable evaluation, our brain makes it difficult for us to assess the emotional effects of future situations.

Fear and anxiety

The next big thing in thinking and feeling into the future is fear. The brain uses these illusions just described to reduce the fear of an unpredictable future. All managers have intuitively used planning in order to provide themselves and their employees with the feeling of control, therefore reducing the fear that accompanies the future. Unfortunately, talking about fear has been, until today, a taboo in executive circles.

Fear is not only an anthropological constant, but also part of every strategy process. In general, fear is triggered by outer or inner threats and induces actions such as attack and defence (fight), or retreat (flight). It can also cause freezing—simulating death. These threats can be real or perceived risks to physical, existential, or emotional intactness. In the context of business, physical attacks do not play a significant role, but existential and emotional intactness are very important. Both deal with self-esteem and thus identity. Existential threats can be around money, home, and health and might also have a physical impact, whereas emotional threats are more difficult to define.

In particular, uncertainty—not knowing what the future brings—can be perceived as a threat. Up until a certain level of difference between the learnt and the new, we react with curiosity and wish for exploration. Yet, when that difference increases to a certain, unpleasant point, initial reactions are to retreat and abandon, which can subsequently lead to existential fear, loss of acting capability, and loss of control.[192] We've seen this in exploring the basic emotional systems where PANIC/GRIEF arise. We can well imagine that decision makers encounter existential fear when facing crisis and long-term company failure. Their own destinies, as well as those of their employees and their families, depend on their success; failure would cause a lot of distress and harm to many of them—a very frightening prospect.

Another fear-creating aspect of strategic decision-making is conflict—every decision encompasses the need to give up one side or idea to pursue another side or idea. Conflict is unpleasant and is perceived by our brain as a threat—which has the capacity to induce fear depending on the size of the threat perceived. The concepts of primary task and primary risk[193] are connected to this conflictual choice. The primary task is the task the organisation is set up to do. We assume for the time being that the organisation has a structure which is good for accomplishing this task. The advantage of using the concept of the primary task is that it blends structural and psychological views of the work—one reacts to the primary task and the task itself represents realities which can be influenced but not completely controlled.

The primary task consists of the ensemble of practices which are leading to the organisation's goals, and it is helpful to differentiate between the stated task and the actual primary task. Finding the right primary task contains the primary risk which is not defining the appropriate primary task. When the environment, the market, competitors, technology, or clients' wishes change, a new primary task must be defined; this is a strategic choice which entails the risk of choosing the wrong task, which cannot be managed as foreseen or does not have the expected results. This is the primary risk of an organisation and is embedded in the environment. The primary risk creates anxiety and fear, stemming on one hand from the uncertainty and on the other hand from the implied conflict perceived as a threat. People shy away from making the final decision; instead they tend to vacillate between the alternatives and show ambivalence.

You have certainly observed that in your own organisation decisions are avoided or taken half-heartedly, which means that they are not implemented. The feeling of ambivalence shows up in the individual and the perception of the conflicting choice, and the resulting indecisiveness, is a simultaneously positive and negative orientation towards an object. Ambivalence includes cognition ("I think about X") and/or emotion ("I feel about X"); ambivalence occurs when cognitions clash, emotions clash, or both cognitions and emotions clash. It is often described as having "mixed feelings", being "torn between conflicting impulses", and being "pulled in different directions".[194]

Let me take a little excursion here to clarify the difference between ambivalence and ambiguity: ambiguity is part of the object, the choices, or in the event—not in the individual—and means a state in which not all alternatives can be described and not all probabilities can be calculated. "Decisions under ambiguity" are real-life decisions, whereas the so-called "decisions under risk" describe decisions where all alternatives are known and all probabilities can be calculated—often applied to simplify ambiguity in strategic planning, yet forgetting the emotional background.

The consequences for strategic decision-making are well known—no decision is taken, the decision is postponed into the future, a half-hearted or unclear decision is taken, the changes and demands for a new strategy are denied or forgotten, one decision is taken today and tomorrow is reversed—there are multiple ways of avoiding facing the primary risk, conflict, uncertainty, and the (often unconscious) fear connected with all of this.

Case study

Decision-making—failure is always an option

Mal O'Connor

A moment that could not be ignored

I was sitting in the back of the room with Orion's board members as day two of the meeting with their sponsoring organisation began. It was eighteen months since Quasar had launched Orion, a new organisation designed to create innovative practices that would help Quasar transform itself.

We started early, hoping to complete everything by noon and head home after yet another work weekend in another time zone. Yesterday, Orion had laid out its progress against three core objectives. Today's focus: how to transfer useful practices from Orion to Quasar's five regions.

Usually buzzing with conversation, the room was quiet. Carl, Quasar's CEO, and his senior leadership team (SLT) had been conspicuously absent after dinner last night. John, my client, the CEO and chair of Orion's board, was about to open the floor for overnight reflections on day one, when Carl stood up. Carl said he had met with his team after dinner the night before, and they had agreed unanimously on a recommendation he would like to make.

I started scribbling furiously as Carl said, "Many of the challenges we anticipated facing a couple of years ago that caused us to launch Orion, and to invite you to become its board members, have been addressed. Thank you for your leadership. We believe that at this time we can bring the work you are doing back in-house and suggest that you wind things down by the end of the year."

You could have heard a pin drop. Everyone was holding their breath. John stood stunned and motionless in front of the room. Somehow, he found his voice and suggested that we take a break and return in twenty minutes to discuss this further. Exhale.

As it turned out, there was no discussion. When the thirty or so participants returned after the break, John suggested that he and Carl meet after the meeting ended. And so it did.

The birth of Orion

Three years into his tenure as CEO, Carl determined that he had three to five years to transform Quasar before losing significant market share to more nimble competitors. The industry was on the verge of major change at the same time as Quasar was coming off its two best years. It was not going to be easy to make a case for change to managers and employees. Quasar was thriving. Who would believe the sky was about to fall?

"Customer experience" was the new buzz phrase. New players, new technology, and flexible-design thinking could turn Quasar's greatest strength, its size, into a major obstacle. They could still trade on economies of scale, and the company had built a strong culture of success. Strong cultures, however, can be the most difficult to change.

Quasar's SLT had two factions. One believed the company faced an external challenge, and that a public relations campaign could shift the company's identity in the marketplace. Carl himself leaned in this direction. Others saw Quasar's major challenges as internal, and believed success would require changing behaviour and practices to meet market shifts.

Quasar decided to pursue both perspectives. At the time, we did not know whether Carl and his team were avoiding making a decision, or if they were making a wise, strategic choice. Perhaps Carl was reacting to pressure from Quasar's board, who had told him, "Failure is not an option." The company hired a well-known public relations firm to design and execute a PR campaign. We, a small consulting firm with expertise in system-wide change, were invited to help work with Quasar to meet three critical, internal imperatives:

- Create and implement practices that help turn a large, bureaucratic organisation into a nimble and innovative one, without losing the advantages of size.
- Develop a framework for identifying, recruiting, and retaining talent needed to create the best possible customer experience.
- Build a technology platform that supports and enhances customer and workforce experience.

How to address these challenges quickly enough? To meet the three critical imperatives above, Carl and the SLT leaned towards creating a temporary organisation, with its own governance and leadership structure, financed for five years to achieve those three objectives. It was a very challenging approach, both exciting and worrisome.

The track record of such parallel organisations is well known. The majority fail, and all face serious "breakup risk". We invited Carl and his team to a pre-decision session to discuss the possible pitfalls of setting up a temporary organisation like Orion. They included:

- Emergence of a fantasy that the temporary organisation will magically save the company.
- Tension with, and resistance from, those who run current operations. After all, the temporary organisation is funded by their hard work.
- Leaders who believe that transformation is something others need to do, but not themselves.
- Lack of ongoing commitment from top leadership, resulting in a fast start that fizzles.
- Failure to transfer new practices back to the "mother ship".

In the end, after much deliberation, Carl and his team decided to go forward. We climbed aboard, first to help Carl and his team create Orion, and then to work directly with Orion to accomplish the three imperatives.

Setting up the Orion organisation

We helped Carl and his team design Orion's organisation and its governance structure, and then focus on boundary relations between the two organisations. We knew from past mistakes that Orion could do great work and still fail if these relations were not clear. Issues of authority and task, when not defined early enough, often result in misunderstandings that require re-contracting the entire initiative with the parent company later on.

We recommended that the two organisations negotiate a written agreement defining Orion's core task and authority, for reference when inevitable misunderstandings and resistance arose later. After much debate, Quasar's SLT and Orion's board agreed on Orion's primary task: to identify and transfer practices that position Quasar for success in an increasingly competitive environment.

Had we stated the task more bluntly, we would have seen the first pitfall embedded in the primary task—the fantasy that Orion alone could save the company by protecting Quasar from losing market share.

In retrospect, as will become apparent later, the agreement helped clarify Orion's authority, but could have mitigated the breakup risk in a more systemic way. The agreement stated that:

- Quasar would transfer a specific amount of money to Orion annually to cover Orion's projected expenses for five years.
- Orion's board was responsible for structuring Orion's organisation, setting milestones and timetables to reach annual objectives agreed on with Quasar.
- The chair of Orion's board was authorised to make decisions for the Orion organisation. Quasar's SLT could make recommendations and critique Orion's work but could not overrule a decision made by Orion about how it ran its own operations.
- Orion was responsible for managing its own finances and authorised to raise additional funds on its own.

The first eighteen months

Everyone applauded progress over the first six to nine months. Quarterly meetings went well. By year end, Orion's practice area teams had identified several quick wins that showed early progress. Orion's multi-year action learning plan for identification and implementation of useful practices met with initial approval at the third quarterly meeting.

Murmurings of dissatisfaction first emerged from Quasar's regional vice presidents (RVPs) towards the end of year one. Their top performers were upset that so much money had been invested in Orion. After one of the regional practice meetings, one of the RVPs complained, "Why are we doing this? ... We could do it ourselves." We had anticipated a first wave of resistance and thought Orion would be prepared to address it as year two began.

By the first quarter of year two, Orion was right on plan, working in all five regions to identify practices that were alive in the present and could be adapted to meet future challenges. Interactive workshops with regional managers and workers to identify and test innovative practices were well received. Excitement in the regions was building, and feedback confirmed the sessions were energising and productive.

Nevertheless, harbingers of push-back were evident. Some RVPs asked members of Carl's SLT, "What was Orion going to deliver and when? Why weren't practices already identified and transferred?" Some members of Carl's SLT started to feel their legitimacy challenged. Some were pushing Carl to bring more of the work in-house. One of his team members said, "My authority is being challenged by the folks running Orion, and they clearly don't understand the complexities of our business." Carl was feeling the heat.

With John's blessing, we offered to work with Carl and his team on ways of managing the increased pressure and resistance they faced, but Carl declined. The next pitfall had arrived: leaders wanting transformation to take place without transforming themselves. It would be just a month or so later that Carl would make his recommendation that Orion wind down its work by the end of the year. Let's pick up the story after that critical meeting.

After the meeting

After others left for the airport, Carl and John discussed Quasar's "recommendation". I stayed to meet with John later, my stomach in knots, wondering what I should have done differently. Breakup risk was staring us in the face.

When we met at the hotel bar later that afternoon, John had recovered some of his composure. He reported that he had committed to get a proposal to Carl within a month. Carl had reiterated his recommendation to close up shop in a few months, but that it was not a command: their authorisation agreement made that clear. Carl chose not to raise the elephant in the room—pulling back funding—and John chose not to ask about it. It was too early in the negotiation.

John and I agreed that our consulting team would discontinue our work until the board responded to the "recommendation". Orion's board needed to come to know its own mind. That would require open and honest debate and could result in discontinuing working with us.

John invited me to continue to work with him in the background over the next three weeks, as he worked with the Orion board to determine the best course to take. None of this unfolded as easily or logically as it sounds. It was a gut-wrenching day.

Consulting to an impending breakup

Orion and Quasar faced serious breakup risk, and so did we. I knew I had to manage my own desires and feelings as the lead consultant responsible for a team working full-time on this initiative, and I was conflicted. We were not quite a third of the way through and had a lot to lose, not least, three years' revenue. A voice in my head said I didn't want the initiative to stop, but I had heard that voice before: it was my own fear of failure speaking.

Intellectually I knew I had set a classic trap for myself. I imagined that if I were the leader I might be able to save the initiative, while at the same time feeling impotent to do so. How could I help John and the board recover its potency? How could I recover my own? Certainly not while bouncing back and forth between fantasies of omnipotence and feelings of impotence.

I usually work with a shadow consultant during difficult consulting projects—a practice I heartily recommend—and I outlined my dilemma to him. I could see the trap I was in, but not how to get out of it. He reminded me that my task was to consult to John and to the initiative, not to save it; in other words, to help them build on their strengths within the limitations and constraints they faced, and my own.

That helped create some space to think. I had focused on the accommodating parts of John's diplomatic leadership approach and desire for consensus. I had ignored, however, his ability to lead with negative capability; that is, John could sit with multiple, conflicting points of view without rushing to make a decision. I was the more frantic one in that moment.

John and I stepped back and mapped out how to use the next few weeks. Why not approach this the way we had approached the entire initiative: listen and learn first—about how it felt to be in the positions of Quasar's leaders. Orion's proposal would fall on deaf ears if it didn't address those concerns. Orion board members held individual discussions with members of Carl's top team and the five RVPs. They learned that in most cases dissatisfaction was not with the work itself. Quasar's leaders felt:

- Disenfranchised in a battle for authority they felt they were losing—“Who’s in charge here?”
- “Their money”, a result of their hard work, was being used by others without their having any say in how it was spent.
- Orion’s existence was an implicit critique of their performance.

Orion’s board members had been struggling with their own feelings of omnipotence and impotence. Would their vision of success crumble if they accepted Carl’s recommendation? How should each manage their feelings of both possible loss and loyalty to Quasar? Learning how Quasar’s RVPs were feeling helped create space for Orion’s board members to think as well.

In fact, the RVPs’ feelings made perfect sense and helped reveal what was missing in the earlier authority agreement. Discussions about authority had been so focused on what Orion needed in order to feel authorised that we had ignored breakup risk as a shared, systemic problem affecting both parties.

This recognition opened an opportunity for John and his board to think strategically and face the risk in front of them more clearly. It was not just a risk to Orion’s future. What risk did Quasar face if the initiative failed? In addition to sunk cost, the entire industry knew this experiment was happening. It was a reputational gamble on Quasar’s part. Internally, given tensions in senior leadership ranks, there could be a talent drain instead of a talent gain.

We had not guided Quasar and Orion in addressing ways to mitigate these kinds of risks, as many firms do when negotiating deals. We had not, for example, recommended making explicit the role that Quasar senior leaders played in Orion’s success or failure. With no incentive, no wonder they felt de-authorised and competitive.

John and I worked on how he could help his board craft a proposal that helped Quasar leaders feel they had skin in the game, sharing the risk of failure and the results of success. Conversations with RVPs revealed, for example, that Quasar had strong, and underused, technology capabilities throughout the company. In addition, Orion’s board now realised that the talent development pipeline could be advanced more quickly if Orion’s team became part of Quasar’s talent department. RVPs were interested in strengthening these two departments.

In the absence of more financial incentives, did it make sense to bring some things in-house more quickly? Perhaps this was a doorway into sharing some of the risk.

Charting a path forward

John and Orion's board held preliminary conversations with Carl and his team to test options. Orion's final proposal included:

- Orion continuing to work on the primary task, but in much closer collaboration with the RVPs.
- Quarterly meetings becoming "Quasar's meetings", with less reporting out from Orion and more focus on the absorption of innovative practices in ways that worked well for the RVPs and Carl's SLT.
- Orion working with systems technology in year three to create a network of tech talent throughout the company with a focus on supporting implementation of new practices; then moving that work in-house in year four.
- Incorporating the Orion talent team into Quasar's understaffed talent department in year three, working with the RVPs and Carl's team to refocus its charter to meet market challenges.

It was not a "perfect" solution, and feelings remained raw. Negotiations between Quasar and Orion were a first step in learning whether trust, once shattered, could be rebuilt. Quasar accepted the proposal, and we all got back to work. As a final request, John asked Carl to commit to no further initiative-ending recommendations for the duration of the initiative. Carl agreed.

* * *

This complex case shows the difficulties of making strategic decisions and the feelings of fear and anxiety involved on different levels and in different stages of this case.

The strategic question emerged at the beginning, when Quasar's SLT was thinking about the problem it was having—is it an identity and thus PR question or has it internal reasons? By asking these two questions, they were most likely avoiding the real question—which is whether and how to change the strategy to adapt to changing markets and by that the need for changing the primary task. The SLT with Carl did not choose between their two options, but avoided the choice and by that also avoided the question for the primary task and avoided feeling their own fears of failure. And to then avoid that primary risk of choosing the wrong task, Orion was founded. Pressure of the board, as it shows here creating additional anxiety, is never helpful and hinders good decision-making. And although the fantasy behind setting up a new organisational structure and its primary task of saving the mother company (and avoiding the real choice) was voiced, Carl and John continued setting up Orion—doomed to fail from the beginning? Yet the capacity for negative capability (see Chapter 2), especially listening to the other side, helped to create a solution which was acceptable to all sides. Whether it will be successful in the long run is still an open question.

Moral choices

An important aspect of strategic and corporate decision-making is morality. Business ethics has been a rising subject over the last thirty years, and together with the discussion of other aspects of justice and fairness has become more and more important. Generation Z at least claims to have and use their moral compass. The climate crisis and the (over)use of the commons, that is, public land, as well as the new quest for sustainability, equity, inclusion, and diversity, are all challenging our moral reasoning and decision-making. Whereas business ethics creates a more general framework and describes what is good and just in a methodological way, moral decision-making focuses on the individual concept of morality and conscience. At the end of the day, moral conflicts in strategy-making must be decided individually if you are the CEO or collectively if you decide together with other people.

What kind of moral conflicts might you encounter? Producing fabrics or T-shirts in Bangladesh under questionable circumstances so as to sell them for a low price, abusing public resources like water or air without using most modern technologies in order to save on costs, manufacturing in a country that violates human rights to increase profit … the list is endless and the conflicts are not that easy to resolve—when the company loses income that can result in laying off people which then results in making their life difficult, also a decline in share price, for example, can impact the pensions of former employees.

The opinion on whether moral questions play a role or not in business decision-making is changing over time. When the social responsibility question came up, Milton Friedman's (1970)[195] counterargument was that the only social responsibility of a business is making profit. His view has been challenged and argued against, but a new wave of arguments have emerged which follow Friedman's direction—from this perspective you shall not allow for any group of stakeholders to be more important than another, and individual moral preferences shall also not play out.

In any case, it is impossible to make decisions with social implications and, thus, without touching morality. Therefore, we are going to dive a bit deeper into this subject, which is often forgotten in the context of strategic thinking but is more important today than ever.

Unmatched in the rest of the animal kingdom, human beings help each other and cooperate with non-relatives at cost to themselves (at an unusual rate).[196] "Social decision making" which specifically "considers and integrates the goals, beliefs, and intentions of other individuals into their decision-making calculus" is always part of strategic decision-making. It relies on the theory of mind—the capacity to attribute mental states such as beliefs, intentions, and desires to oneself and others—and is by nature often constrained by social norms and the imagined penalty, which is to influence the expected value of decision outcomes. The imagined penalty is presented by, for example, conscience, the superego, God, or maybe even the legal system and a judge. Giving an account or giving a response to someone or something is considered taking up responsibility. Most humans know how to behave appropriately and also how to lead a good life, and are deeply concerned with morality, justice, and fairness. We create and design cultural organisations for social norm enforcement.[197]

This moral or social decision-making presupposes freedom and voluntariness which demands responsibility and accountability. So, the question is, how do we as humans develop our moral compass? A model for child development assumes the three levels of pre-conventional,

conventional, and post-conventional thinking. The child develops, in the first level, from obedience and punishment orientation, to, in the second level, self-interest and conformity, and, in the third level to adhere to social contracts and universal ethical principles (e.g. Kohlberg[198]). At the end of this development (hopefully) stands the individual as an independent subject who follows their free moral choice based on universal ethical principles.

Kohlberg's theory of moral development builds at its core on the morality of rights and justice. It was furthered in the last century by introducing an addition focus—the morality of care. Therefore, Gilligan[199] differentiates between justice and caring as alternative perspectives. She argues that all human relations can be characterised in terms of equality (justice) and attachment (care), and that inequality, separation, and complacency pose moral problems. We are then able to say that "acting unfairly" and "not helping somebody in a time of need" pose basic yet important moral questions. By including care, she integrates the female perspective into moral philosophy and ethics.

The following Figure 24 gives an overview of the main differences between the two moral principles.

	Care	Justice
Framework	Attachment	Equality
Postulate	Help in times of need	Fairness
Prerequisite	Social context	Freedom
	Socialisation/education	Voluntarism
Dominant feelings	Affection and empathy	Need for justice
Reason for moral problems	Separation/indifference, complacency	Inequality
Gender attribution	Rather female	Rather male

Figure 24: Characteristics of the moral demands of care and justice (author's diagram)

The reflection of justice and care, of equality and relatedness, are central to our human way of being: they belong to "our human nature". Therefore, they should be integrated into our strategic decision-making realm since both of them are more or less consciously prevalent in the social, and thus moral, character of our decisions.

That also means that our more social emotions such as empathy, guilt, and shame are to be carefully observed since they contribute to the moral quality of the decision-making. When people see another person suffering pain or distress, this motivates them to carry out pro-social behaviour in an effort to ease the other's suffering, and also to criticise or punish harmful actions when they see them. Research also shows that when having experienced a secure attachment in early childhood, moral reasoning and authenticity develop, whereas insecurity leads to the opposite and is linked to dishonesty.

What we have seen so far is that conflicting goals create difficulties for decision makers which cause unconscious mental biases, social defences, and other psychological fear-avoiding answers. They may also confront us with moral choices or even dilemmas.

What can you do?

In the grip of all the difficulties strategic thinking entails, we might turn to techniques or ways of reflecting based on paradoxical thinking because the conflicting choices are very often connected with each other as if they were two sides of a coin. A paradox (for example, stability vs change, exploration vs exploitation) is characterised by a tension of opposites and is defined by persistent contradiction of interdependent elements.[200] In Chapter 14 we will explore dealing with paradoxes in more detail, yet some basics are at this point helpful.

Paradoxes are often confused with dilemmas, yet they differ because paradoxes persist, being impervious to resolution, whereas dilemmas can be resolved with either/or decisions requiring a trade-off.[201] However, these concepts overlap, and whether a conflict can be said to entail a dilemmatic or paradoxical choice depends mainly on the time horizon.[202] An important and always present paradox is stability vs change. They seem to be contradictory, yet they are obviously both necessary for organisations to be successful. Stability stems from the need to invest in strategic long-term investments to create a purposeful resource base such as a production site. Investments in the resource base always lead to a certain level of determination, sometimes also resulting in rigidity and turning them into sticky resources. An organisational and structural inertia stemming from the tried and tested plays, also, a role, since most people resist leaving their comfort zone. Yet, in the organisational context, clients and their changing needs, technological development, changing competitors and suppliers, and their behaviour change is necessary to survival and growth.

Nowadays we need to think even more about paradoxical choices, since with increasing technological change, globalisation, and diversity disruptions appear and expose tensions which reveal paradoxes on all levels—individual, team, and organisation. Some quotes illustrate what kinds of paradoxes exist:

- "Art is a lie that shows us the truth"—Picasso
- "One thing I know: that I know nothing"—Socrates
- "Life is a preparation for the future; And the best preparation for the future is to live as if there were none"—A. Einstein
- "Whatever you do will be insignificant, but it is very important that you do it"—Gandhi
- "Some of the biggest failures I ever had were successes"—Pearl Bailey.

I really enjoy what Niels Bohr once said: "How wonderful that we have met with a paradox, now we have some hope of making progress." I would add: "when we deal with it appropriately". Freud formulated it the other way around, saying: "Neurosis is the inability to tolerate ambiguity."

For many people, paradoxes are difficult to deal with since they seem to force you into a decision. This is why they often develop a vicious dynamic, because the more a manager, for example, wants to resolve the paradoxical tension by choosing one side of the coin (such as wanting to achieve change), the more the other side of the coin creeps through the back door into the forefront.[203] Denying, overlooking, rationalising, or repressing are part of shielding against the unpleasantness of this tension. However, it is a typical neurotic reaction to the incapacity of holding the emotional tension and integrating the polarities—the more one side is rejected or suppressed, the more it pops up at unexpected moments. A lot of energy is lost and paranoid reactions can occur with this defensive way of dealing with a paradoxical tension.

There exists, also, a non-defensive way of dealing with fear and anxiety resulting from strategic choices and paradoxical situations—which needs more attention and patience.

For the individual leader it entails actively dealing with the emotions, tuning into the personal reasons for the perceived anxiety, and cognitively understanding and dealing with the conflicting elements of choice. First, one has to perceive the paradox as what it is—a paradoxical tension which (paradoxically) can only be solved by not solving it immediately. From an emotional perspective, it is best described as holding the tension of the opposites instead of avoiding the problem. It demands high emotional maturity and the capacity to undergo a personal quest for the anxiety-provoking aspects of this strategic choice situation, associations accompanying the strategic choice, and expected results and outcomes. What exactly it is that provokes these feelings must be explored. The difficulty here is detecting and admitting one's own defences. A self-experienced manager can handle this intrapsychic personal process alone, but it would be better to deal with it in the management team and maybe using the service of an external facilitator to frame and manage the conversation.

On the cognitive level, paradoxical thinking is the ability to juxtapose, explore, and integrate contradictions in actively thinking of these opposites or antithetical ideas as equally true. This capacity is also the basic resource for creative innovations.[204] We will talk about that in the next chapter.

Successfully managing paradoxes can be best achieved through the interlinked capacities of accepting, confronting, differentiating/integrating, and transcending.[205]

Accepting paradoxes means "learning to live with the paradox"[206] and working it through in the following steps. Confronting consists of discussing the tensions, the opposite poles, their logic, and the questions and concerns connected to that tension. This is quite difficult, especially when you talk about the paradoxes in a team. Humour helps to overcome the emotional tension of the cognitive tension, and it could be an idea to have two team members advocating for each pole whereas the other members are already creating first associations and connections taking the thinking further. This discussion prepares for the next step of differentiating, which involves the separation of distinct elements and the honouring of their differences, whereas integrating involves creating linkages and synergies.[207] Transcendence is the ultimate way of dealing with a paradox—it requires the capacity to think paradoxically. We will look at an example of transcendence in Chapter 14. Paradoxical thinking techniques such as "Janusian thinking" consist of creatively and simultaneously formulating antithetical elements so that something new, a real third position, develops creatively, transcending the ordinary logic.[208] For all human beings—in strategy or in ordinary life—the task of life is to continuously progress through balancing, integrating, and creating new possibilities as a possible third position. The dialectical tension and its inherent ambivalence can thus only be experienced consciously so that a creative new way of dealing with the ambivalent situation will appear.

When the paradoxical tension lies in the use of resources, it may be more helpful[209] to try to focus on the ability to combine and connect the resources instead of focusing on the resources themselves. In addition, you could add a kind of monitoring system: a group of people watching for the emergence of paradoxical patterns. This is called "institutional reflexivity". Both share the separation of the creation of patterns from the creation of dynamics. As we will see later, the paradox is and must be unsolvable when the human side of the decision maker is taken into account as an important root of dynamic capabilities.

KEY LEARNING

- In decision-making, where you have to imagine an uncertain future, fear and anxiety are normal human reactions, but often they are suppressed, denied, or kept at bay by a number of social defences. Knowing them helps to overcome them.
- Male leaders, in particular, prefer to avoid thinking about fear, and certainly do not want to talk about it. Yet fear is an anthropological constant with an extremely important signalling function—naming one's fear should be part of every larger strategic decision-making process, because it contains important indicators for conscious decision-making. And if it remains unconscious, it can have disastrous consequences, especially in long-term decisions, because (not only) the tunnel vision that develops can lead to the overlooking of strategic building blocks that are essential for survival. Moreover, evolution has not eliminated anything that would not be of use to us in some way—so take heart in fear.
- The social influence or better moral impact of decisions is underestimated. Since human beings are by nature moral, this capacity for morality has to be used to make decisions which adhere to two moral systems: they need to be fair, and they need to care for others. This is sometimes difficult when choices seem to be paradoxically intertwined. For that, the capacity for holding the tension of opposites is essential to getting into the paradoxical thinking mode.

CHAPTER 11

Being together in the locker room: creativity, conflict, and divergent thinking

One of the key activities of business leaders is to constantly reflect on how to improve their existing product or service, how to develop new products and services, and whether and how to change their business model. Yet the sheer amount of management literature on how to achieve innovation seems to point to some difficulties in this area. In reflection on what we have talked about thus far, a couple of aspects are obvious: people enjoy stability, comfort, and familiarity; most like to stay in their comfort zone and enjoy only incremental changes. Everything else—bigger changes, new business models, new ways of doing things, etc.—creates uncertainty and by that anxiety. Exploitation would be thus in the focus. However, you need to think exploration also. So, creativity and innovation must come into play. Of course, these attributes were also essential to getting the business off the ground when the entrepreneur built the first stage of the business.

There is something special about them—creativity and innovation are on the one hand difficult to achieve in organisational settings, yet on the other hand are deeply engrained in us humans, serving to allow us to cope with life every minute of every day and as a life moving-forward force. If we did not have this force, we'd still be sitting in our caves.

In a way, achieving innovations must therefore have to do with the organisational setting which makes them so difficult to achieve. But let us first have a look at the built-in innovative capacity of human beings.

Creativity is needed for survival, and more so if one is to lead an efficient life (the brain is always striving for lowering the energy consumption of the whole bodily system) and adapt to changing life circumstances in reacting to its challenges. This is mirrored in the seven basic emotion systems, where creativity plays the most important role in three basic emotions: SEEKING and PLAY and RAGE.

SEEKING makes us search for everything that we need to survive and live: food and shelter, social relationships, friends, a partner. It is also our sense of curiosity which makes us go beyond given answers, boundaries, routines, and rituals. SEEKING does not exist without creativity, since the world of today is not the same as it was yesterday—the prey has moved, people have moved or disappeared. Without imagination and fantasy the continuously changing world cannot be met and thus our needs would be unmet. SEEKING can be integrated into PLAY when two human beings come together to imagine and play out social hierarchies in "playing as if". Since there are no rules or self-invented rules in this act of playing, without a sense of creativity it would not be possible. Not so obvious is the connection to RAGE, which results in the furious destruction of what is hindering the fulfilment of a need. Since this aggressive destruction is not always possible or desirable, we need to find other ways to appease our frustration and rage—for that purpose, creativity is needed as well. You can find a necessity for some kind of creativity in every basic emotion system. These three are the main emotions which play a role in organisations.

The question here for us is now, how and when creativity develops in the human being—so that we may deduct some ideas about how to support its development and flow in later life and in organisations.

At the beginning of life, an infant feels unity with the mother, as if they were one and as they were while the child was still in the uterus. Over time the infant learns and understands that the mother is "not-me".[210] For a very long time the infant needs the mother or another caregiver to be present in order to feel secure and safe. To help this process of understanding that there is a "not-me", the child uses, in this so-called transitional phase, transitional objects. At the age of four to twelve months the infant might be grabbing a blanket, napkin, or handkerchief while sucking a thumb. This later changes into a soft object like a doll or a puppet (and it is so important to the child that they carry it around wherever they go, especially when travelling). They often want to keep this object the whole life long, even as an adult. It is a defence against anxiety and needed for consoling and for falling asleep. This object, as the first "not-me" but extremely closely tied to the me, plays an important role in the development of early creativity and imagination, and helps to bridge the gap between inner reality and outer reality as a space for primary creativity.

This space is the base for the child to develop thinking and feeling in symbols and images: things which are represented but not there at the actual moment—this is called the symbolic function and lays the ground for creativity in later life. Creativity is a process which meanders between conscious and unconscious thinking, between fantasy and real life, between the known and the new third. The new third is like a new and creative solution or idea which emerges from this process of bringing the conscious and the unconscious together—one can call the space in which this thinking develops the *potential space*. It is about experiencing life in its multiple facets, creatively and imaginatively.

This potential (or transitional) space is helping us to manage the tension between different needs and wishes. It is the space where ideas can be imagined, and alternative solutions can be dreamt. Without tension, without unmet needs, without conflicting aspects, no creativity is needed; everything can continue the way it is. Conflict can lead to creative thinking, involving different modes of thought, as in the potential space where the boundaries blur.

The following case study describes an individual in his transitional space.

Case study

A creative mind—an efficient transitional space

Gilles Amado

The Roland Garros tennis tournament, which took place in June 2021 in Paris, gave rise to a phenomenon that intrigued both spectators and sports experts: the incredible resurrection of the No. 1 player, Novak Djokovic, who was severely dominated in an unpredictable manner at the beginning of his match against the Greek Stefanos Tsitsipas, in the final of the event. The surprise was all the more intriguing because this resurrection occurred after the player had requested a break after losing the first two sets.[211]

What could have happened during that time? Djokovic, who was previously down two sets to one in the fourth round match against the Italian Musetti (only ranked 76 in the world), had already asked for a break at that time, but according to Djokovic, a simple shower was enough to get him back on track. But against Tsitsipas, a top-ten player at the peak of his form, the case was much more difficult, as Djokovic seemed to be out of sorts in the final game of the tournament in front of 5,000 spectators. Moreover, the defeat that was about to take place had a "dramatic" dimension insofar as a nineteenth Grand Slam victory would have brought him to within a single unit of the titles of his great rivals, Federer and Nadal, thus propelling him towards a possible title of best tennis player of all time.

Although the breaks were tightly controlled by the officials, wild rumours spread, perhaps spurred on by the conspiracy (pandemic-related) climate of the time. Especially since Djokovic's three-set win on his return from the locker room had left his unfortunate opponent with little chance. After the match, Tsitsipas said: "I don't know what happened in the locker room, but he suddenly became a different player … I'd like to understand … the physicality, the anticipation, the movement, everything seemed better when he came back."

Djokovic himself tried to explain this "miracle". Very religious, he first attributed it, with his usual humour, to St. Sava, the father of the Serbian Orthodox Church. Then he spoke more seriously about the importance of the "inner dialogue" that was made possible by this pause. As he told a journalist, two opposing voices were talking in his head during the game. The loudest voice predicted failure, the other one gave him hope for a turnaround. "Usually," he confided, "this voice stays inside, I don't externalise it. But there, I had to verbalise all that aloud, that I become this other voice which wants to make silence the other one. I encouraged myself, I told myself that I could do it, that it takes possession of my whole being." This statement allows us to understand the necessity of the closed-door setting, as this sonorous monologue could hardly have taken place in public, especially if we know that one of the assets of champions (of tennis in particular) is their ability to hide their negative emotions from their opponents. His cathartic outburst produced a kind of new incarnation, if we are to believe his words: "In fact, in the locker room, I changed my skin!" However, the emotional dimension does not constitute the only aspect of its transformation. The protective space thus found gave him the opportunity to reflect on his "work", to analyse the game he had produced until then as well as that of his opponent, and then to develop a new strategy that the former Swedish champion Mats Wilander described very accurately: shorten the exchanges (four strokes in the last three sets instead of six in the first two) so as to deprive Tsitsipas of time to organise his game.

If we follow him, it was this retreat, this emotional and mental isolation, that allowed the Serb to become an unprecedented opponent.

Djokovic used this "toilet break" again in his quarter-final at Wimbledon (5 July 2022). Dominated by the young Italian Jannik Sinner, who was still inexperienced at this stage of the competition but was unstoppable in the first two sets, Djokovic took a short break, after which the young Italian's game inexorably faded. Interviewed on court after the match, Djokovic recounted the "mirror" scene in the locker room, where he once again spoke his truths out loud. The thousands of spectators seemed incredulous at this account, and Djokovic felt the need to insist: "But it's really true!" This new exorcism session was accompanied by the unlocking of his analytical skills, his precious insights, one of which was decisive: "I feel like Sinner came into the match with not much to lose, but he had a lot to lose when he led two sets to zero. I could feel it … I was able to get inside his head." In other words, rather than internalising the pressure, or even allowing it to overwhelm him, his empathy allowed him to imagine the process that sometimes grips the player on the brink of success: "the fear of winning", an expression that is well known in this sporting world. No change of strategy was needed this time, just a renewed serenity to show his opponent that he was still there, sure of his strength, always ready for a fight far from over, betting on the fear that could gradually invade the young Italian. This happened and opened the way for Djokovic to win the tournament.

Of course, Djokovic is known for his analytical skills, which are matched by a precocious ambition (didn't he declare in his early days that he would be No. 1 in the lifetime of the two current tennis "giants", Nadal and Federer?) and a particularly supportive family and professional environment. But it is quite possible that, without the reflective spaces that he offers himself from time to time in the course of the activity, he would not have won so many decisive matches.

Some will argue that such a break in the game is intended to destabilise the opponent and is therefore not fair play. It is possible that this is sometimes the case with some players. Many players simply hide their faces under a towel during side changes when they feel the need for protected concentration. But most professional tennis players regret the reduction of this break time (from one minute and thirty seconds to one minute), a measure imposed for essentially economic reasons, as too long a match duration disrupts television programmes.

For it is these reflective psychic spaces that allow the overcoming of obstacles and the adjustment to reality, as in the example given by Djokovic.[212]

* * *

In this case, the locker room is the transitional space; the inner dialogue needed a safe space to allow for it to happen. That metaphor can be translated to the team level as well. When a board comes together for a decision-making process, they are also in the "locker room", preparing and reflecting on strategy and tactics, analysing the opponent, licking wounds, reflecting, and creating alignment.

This divergent mode of "emotio-reflecting"—since it involves both emotions and thinking—can lead to transcendence, a new third, and synthesis—this is then creativity. Interestingly, there is a personality trait found in many highly creative individuals that may both result from but also in turn lead to these tensions between modes of thought.

This trait is sometimes called "the preference for complexity".[213] It not only allows the individual to tolerate situations full of tension, but in fact the individual with this trait may have learned that from tension comes the satisfaction of creative insight. The individual learns to prefer complexity, even if there is a tension felt because of it. They know that the tension is indicative of the creative process.[214] Creativity requires effectiveness as well as originality.

If we now turn to the organisational setting, what do you think hinders the appearance of creativity? I think there are a multitude of aspects interfering here:

- As mentioned before, people like their comfort and dislike too much change.
- People are afraid of being shamed by sharing "stupid" ideas.
- Ideas can be claimed by somebody else and can be "stolen", taken away from the idea owner, so there is a bit of a narcissist defence in that.
- People are not (implicitly but also explicitly) allowed to bring in their creative ideas and minds, because the leaders think they may not be good enough, not the right people, or they may be afraid, thinking they should have had that idea themselves.
- Some issues are so complex that people shy away from the size of the task.

A social network is important, yet it is not so easy to find your role and place and to adapt the network if needed. When organisational and individual identity meet, then some kind of struggle takes place at that intersection, a struggle about resistance and adaption to change, about curiosity and fear, about the proven and the new and untested, about old networks and new relationships to be built.

The complexity which is at the heart of the matter of the intersection mentioned, as well as the organisation and its context, can be distinguished in three different forms, which add to the rising need as well as the rising resistance to creative new ideas:

- Dynamic complexity—indicates the extent to which cause and effect are disconnected time-and-space-wise

- Relational complexity—the extent of the differences between the mental models, values, and political interests involved
- Generative complexity—the extent of the connection between knowledge, self, and reality.[215]

The last is particularly important for identity building. No longer is identity so much defined by profession, as it once was; we have to find, create, and design our identity by ourselves, which is demanding (with all the religious, spiritual, gender, job role opportunities we can choose), needs energy and attention, and maybe does not leave so much space for thinking beyond that.

From the organisation perspective, a creative idea is not an innovation if it is not implemented. That adds to the difficulty—to find applicable ideas and solutions. Creativity requires originality and effectiveness. This is especially true in organisations, which need innovation to survive. "That means that an idea must not be simply original; it must also work. It must be practical. It should lead to implementation. It would be good if it could sell."[216]

How does one get to these wonderful original and implementable ideas? The basic answer looks like the following—create a climate, which we've already labelled a safe psychological space, that:

- Allows for mistakes
- Gives room for experiment, yet also gives a framework to experiment within
- Allows for creating trust and
- Gives people autonomy and freedom for independent decision-making.

You also need (like in a cookbook) a bit of:

- Diversity, but not too much (novices and experts, men and women, different cultural backgrounds)
- Motivation (willingness to work on the creative question)
- Purpose (what is it good for?).

This is nothing new and you probably know all of this already. But something, an ingredient or two, seems missing. If everything is *hygge*, nothing new will develop. If there is no curiosity and no playful competition, and especially no conflict—it will not work out.

What is the nature of this conflict? Which type is helpful, and which is a hindrance?

Research has found that task conflicts are good and relationship conflicts are bad for creative thinking.[217] What does that mean? It is better to have a conflict around some content aspects than to have a conflict with a person you do not like, for example.

In addition, certain skills or competencies have proven to be useful.

Divergent thinking, in contrast to convergent thinking, is one core capacity for creativity[218]—it stands for generating multiple solutions translated into fluency (produce a great number of ideas), flexibility (propose a variety of approaches), originality (produce new and original ideas), and elaboration (organise and systematise the details of the ideas and apply them).

Different thinking processes may lead to idea generation:

- Using knowledge in the form of schemata: images, metaphors, analogies
- Associating using creative areas in life, such as music, art, poetry, to start with
- Using emotional imprints of existing experiences with the actual product or service from different stakeholders
- Design thinking which puts the user at the centre of attention by sketching, prototyping, and storytelling around the user's experiences
- Using symbols to develop moments of deep insight (see Chapter 13).

Once ideas are generated, they have to be evaluated for their applicability, effectiveness, and implementability.

One more interesting facet is important and for some time we have been able to observe that it is changing as well. Many years ago we could have said that we live in a global economy, and globalisation has become a day-to-day term for most, but a frightening term for many others—because of the risk or fear of not being able to "catch that train". In addition, due to Covid, the war in Ukraine, and the power struggle between China and the US, this globalisation is under threat. However, it was for a very long time a source of inspiration and creativity.

International understanding has opened up through it and has created international encounters which were the inspiration for new and creative ideas.

KEY LEARNING

- Creating innovation requires a lot of your attention as a leader. Only strong personalities are able to introduce the new and manage the opposing wind from comfort zones and inertia. Only in leaders ready for the new can the new and the foreign come together.
- Good leaders will also see the need for change early enough. It is for you to create the space, the locker room, where your team can get together and develop the organisation further by not avoiding, but looking for, conflictual tensions on the content level. Relational conflicts could yet hinder the process of creativity and innovation.

CHAPTER 12

Thinking together—and how to get there

Thinking together is a crucial capability for organisations and for their leaders who are responsible for enabling that thinking process. Thinking and innovation are closely connected. What does it mean then for the leader, the team, and the organisation to think together? What is needed? What are the hurdles to overcome?

Before we answer these questions, we need to clarify what thinking together means. It consists of just two words—but they entail a whole world. Thinking about thinking suggests a mostly cognitive process, yet as we have seen, thinking without feeling is impossible, and intuition is also an important aspect of thinking. Emotions and intuition interfere with or without us realising it, both within the individual and between team members. This brings us to the second aspect of togetherness. Thinking *together* is particularly challenging since it means that the thinking process has to happen on three levels within the team and within the individual and between the team members—all at the same time—and emotions may interfere on all levels. We will start to look at the details of this challenge in the next paragraph. But before we do that, we have to answer the question: what is this thinking for? When do you really need to think together? Many problems in organisations can be looked at and talked about in a group of people coming together temporarily and thinking in terms of "if this, then that" relations. They need to solve simple or even complicated problems which may require the knowledge and experience of a number of people. Complicated problems have many if–then relationships and for these relationships there exists at least one solution, sometimes even with alternatives. Yet the alternatives, their dependencies and probabilities are known—it happens, so to speak, in a completely predictable universe.

But what I mean here by talking about thinking is solving complex problems together—problems where the number of potential solutions, as well as their probability of success, is unknown. Complex problems are puzzles; they need more than linear if–then thinking and more than the prescriptive input of experts. Their solutions entail a creative and unpredictable element, something very new and different which goes beyond expertise and factual knowledge. Such solutions are therefore difficult to attain as they need more time and attention to develop. Furthermore, when people are coming together in such a way for the first time, they would also need meta-reflection. By meta-reflection I mean a process in which emotions that occur during the process are shared and the group tries to make sense of these emotions by exploring them and even working them through, when necessary. The leader plays a particular role in this process since he allows for it, enables it, and creates the space. Often, when many different values and interests interfere and conflicts are to be expected, it makes sense to progress with an external person who helps guide the process (see the case study in this chapter).

The problems to be solved are mostly strategic questions of some sort, where a look into an uncertain future implies the different emotional reactions we have already discussed (see also Chapter 10).

In management theory you can find two streams which look at this special situation: high-performance teams, and behavioural strategy combined with dynamic capabilities. Especially in the latter, the interfering aspects of that process of strategic thinking are discussed, whereas in the first, the special prerequisites which make a team a high-performance team are explored.

High-performance teams are those which under very special circumstances are capable of producing extraordinary results. These special circumstances can be best described by the level of uncertainty, the complexity of the issue, and the need to share and work together. These three factors determine which working model makes most sense.[219]

Let us here imagine a board of executive directors of a food production company.

Some problems are simple puzzles: they need the attention of just one or two board members and can be best described as easy to solve without the need for a lot of creativity or cooperation—a standstill on one production line because of a fault, for example. For that kind of work, only basic social skills are necessary. More complex problems, such as reinvesting in an existing production line or upgrading it with new technology, which entails not only major financial investment and a partial product strategy change because of additional or different product features, first require more exchange of information and, second, more cooperation between the different management functions. At this level, one needs more well-developed coordination, negotiation, and cooperation skills.

The highest level of collaboration and thinking together is needed when the level of uncertainty is extremely high. Imagine the problem of newly structuring the organisation along the value chain, focusing on the customers and their needs, which then also entails digitalisation of processes as well as cross-functional teams, a new performance measurement system, new payment systems, various new people development tools and methods, etc. This is a huge shift in culture and strategy, and whether and how it works out and whether the client will reward this shift is extremely uncertain. In that kind of situation, the board has to function as a high-performance team for which the highest interpersonal skills are needed—as only they allow for real collaboration. A team being confronted with a difficult choice meets the emotions of fear and anxiety on both an individual and team level. Therefore, it is key to be able to go beyond individual fears of exposure and share worries, since they may become part of the solution. Shared mental models on the cognitive level and shared representations of the future organisation are the goal in this process; a kind of shared map of the future of the organisation, also on the more implicit level, should have been achieved.

Here, the reflective and reflexive systems are at work simultaneously. The art to it is to be inspired by the differences in what people think and feel and not to be put off by them or the difficulties in reaching agreement. The reflective system of a team produces shared mental models about the task and the team, whereas the reflexive system uses implicit attitudes, subconscious goals, heuristics, and implicit stereotypes. It is easier to coordinate a team where similar mental models and representations of the reflexive system (i.e. emotions, associations) prevail. Dissimilarity hinders it, but when well managed may lead to more innovative solutions. A bit of discordance is good for creating conflict and creative solutions, yet too much will most likely shut the process down. I would argue it is important to not only acknowledge, but also make use of, the different representations (thoughts, ideas) on the reflective and the reflexive level to stimulate debate on the future of the organisation. The key competency in creating this thinking space for shared reflexion and reflection is "cross-understanding", which means understanding another person's mental models and implicit assumptions.

The capacity for empathy is fundamental, whereas introspection, self-reflection, and a willingness to communicate insights gained is necessary. In this shared thinking space, different perceptions of strategically relevant facts need to be open for discussion: their individual and group interpretation, their underlying assumptions, as well as the hopefully shared conclusions about how the actual reality and future developments are seen and evaluated, so that a shared conviction can lead to a strategic choice and a shared strategy map. Allow yourself and others to share emotions, interpretations, and assumptions regarding the future and the respective interpretations. For that, containment and a safe psychological space are needed—not the easiest thing to achieve at a board level, where you find many alpha personalities who are often not used to listening attentively and with an open mind. Taking all this in together, a high-performance team would be able to create a special "thinking space for the future".

The following case study shows how this shared thinking space needs time to develop, but also proves it to be a useful concept.

Case study

Shared thinking—a joint venture between failure and hubris

Martin Ringer

This is in part a story of a dance between fear and hubris. All participants, including myself as consultant, were immersed in a project of greater size and significance than anything that any of us had done before.

The client group was an international joint venture that was tasked with establishing a new mineral extraction, processing, and shipping mega-project. I will call this the Biggerore Project, in order to maintain confidentiality. The proposed budget was astronomical in that, in the words of one participant, it matched the GDP of some small countries. I was at the time a sole charge consultant and normally worked with smaller enterprises. Consulting to this project felt like a massive exposure. My sense of vulnerability arose partly because there had been several previous attempts to launch the project and partly because it was a project that attracted regular exposure in financial and public media. At the same time, I was proud because I had been chosen to facilitate the kind of project that normally only the big players—like Deloitte Consulting and McKinsey and Company get to work with.

There was also a sense of pride among participants. Each had been chosen by his or her company to conduct a high-level internationally significant negotiation. They all stood to gain significantly in status within their respective organisations if the negotiations to fund the project proved successful. However, they, too, were aware that any form of failure could be very detrimental to their careers at an international level.

My role in the project was to facilitate four or five two-day "off-site" meetings per year until the joint venture partners agreed on an outcome. In the end, the process took five years, but I was not to know that at the time I was first engaged.

I proposed that my role would be that of "helping you to think together". The representatives agreed to this and in fact this frame was to persist throughout the whole period of negotiations. We established a pattern of work for each meeting. First, I held individual and confidential in-depth interviews with the three joint venture representatives and their deputies—six people in total. From the patterns that emerged from the interviews, I proposed a few topics for "deep-dive" conversations. These topics were then approved by the three senior joint venture representatives, or else they would propose alternatives. I then developed a more detailed agenda in collaboration with a senior administrator in the lead company for the project, who was designated project manager. The six-person joint venture representative team was designated as the project development team (PDT). It was this PDT that I was designated to facilitate.

The initial interviews surfaced high levels of doubt and cynicism about the project and so the original assessment I did when I first met with the group was to ask each pair of company representatives to pour water into a glass to indicate their level of hope that the joint venture team partners would reach a successful collaborative outcome—whatever that might be. Each pair then explained briefly to the others why they had chosen their particular level. Two glasses were less than half full and the other was just over half full. The fear of failure was palpable. This exercise was an opener for the first "deep dive" which was a clarification of the participants' goals and roles. I wanted to clarify with the joint venture representative whether their goal was primarily to achieve approval of the project or, on the other hand, to arrive at the best financial, economic, and environmental decision, even if this meant not proceeding with the project. The second part of the deep dive was a close look at the roles of the team participants. For instance, to what extent did they see themselves primarily as advocates of the interests of their respective companies and to what extent did they see themselves as promoters and supporters of a collaborative joint venture? From their responses, it seemed that they had been instructed by their respective head offices to determine if the project was a viable option and only then would the negotiations start to actually develop the project. However, each head office had already forecast billions of dollars of expenditure in their forward financial estimates, which seemed to contradict the idea that the project development team (PDT) was free to decide that the project was not viable.

Early on in the first off-site meeting I got the feeling that conversations were mostly guarded. It took some time to uncover why this was the case. A participant disclosed that a recent redistribution of ownership of mineral rights between participating companies had caused significant anger and frustration for the two representatives of one of the participating companies. I wondered what then were the levels of trust between the companies, and asked how they might work together to enhance trust. An important agreement emerged: the participants agreed that there were significant figures, assumptions, and calculations that each company used to determine the viability of the project and none of the companies wanted the others to know these figures. This was because all three companies were involved in other mining operations around the world that were in direct competition with the other joint venture partners' companies. The agreement then was to "disclose in general terms what is not being disclosed or shared". I used this opportunity to observe to participants that when we know that something exists but we don't know enough about its exact nature, we will fill in the blanks by imagining. This principle proved to be a useful encouragement many times during subsequent debates for participants to provide enough information to avoid the others filling in the blanks with negative imaginings.

Frustration levels were rising by the end of year one. Also, the initial hubris was no longer apparent as participants became worn down and demoralised by incessant challenges that emerged in the process of attempting collaboration. During a pre-meeting interview, one participant said that he did not want to go to the next off-site meeting because of the overall negative atmosphere between those in the project development team. All other members of the PDT made similar comments during pre-meeting interviews.

Nonetheless, we did meet and I opened the off-site with the observation that there seemed to be an atmosphere of disappointment, perhaps of some distrust, and of a wish to withdraw—everyone into his and her private corner. Participants were a bit surprised by this level of confrontation and it took some time to reach an understanding that the foundation of the capacity to think—and hence negotiate—together was in fact a network of adequately trusting and respectful relationships. I suggested that we pause the substantive work and spend some time rebuilding our capacity to think together. Some expressed a fear that exposing differences could cause "an explosion". During the ensuing discussion the project manager spat an angry and hostile response to a comment by another company representative. I called a pause, and asked the manager to say in his own words what he heard the other representative to have said. The other person was shocked by the manager's interpretation of what he had said and so I facilitated what could be called a "slowed down" conversation where each participant reflected back the meaning of what he or she had heard the other to say. The subsequent exchange not only clarified the immediate misunderstanding but my direct confrontation of the project manager also built trust in the PDT that I was adequately neutral and was not favouring the project manager and his company. The residual mistrust had persisted despite the fact that I had been completely open with the PDT that I had worked as a consultant with that company on previous occasions and had discussed my determination to be neutral.

Near the end of these two days, one of the company representatives proposed that we regularly check in as a group about the level of "relationship capital" that existed in the group. He observed that tough negotiations on highly contestable items "used up" relationship capital and that it was important to spend time together enjoying meals, excursions, etc. to rebuild relationship capital. One subsequent activity that was popular for a few off-sites was an after-dinner game of petanque/bocce with representatives from each company divided into different teams. The emergence of the idea of relationship capital was also a good reminder that it was important for the company representatives to develop their own shared methods and language rather than seeing me as the only one who would introduce ideas and techniques. Over time, other representatives became more confident in suggesting ways of working and hence started to become active supporters of the facilitative process.

One morning during the second year of off-site meetings, one of the company representatives started the routine morning reflection session with the comment that he and a representative from another company had moved through a "stuck" conversation that had occurred the previous day during the formal meeting. He told the group that this breakthrough had occurred during a dinner conversation and a subsequent one-to-one in a corner over an after-dinner drink. This disclosure was almost an apology because the participants had all learned from previous facilitators the pair of rules (1) "What goes on in the group stays in the group," and (2) "If it matters it must be discussed in the group." In fact, the idea of "circuit-breaker" conversations over dinner and sometimes in small break-outs proved to be a vital element of subsequent off-site meetings. Again, this was not my initiative, it emerged from the team.

As the second year of meetings progressed, it became apparent that fear levels were diminishing and the concerns about reputation and career trajectory had faded into the background. It appeared to me that we had matured as a group and the initial power of the see-saw between pride and fear had largely been replaced by immersion in the task at hand.

Because all participating companies were experienced miners on an international scale, they all had particular licensed technologies for specialised techniques in extraction, processing, handling, and shipping of minerals. For each of these technologies that the joint venture adopted, the company that owned the rights or the technology would receive royalty income, and hence the project would become more profitable for that company. In one case, a company representative was particularly stubborn with her insistence that the joint venture adopt her company's transport and shipping technology. Other company representatives put up robust counter-arguments and the team reached an impasse that lasted for six months. In a subsequent pre-meeting interview she revealed to me that she was not personally convinced that this was the best solution but she was obliged to fight for it because her head office had directed her to ensure that this technology was adopted by the project. I asked her to disclose this dilemma to the project development team at the next off-site meeting. This was to lead to another important breakthrough.

Her disclosure of the dilemma resulted in other company representatives exploring with her how she—and the negotiating team as a whole—might work through this impasse. All representatives disclosed that they had similar issues from time to time with their head offices and that some head office directives had earlier triggered high levels of tension in the negotiations, but nobody had previously disclosed the origins of the tension. The result was an agreement between PDT members first to disclose when they found themselves in this situation in the future and second for them all to work together to provide a "push-back" on the parent company when head-office directives proved to be problematic for the negotiations. This agreement depersonalised many of the potential conflicts that emerged during later negotiations and helped the team behave as a team rather than a set of six hard-nosed company representatives. It seemed that the pervasive fear that the negotiations would fall apart started to diminish, partly as a result of this newly enhanced commitment to collaborate.

Over time, the team became more adept at managing difficult moments, recovering from painful interactions, and creating a "thinking space" that eventually led to their constructing robust business cases that resulted in all three international head offices agreeing to fund the project. In an informal review process, all participants reflected that the key element of my role had been my focus on building, using, maintaining, and repairing the thinking space.[220]

* * *

This example of a rather transformative strategy process describes how the shared thinking space is developed and what it is needed for. Of course, openness and trust are the key ingredients, and sharing dilemmas can result from that. We will explore these ingredients together in the rest of this chapter.

The strategy process as a thinking space

To help to understand what happens in important strategy processes, a model can be used which separates three phases taking place consecutively and in parallel: sensing, seizing, and reconfiguring.[221]

The first step involves sensing opportunities and is based on processing information by constantly scanning, searching, and exploring the context of the organisation across technologies and markets. To do this well you need to have access to and properly process the right information, as well as possess the right cognitive capacities. Being able to add subjective mental models and the interfering judgemental, defensive, and emotional reactions to the information gained is helpful. Of course, all kinds of biographical experiences and personalities influence the sensing process, not only via mental maps, but also via unconscious emotional reactions to fear and anxiety. When the process of sensing opportunities starts, there is normally a feeling of "we need to change something" prevalent in the leadership. Therefore, anxiety might have already developed (unconsciously) and psychic defence mechanisms started to work. Imagine you are a board member and information to which only you have immediate access informs you that future markets are threatening the product line for which you are responsible—how will you react? Maybe you'll deny, overlook, or even just ignore it, hoping that the rest of the board might not even learn about it. The quality of sensing thus depends on how well one can deal with the emotions arising from the need to update mental representations.

The next step, seizing, is about strategic choices: deciding which services, products, technologies, and markets clients will be focused on, selecting innovations, changing or adding new business models, as well as choosing an investment path. Decision-making skills, consisting of managerial judgement after thorough analysis, are the key competencies for managers in this phase. Biases can undermine rational choices and make them appear irrational.[222] Overcoming biases, however, seems to be possible and "almost always requires a cognitively sophisticated and disciplined approach to decision-making".[223] Decision-making needs to be embedded in the respective structures, procedures, designs, and incentives for creativity and good thinking.

You also need emotional capabilities to overcome biases and inertia.[224] The feeling attached to the imagined future outcome influences the decision more than estimated probabilities and likelihoods. Managers can be emotionally attached to the past and past achievements or can be overly committed to a new direction. Yet a certain emotional commitment is needed to create the ground for new investments to develop and grow positively.

In the next phase, having chosen the strategic option and the strategy, implementation should take place through a process of asset orchestration by creating, extending, upgrading, and protecting the enterprise's unique asset base.[225] In this asset orchestration, the leaders of the board function like orchestra conductors, while the assets/instruments are newly combined, created, renovated, and/or replaced. On this level, another filtering process takes place—this time on the level of the organisation or subunits. Here, corporate culture, corporate trauma, and social defence mechanisms may interfere.

The next figure gives an overview of this process and the interfering human aspects stemming from past or present emotions and their associated cognitive and emotional structures and models translated into organisational structures, processes, routines, values, etc (see Figure 25).

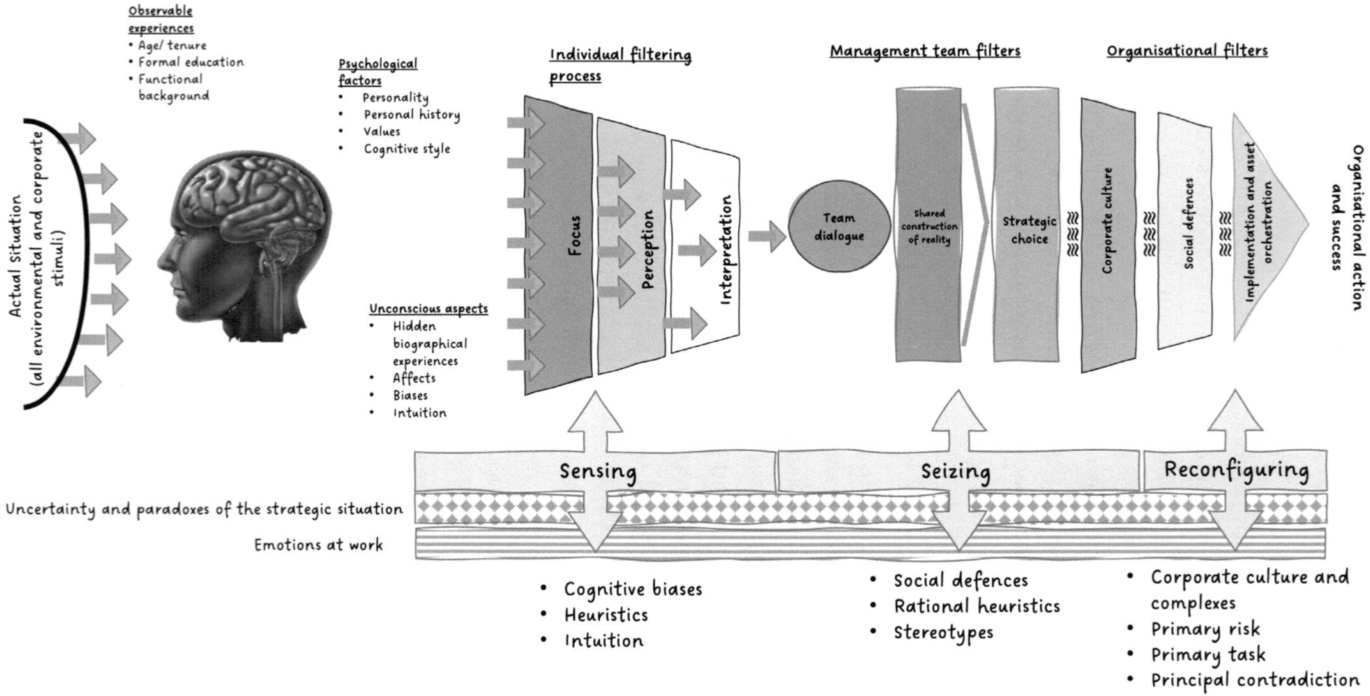

Figure 25: The organisational strategy making process (author's drawing)

As you can see, all the factors which we have discussed so far are influencing the strategy process—from the very first perception of the actual situation until the implementation. On different levels and in all steps psychic events influence the thinking.

KEY LEARNING

What is now needed to overcome these shared-thinking and thus strategy-process fallacies?

- Understanding thinking not as an individual but a shared process, where one idea or question contributes to the next, back and forth, until the sum is more than the parts.
- Developing a willingness for holding each other accountable.
- Supporting the development of trust by getting to know each other as human beings—giving space for humour and pleasure/joy/fun.
- Openness and honesty, fairness and mutual respect, listening and communicating are important ingredients.
- Only with trust can teams work well. It is even more needed when working together virtually.
- Only with trust can you overcome the idea of knowledge being an instrument of power.[226]
- Create a transitional space—to test out different ideas.
- Trust also allows for meta-reflection on what happens on the hidden, emotional, partly unconscious levels of the process—trust and meta-reflection enhance each other mutually.
- Let process improvements emerge from within the team. The consultant or the leader does not need to know it all—which means allowing the process to unfold without controlling every detail.
- The team needs to be able to live up to what we have already discussed—negative capability, managing the not-knowing, and the inherent tensions.

It is the leader's task to create the thinking space and contain this process, which is emotionally as well as cognitively demanding. This can be supported by internal or external facilitators.

CHAPTER 13

Understanding hidden feelings and culture

Organisational culture has been a buzzword for many years, but it is often confused with organisational or corporate climate. Organisational climate is concerned with how people feel towards each other within an organisation, whereas organisational culture deals with lived and implicit ways of doing things in an organisation. In his famous article, Edgar Schein explains:

> Organisational culture is the pattern of basic assumptions that a given group has invented, discovered, or developed in learning to cope with its problems of external adaptation and internal integration, and that have worked well enough to be considered valid, and, therefore to be taught to new members as the correct way to perceive, think and feel in relation to those problems.[227] (see Figure 26)

In his definition, you find all the elements we have discussed so far. The question is, how do you get to these basic assumptions which concern the nature of reality, time and space, human nature and relationships, and our relationship to the environment?

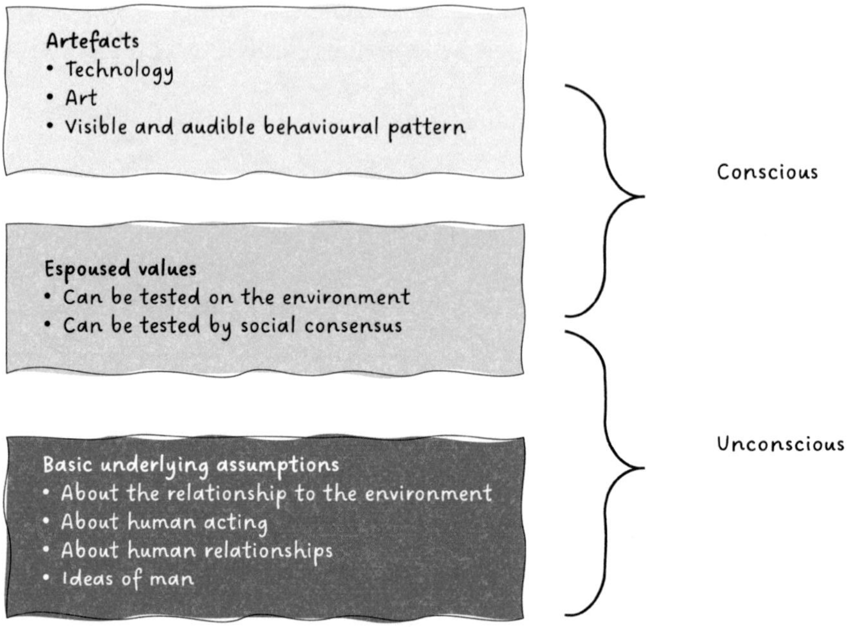

Figure 26: The three levels of organisational culture[228]

You can approach it by looking at organisational artefacts such as building architecture, symbols like the logo, uniforms, interior fitting, etc. Yet, it is difficult to ascribe meaning without delving a bit deeper and connecting the artefacts with values, which can be both open and claimed, or hidden, implicit, and espoused. This is not yet deep enough, however, as we need to get to the underlying assumptions which are by their nature more unconscious. It is also obvious that the organisational culture cannot be viewed independently from the context culture. A particular influence on the corporate culture stems from the founders, their personality, their way of communicating and relating, and the way they do their work.

In addition to the organisational culture, we can have a look at organisational complexes. These complexes on the organisational or even team level contain former traumatic or discrimination experiences—which may result from painful ordeals during mergers, joint ventures, or takeovers.

Approaches to understanding the organisational culture can take many forms and have different focal points. I will present some of them which are not yet part of the mainstream leadership literature, but are very helpful for getting closer to these cultural basic assumptions Schein is talking about (and which are not to be confused with the basic assumption modes of Bion and others, which we talked about in Chapter 9).

The inroad to organisational culture you choose depends on what you are looking for: one can look for unconscious dynamics, symbols, narratives and stories, or archetypes—all of them need to be analysed and interpreted. An important inroad into the unconscious aspects of culture is the use of semi-structured or open interviews with people at different levels. Other techniques are more creative and/or they appear less rational in their approach, for example, using drawings, dreams, or even photos.

But before we start diving into the culture, we need to understand how symbol interpretation works, since this is at the core of these methods.

Symbols are said to be the language of the unconscious and the soul. Symbols, as well as images, transport unconscious material, emotions, memories of experiences and events, insights, conflicts, and other psychic content. Working with symbols helps to gain new insights in difficult situations as well as in basic personal or organisational issues. This often brings a different and new perspective. Symbols can be understood as vehicles for psychological diagnostics due to the fact that they can also reflect difficulties and central queries, either in the person or the organisation using them.

We can attribute a symbolic meaning to almost anything yet must be careful not to over-symbolise. When studying organisations, it makes sense to look at both inner symbols from individual organisational members and those which are developed collectively, such as social dreaming (I will explain this further below) or drawings, and outer symbols which stem from society and culture, art and religion, such as myths and fairy tales, paintings, sculptures, and objects of desire, of collection, of phantasy, etc.

There are several possibilities to enter work with symbolic meaning. We will take a look at these after first understanding the process of how to work with symbols.

How to interpret symbols

A symbol has complex, multilayered, infinite meaning and invites many possible dimensions of interpretation—it is never a clear sign or a precise equation, it is blurry, mysterious, unclear, and can only be explored intuitively by using cultural knowledge of the background, or history of the symbol that can support and amplify the exploration to facilitate additional insight. The symbol interpretation is not a linear but a multi-step process that moves backwards and forwards until an "a-ha" moment is reached from which one can take the reflection further into sharing with others, or even acting upon it.

The symbol interpretation process can go as follows (see Figure 27):

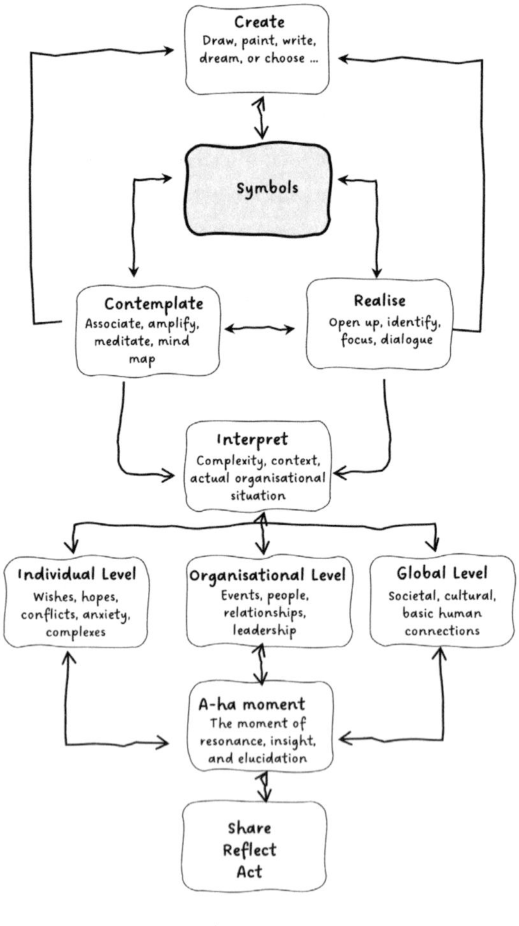

Figure 27: Working with symbols[229]

We begin with an object which is either created on purpose, like a drawing, a photo, or dream matrix. We can also take one from the organisation; for example, a logo or the outer structure of the building. The first step is wanting to understand it symbolically—which means wanting to enter into the multidimensional meaning. In a group process this needs to be explained, and it helps to open the thinking and feeling space when appealing to intuition. There is no right or wrong in understanding meaning; each participant is allowed to understand it in his or her own specific way. Yet, in most cases a shared sense evolves with time. Realising the created object as a subject of significance, focus on what is there and create a safe space for reflection, imagination, perceiving, and feeling when diving into it. This entails also contemplating and freely associating what comes to mind without censoring; it is also helpful to walk around it together, either inwardly or, for example, when it is a drawing, walking physically around it. Then you can look at it from different angles and perspectives. When starting, spend a moment with the complex, paradoxical, and multidimensional nature of the symbol, then begin the interpretation by exploring, first, ideas or insights that may connect the symbol with the individual's situation within the organisation, such as memories, feelings, and experiences in work life, similarities, analogies, etc. Then look at the organisational situation. Imagine it and connect it to the context of the organisation, its people, critical incidents and events, and the leadership of the organisation.

We can rather easily access the symbolic meaning when it is part of our own cultural context. This has very much to do with the notion of the collective unconscious, which assumes a connecting unconscious layer between people in a certain cultural group. In this linking unconscious layer you can find collective patterns and symbols which are part of our culture and art, in myths and fairy tales, plays and movies. The meaning of these collective patterns is often intuitively understood by everyone being part of that culture and without the need for further explanation. It is also helpful to look at a symbol from a cultural or global perspective, looking into, for example, when and how it was incepted or turned into something meaningful. Here it can be helpful to refer to anthropological, theological, or mythological literature as well as etymological encyclopaedias.

This process will hopefully lead to a shared a-ha moment, when suddenly an insight, a deeper and new understanding develops which resonates so well that one feels enlightened. This emotional feeling of approaching an understanding without claiming that it is yet fully understood is an important part of working with symbols.

It is always a great moment when a group of people reach this a-ha moment after a meandering process of trying to make sense of something. When this moment has been reached, then further steps can be taken. The meaning can be shared with others; what it means for the future of the organisation when this interpretation mirrors the actual situation can be reflected on, and of course action can be taken, depending very much on the outcome and the organisational situation.

How to elicit symbols and symbolic meaning

A very basic technique which can be used for eliciting meanings from symbols is asking people to make drawings, either individually or as a team. These drawings can represent the culture, the way people work together, the idea of the organisation as such, the future, the past, or both in one—there are no limits. What's important here is to allow for anything that comes up and not to tell people what to do or how to do it. Drawing is best done with colour pens; my favourites are colourful wax or gel crayons.

Similar to drawing is social dream-drawing, which will be explored in the following case vignette. Instead of drawing, you can also use photos (taken for this occasion or pictures from magazines, etc.) and make a collage of what people see when they imagine the organisation. When we work as consultants or coaches with organisations, we also use active listening in explorative interviews. Social dreaming is another technique which explores dreams in a group as an expression of the unconscious of the group or the context. For that, the dream needs to be detached from the dreamer, and one is allowed to associate freely to the dream or bring up new dreams—but not analyse the dream. The meaning develops from the different associations and explorations. The shared dream belongs then to the group of people with which it is shared and no longer just the individual. It is a powerful technique for understanding what goes on underneath the carpet in an organisation and in the respective context.

Case study

Social dream-drawing—healing generational conflict

Rose Mersky

Those of us working as consultants using a psychosocial approach to organisations are often asked to help groups function better. These work groups are of any sort, such as colleagues in peer supervision, small project groups, management teams, executive boards. Some of these groups are comprised of more than one level of authority, for example, a CEO and his management team. Others are comprised of organisational peers. Their tasks can be the implementation of a new marketing strategy, the exploration of a particular case presentation, or the daily review of patients to be treated during the course of the day. Tasks vary, but when groups cannot manage to complete their tasks, work satisfaction and effective functioning suffer.

Those of us using creative methods to create awareness of underlying causes of such dysfunction are often called in after more familiar techniques of organisational intervention (e.g. questionnaires) did not solve the problem. Our work enables the deeper root causes to be illuminated and discussed openly, so that problems can be solved. The need for this approach is due to the fact that conflicts and differences in groups are often suppressed or denied. As a result, energy is dissipated, innovation stalls, and creativity is lost.

Very often, therefore, our approach to working with a group in trouble is to propose a method that brings that lost creativity back into the group experience. There is a set of methodologies that can be utilised, all of which help groups to face their key deeper issues in a way that sparks positive interaction. These methods use physical objects created by participants as catalysts for learning. These creations include drawings, photographs, poems, and sculptures. Mostly they are visual representations shared with the group by their creators.

When using these methodologies with clients, the consultant is not under pressure to "figure out" the underlying problem. Instead, the role of the consultant is to facilitate in a safe and clear way a creative method and, with the group itself, to "discover" what is going on at a deeper level. The group must feel safe enough with this consultant to take the risk of working this way, and the consultant must have a very clear notion of why a particular methodology would be appropriate.

It is important that all group members agree to participate, and that the consultant describes very clearly what the steps in the process will be. Even the agreement of a group to engage in such an experience is already an act of healing and learning.

In order to illustrate such a method of working, I want to use the example of a method called social dream-drawing (SDD), which I have developed, researched, and used with many different groups. SDD was the subject of my doctoral studies. I was able to demonstrate that this method helps groups become aware of their unconscious conflicts and, as a result, to better function and fulfil their tasks. My book, *Social Dream-Drawing: A Handbook for Professionals* has just been published by Routledge.

During my studies, I was invited by the instructor of a course called "Researching the Unconscious" to offer a social dream-drawing (SDD) workshop to the participants. As one of the participants myself, I welcomed this opportunity to share this new way of working with my fellow students; however, I never anticipated how significant its impact would be.

The class consisted of six women (including myself). We spanned generations. Two women were in their twenties, one was in her middle thirties, and the remaining three of us were over fifty years old. Our older cohort was the same age as the mothers of the younger ones. This fact would become very important for the subsequent work of the group.

When using SDD, I always choose a theme that reflects the question the group is working on and the potential dilemma they are struggling to solve. In this case, I asked the group if someone could suggest a theme. Immediately the youngest member offered: "To what extent does generation play a role in research?"

The fact that a member of the youngest cohort put forward this theme already indicated that generational dynamics in this group was a key issue. Here again, we have more data to suggest that the group's dynamics must be related to the age differences between participants.

The task of the group, as assigned by our male instructor, was to develop and present a small project related to the unconscious. We were completely free to choose one for ourselves. At this point in the course of the class, however, a number of participants had still not been able to come up with a viable idea for a project. In particular, the younger participants had made no progress on this assignment.

Could it therefore be that the dynamics in the group were somehow inhibiting the younger ones from undertaking this assignment? And if so, could this also be the case for older participants as well?

With this theme in mind, all participants were invited to bring a drawing of a dream they had the night before to class the next day. Of the five participants, only two (the second youngest participant and the participant in her thirties) brought dream drawings to the workshop.

Just to give a short introduction, the method of social dream-drawing (SDD) is based on the theory that dreaming itself is a form of thinking which contains information about what is happening in the unconscious of an individual or a group. People dream about personal issues (relationships, children, health), but they also dream about social issues (organisations, society, work). And while each individual in an SDD workshop may have his or her own issue relating to the overall problem in the group (i.e. not able to do the assignment), any dream drawing that is brought by a participant can be helpful in illuminating what collectively is hindering the completion of a task. The pre-identified theme (in this case "To what extent does generation play a role in research?") provides a context for what dream material will be brought.

The social dream-drawing method involves six steps:

1. The dream drawer shares the dream with the group (before showing the drawing).
2. The dream drawer shows and explains the drawing of the dream.
3. Participants ask questions to be sure they understand everything the drawer has explained.
4. Everyone offers free associations to what they see in the drawing.
5. The dream drawer responds to what is said in the last step and discussion follows.
6. The group reflects on the theme of the workshop and sees what new insights have emerged.

During the course of the workshop, we worked on both of the dream drawings brought to the class, each for one hour. As the workshop was recorded, the following description includes actual quotes from the event.

Here is the dream drawing of the participant in her thirties, who went first (see Figure 28):

Figure 28: Dream drawing 1—Rose Mersky[230]

This drawing depicts a very big space, with hospital beds suspended from the ceiling. The dreamer is lying in one of the beds. When her doctor enters, she starts to feel "uncomfortable" and "vulnerable". In real life, this doctor is actually the dreamer's therapy client, who is older than the dreamer.

Several associations by group members to this dream drawing referred to this lop-sided intergenerational relationship, such as: "inferiority", "mother and child", "parent and child", and "the mother putting you to bed". In this dream drawing, the doctor is both patient and healer, and the dreamer is both patient and healer. There is a "role reversal". It is "spooky", "complicated", and "awkward".

The discussion following the free associations helped to finally acknowledge one of the major characteristics of this group, that of the generational differences between the two subgroups, with one person (the dreamer) finding herself in the middle. As one of "the oldies" noted, "We are at the extremes, really."

There followed various comments about the advantages and the difficulties of each generation. On the positive side, for example, an older member noted: "One of the things you learn as you grow older is that you can survive what you didn't think you can survive." On the other hand, another said that it is "hard to be an older learner".

Younger participants shared their perspective, for example: "Just because I'm younger doesn't mean I don't know what I want." They wanted to tell their elders "You don't know how it works!" They were resentful that our generation was able to go to university and get support to start our professional lives, while these students would be burdened for years with educational debt.

Exploring these differences was not easy for everyone. As an older participant said: "There's some reluctance to, to think about you as being different because you're younger … Maybe it's just my, my reluctance to acknowledge difference … 'cause difference can lead to conflict." Perhaps this could account for why none of the older participants brought a dream drawing. The intergenerational topic was just too threatening to face.

The second dream drawing was by one of the youngest participants and depicted her in a swimming pool with a shark nearby (see Figure 29).

Figure 29: Dream drawing 2—Rose Mersky

Here, perhaps the conflict was more out in the open. For example, an older woman noted: "You could be out of your depth in certain ways."

Further comments (one by a younger member and one by an older one) crystallised the situation:

> I really enjoy people that are older than me talking about their experiences, what they've learned, how they've dealt with situations, because I can really learn from that. But on the other hand, I kind of feel sad because although I can still live it, like that time is over for them … I kind of feel sad or guilty that I like can do it now, but that time is gone for them.
>
> I really know what that phrase being "over the hill" means. I really have that experience inside, you know. The feeling that actually I've reached my zenith and now there is no other way but down, down all the way to the bottom … which is a scary sort of feeling … I can't actually go back, you know. It has to carry on to the end of that arc, wherever that may be.

In other words, the older people had the experience and wisdom, but less time left. And the younger people had all the time in the world, but without the advantages that we had enjoyed. It was a no-win situation.

As I realised later, it seemed that we as a group had participated in creating a split between the generations. We all colluded in having the participant in the middle (presumably the safest one of us) present the first dream drawing. She served as a mediating figure in that sense, and perhaps it was easier to work first with her dream drawing, rather than the one by the younger person. Nevertheless, although the first dream drawer was easily ten years older than the two youngest members, we lumped them all together as the "young" group. She herself colluded with this that as a group participant, she was "feeling myself a lot younger than I was".

Thus, I would say that these extreme tensions between the generations (the humiliation of being an older learner, the resentment of not getting a good deal in society and being dismissed by the older generation) were so strong that they dominated the system at the expense of the course. The potent generational issues were impeding the group's ability to get on with the task. For the younger ones, it felt especially risky. And while before this session, most participants were having difficulty identifying a research question, following the session, almost all were able to.

Just to conclude, it's important to note that this method is not for every group. Sharing dreams and doing drawings make people feel vulnerable. This group was willing to take the risk to try a new method for learning. Since it is generally accepted that the content of our dreams is not under our conscious control, participants do not have to fear being criticised for unwelcome thoughts or ideas. We work with the content of the dreams and analysing or interpreting the dreamer is not permitted. We confront problems and not the person. Now that neurological research has finally caught up with Freud's original theories, there is wider acceptance that dreams can be the royal road to discovery and learning and—in some cases—to healing, as in this example.

* * *

Dream drawing is a sophisticated method which requires a lot of trust between the participants. Yet the interpretation of dream symbols in the drawings, or even symbols in general drawings which, for example, represent the culture, are very similar. Instead of drawing dreams, one could also suggest drawing the organisational culture. One can also draw a team and its culture, or the impression and feelings about leadership in the organisation. It also works to ask for symbols such as an animal representing the organisation or the team, and is as well another way to use drawings.

Storytelling, myth, narratives, and archetypes as symbolic expressions

Over the last two decades or so, storytelling has been used to influence culture, strategy, and communication through the telling of specific emotionally charged stories about, for example, how the future of the organisation shall look. But for our purposes here I would like to shift the focus to already existing stories.

Narratives and stories can be researched by picking them up from different parts of the organisation and analysing them. Listening to stories which are already there, connections with myth, mythology, and archetypes, can reveal undercurrents and unconscious aspects in the life of an organisation. Founder and foundation stories, stories about managing a crisis or countering a competitor attack, and stories about the leadership team are there to create a common ground for people, a common framework and cognitive map which stabilises the organisation and its culture for better or for worse.

In organisations, stories and narratives can be shared at any time and place—at the water cooler, in the kitchen, over lunch or coffee, in the boardroom. "If accounting and finance are the backbone of organizations, then the stories which permeate all organizations of any size are their lifeblood. Stories are so central to organizations that not only do organizations depend on them, but stronger still, they couldn't function without them."[231] Stories are shared, they have mythological qualities, they serve as instruments of organisational socialisation, they offer problem-solving recipes, and they often express unconscious wishes. Stories are there to help us make sense of things—mostly after the fact. By that, they help us to understand and digest our experiences and to share them further with our own amendments—thus contributing to personal and organisational identity.

Narratives can also have counter- or anti-narratives, as critical stories that don't necessarily please the leadership of the organisation. Narratives and stories are also seen as expressing organisational identity, which becomes more necessary the more fluid organisations become, and the more people have to be flexible and on the move between different jobs.

Narratives can also be comic, tragic, cynical, or fun; they can share devaluing, humiliating, discriminating, and dismissive acts, as well stories of heroism, glory, and the joy of working together.

There is never only one story or narrative in an organisation; it is always a web or landscape of stories which can be contradictory or even paradoxical, and, by that, represent the different realities organisational members experience—depending on their task, their role, and their hierarchical level. These stories are part of reality inasmuch as they constitute reality. The ruling group may try to suppress unwanted and negative stories and support one strong corporate narrative—yet these anti-narratives will always develop as a form of resistance; as such they are an organisational defence. Instead of fighting them, it would be more helpful to understand their issues and the reasons they give, and learn from what they are telling us is going on in the organisation.

Personal and organisational narratives as well as their connected identities are intertwined—we have seen this (see Chapter 1). The personal identity could completely identify, ambivalently or temporarily identify, or even dismiss the organisational identity.

The personal identity of the leader often becomes infected with an archetypal leader identity. These archetypal patterns or deep roles are connected to our basic social family structure—mother, father, son and daughter—which can have good and bad aspects. They resemble what we know from fairy tales and myths which also use these archetypal roles to present us with a story about life and death. Moxnes[232] developed the concept of deep roles for this. They are helpful for understanding the dynamics on team and leadership levels.

The archetype of the father is God or the Devil, the mother the queen or witch, the son the crown prince or black sheep, and the daughter the princess or whore. As in fairy tales (or in the Bible), one can also identify secondary or helper roles: two transcendent or spiritual roles, the sage and the false prophet, who support and advise the other characters, and two material helper roles, who win or lose battles. This leads to a colourfully extreme overview of the roles people, especially leaders, receive as projections and sometimes also identify with (see Figure 30).

Archetypes	Father	Mother	Son	Daughter	Helpers		Change
Good	God	Queen	Crown prince	Princess	Sage	Servant	Hero/ winner
Bad	Devil	Witch	Black sheep	Whore	False prophet	Betraying servant	Fool/loser
Type	Primary roles				Secondary roles		

Figure 30: Mental matrix of unconscious roles[233]

These deep roles recur regularly, and real individuals come to occupy these roles in specific narratives, thus drawing on the symbolic power of the original archetype. A leader can then be experienced, after the father archetype, as a benevolent godlike father or, alternatively, as a devil; or he or she may be experienced (and feature in stories) as a prince (hero or clown), or indeed in any of the other deep roles.

The negative archetypes also point to the group or organisation shadow. There you find the dark character traits, the undesired and reprehensible aspects. Often, a group or organisation can be said to be in the grip of the shadow, because it contains facets and dimensions that are collectively suppressed; they do not fit into the attitudes, preferences, and behaviours of those who have determined the values and playing rules of the organisation. Yet these suppressed aspects have the tendency to come in through the backdoor at unexpected and rather unpleasant moments, when they are not at all wanted. The shadow can be better seen from the outside than from within—you see the mote in the eye of others better than the plank in your own eye. The problem is that the defence of the shadow's content uses energy that could be released and used elsewhere when the content is dealt with consciously.

Understanding an organisation as representing an archetype contributes therefore to a deeper understanding. We can often connect an organisation with one human archetype. According to Corlett and Pearson,[234] there are four overarching themes in two paradoxical pairs: developing and nurturing people, which is in tension with achieving results, and learning, innovation, and transforming, which is in tension with stabilising and maintaining traditions (see Figure 31).

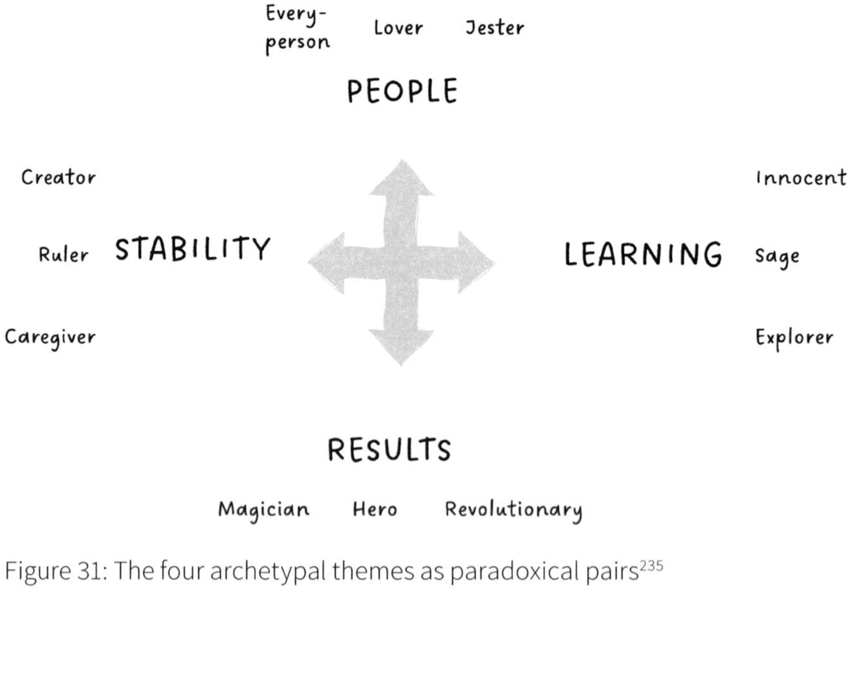

Figure 31: The four archetypal themes as paradoxical pairs[235]

An organisation often represents one of these archetypes explicitly.

A healthy organisation could be represented by archetypes from each of the four themes (see Figure 32).

Archetypical area	Face of the archetype	Organisational specifications	Example
People	Every-person	• Everybody is important • Nobody is treated exceptionally well, everyone the same (poorly) • Heroes/hero-worship is condemned	Snapple
	Lover	• Democratic structures • Employee ownership • Feelings, honesty, loyalty are valued	Victoria's Secret
	Jester	• Value spontaneity, new impulses, humour and fun • Little tolerance for formal rules, structures, bureaucracy	Pringles
Performance and result	Hero	• Is committed to an important topic or helps his or her customers to achieve the best possible results • High expectations made on the employees; they have to do everything in order to be successful	Nike
	Revolutionary	• Nobody is privileged; everything is fluid, always in motion	TikTok
	Magicians	• Focused, flexible, innovative organisations • Extremely fast and flexible reaction to changes	Zara
Change and growth	Innocent	• Benevolent • Centralised, hierarchical	Disney
	Explorer	• Value individuality, fewer rules and hierarchies • Allow the employees to individually regulate their working hours and workload	Starbucks
	Sage	• Learning organisation • Always looking for feedback • Values excellence, planning, analyses, strategic thinking	Oprah Winfrey
Structure	Caregiver	• Altruism • Service orientation • Cohesive values such as harmony and cooperation and trust in one another	Maggie
	Creator	• Extensive freedom, experience creative potentials • Value of the work is more important than the financial results	Early stage Apple
	Ruler	• Stable, productive, orderly, and bureaucratic organisations • Function on time and without a hitch	Siemens

Figure 32: Examples of organisational archetypes[236]

The idea of using archetypes is to approach a deeper understanding of what is going on in the organisation, discovering which tensions are only felt but often not expressed since they are at work underneath the carpet. Using the archetypal perspectives helps to take away the feelings of guilt and shame when talking about difficult developments in organisations, and people can connect with them quite easily since they appeal to rather basic functions in us.

KEY LEARNING

- Organisational culture is a complex concept which you can best approach via symbols.
- Archetypal roles play an important part in better understanding leadership, and both symbols and archetypes are helpful intermediaries between the unconscious world of organisations and their dynamics and the real world.
- Using creative techniques, make meaning of what is managing us from underneath the carpet.

CHAPTER 14

Leading networks and ecosystems

Leading in systems

Living systems

Organisations are more than people, processes, and structures. In the late 1950s, a new theory about systems was developed based on understanding an organisation as a whole and not only as separate parts or building blocks. This theory has laid the foundation for our contemporary understanding of organisations, hence we will now take a look at how this thinking developed over the last one hundred years.

This highly interdisciplinary theory was developed by the biologist Bertalanffy as the so-called "general systems theory". The aim was to better understand complex phenomena in nature which could not be explained by the prevalent closed system theory.

> The present author, in the early [19]20s, became puzzled about obvious lacunae in the research and theory of biology. The then prevalent mechanistic approach … appeared to neglect or actively denies just what is essential in the phenomena of life. He advocated an "organismic" conception in biology, which

> emphasizes consideration of the organism as a whole or system and sees the main objective of biological sciences in the discovery of the principles of organization at its various levels.[237]

Bertalanffy's main contribution was to understand living systems as open systems which maintain a "time-independent dynamic equilibrium of steady state" (*Fliessgleichgewicht*) that remains irreversibly constant at a macroscopic level, holistically, while the system simultaneously evolves over time with continuous flux of matter, energy, and information. This general living systems theory is especially helpful in explaining the nature of life. Arising out of biological and ecological sciences, it attempts to map general principles for how all living systems work.

Living systems are open self-organising life forms that interact with their environment. These systems are maintained by flows of information, energy, and matter.

Organisations as well as groups, societies, or communities can be understood as living systems. This idea presents a paradigm which provides us with a specific lens through which to better understand what leadership means in and for a living system, because it takes the complexity of systems into account. Simple if–then connections are complicated but not complex. Complex problems, for example, entail multiple dynamic relations: there is no one single solution. Solving them requires masterfulness (and not expertise), and it is incalculable and unplannable. (Complicated problems might need time, energy, and effort, but they are manageable and controllable and can be analysed rationally.) The living system theory can therefore contribute to developing a deeper understanding of the complexity of today's organisations as well as the complex requirements for leading them.

Other living systems are cells, organs, organisms, and supranational systems. Living systems theory[238] deals with understanding these self-regulating or self-organising open systems. Living systems have some interesting characteristic features which will help us to understand how to lead teams and organisations as systems. It is important to understand how they maintain themselves, which means how they survive and propagate in a changing environment and how they change and develop—to be alive and living. The essence of life is processes;

without them life stops. These processes are for interacting with the environment via information exchange and material/energy exchange. The characteristic of life is a longer steady state in which the system's entropy (disorder) is lower than in its environment. Interaction and emergence are fundamental to living systems.[239]

Let us go back a step in history: Kant had already recognised that the whole, for example, a tree, only comes into being in a self-organising way by the fact that its parts (trunk, branches, leaves) let it come into being as a whole. The parts fulfil in each case an own purpose, so that the whole comes only thereby into being.[240] However, in Kant's systemic thinking, people are not self-organising systems because he thought that they can decide autonomously and because they have a soul. Moreover, the crucial question for him of how the new comes into being and how innovations occur, remains open, because his notion of purposiveness is shaping and forming ("formative") but not transforming ("transformative"). Between 1945 and 1968, Bertalanffy, in particular, researched and developed the idea of organisations and societies as open systems.[241] The further systems theory view of organisations, which developed on the basis of biology, cybernetics, and epistemology, is today strongly influenced by Luhmann's social science approach.

According to this, systems are wholes consisting of elements that are interconnected in a unique way. They are in an open relationship of adaptation and exchange with the environment but have a boundary by which they are distinguished from the environment.[242] Each enterprise system is made up of people who have roles, perform certain actions, and relate to each other. Within a (sub)system and between (sub)systems, materials, labour, money, information, and feelings are exchanged. Because technical and psychosocial subsystems are so closely intertwined, separating them makes no sense. The relationships at the boundaries are constantly changing, so the boundaries have a regulating function; they protect the system from the influences of the environment and transport messages into the system from the changing environment. The role of management in a company as a system and as its own subsystem is to manage the boundary of the system so that it is protected and yet adapts accordingly to the extent necessary; this means, above all, influencing the adaptability and persistence of the system. Behind this is the widely held basic assumption (already formulated by Kant) that leaders as agents of a system are autonomous and can act individually. To do so, they must be able to stand outside the system and observe it objectively. This, in turn, would require that the system has an objective reality, and that the reality of the system can be modelled and shaped so that leaders can control this process. They must therefore be concerned with the functions of the system, predict its behaviours, and then respond accordingly. In particular, clear roles and clear tasks, appropriate rules and structures, and high personal maturity and autonomy help.[243]

Complex adaptive systems

We now take this thinking one step further to complex adaptive systems theory. This theory does not assume any longer that individuals are autonomous and decide on their own. It claims that complex adaptive systems (CAS) consist of a large number of components called *agents*, which interact with each other, adapt, and learn. Heterogeneity is an important characteristic, allowing CAS to evolve on their own without any external cause. Another important assumption for this is that human actions are not driven by universally valid rules, but that the rules are constantly changing as humans learn. Complex responsive processes prevail *between* people because people are not—as assumed in the previous system-theoretical model—autonomous and independent individuals, but are supremely and inevitably interdependent, because the individual self is social. People are shaped by social interactions, so they shape them equally.

An organisation can therefore be understood as a complex responsive process, a self-organising process of being-in-relation (self-organising process of relating). It consists of temporary processes of interaction between human bodies through symbols that result in emergent patterns of these symbols giving rise to themes in communication. The basis of the system is relational, and since it happens between two people, it is a local interaction. We can state that the system is created only through relationships at the local level. The multiplicity of interactions at the most diverse levels leads to the emergence of patterns and themes. Change develops only through a new reaction of a local individual as a new response in an interaction.

By the fact that the system emerges only in the interaction, one must assume that values and strategies are not kept on paper but created and constructed again and again in the public interaction or in the inner communication of the individual. An individual changing focus, or perspective, means the orientation of his or her actions presumably changes, and so does the interaction.

This CAS theory has consequences for leadership. Under the assumption that a system consists of local interactions, leaders can only exert influence on a local level of interaction, and management is then no longer a process of designing and controlling, but of participating and constantly asking oneself the question of *what* should be done?

Complex systems are characterised by paradoxical dynamics; they are simultaneously stable and unstable; movements are regular and irregular—all living phenomena seem to exhibit these paradoxical dynamics. We can see here again the crucial role of paradoxes. There does not seem to be a stable equilibrium, as expected by previous system-theoretical considerations. This raises the question of the significance of instability for organisational vitality. Also, the idea of manageability of a system as a whole is fundamentally questioned, and it challenges the basic idea of harmony and agreement that underlies general systems theory. Very interesting is what is happening in the interactions at the edges of the system. For leaders, it means that they must be in constant dialogue with the various levels of the company in order to form their own judgement about what issues are emerging in the interactions. And leaders must ensure that those who interact with the next levels in the organisation on its behalf have understood the common basic idea of the company.

Since nothing is fixed, but reality emerges in each relationship, this is an ongoing process through which the individual leader may also change. Therefore, it is important to pay attention to one's own inner voice as well as to the content of the local interaction. Active listening becomes a particularly important leadership quality. This also includes intensive dialogue at the management board level. This is because local interactions at this level enable reporting on issues in other areas and can help to jointly interpret and thus better understand emerging issues in one's own area of business. In the permanent tension between the paradoxical forces in the company, top management is called upon to pay attention to which changes it attaches what significance.

In addition to complex adaptive systems theory, systems psychodynamic theory focuses on the interaction between collective structures, norms and practices in social systems, and the cognitions, motivations, and emotions of members of those systems.[244]

A further perspective of how to understand organisations as systems has been developed more recently by understanding them as well as placing them into (social) networks and ecosystems. Networks and ecosystems can be understood as higher-level organisation.

Social networks

When looking at an organisation as a social network, this has additional consequences for leaders, which we will explore here. A (social) network is a loose system of interactions between different individuals—physically as in organisations when people meet, but also online when people interact via specific platforms—and also between larger entities such as groups and organisations. Social network theory is part of network science which is "the study of network representations of physical, biological, and social phenomena leading to predictive models of these phenomena".[245]

Social network theory focuses on what happens in the relationships between people within a system and is therefore linked to CAS—which can be one organisation or several connected ones. From that theoretical perspective, the embeddedness in social fields and interpersonal relationships of individuals is crucial, as is understanding the patterns in the relationships, their connections, as well as the splits and breaks, and open or close ties. These social ties are understood as social capital which has value, especially economic value.[246]

Leadership embodies these ties. Leadership is about creating interpersonal relationships which will then accumulate social capital. Understanding the informal social structure is itself social capital and creates a power base. Leadership understood as a social network makes again very clear that a social network structure cannot be controlled by one individual.

Three social networks can be described as: the individual leader's network, the interorganisational network, and the organisational network. All three need your attention and will influence your effectiveness as a leader (see Figure 33).

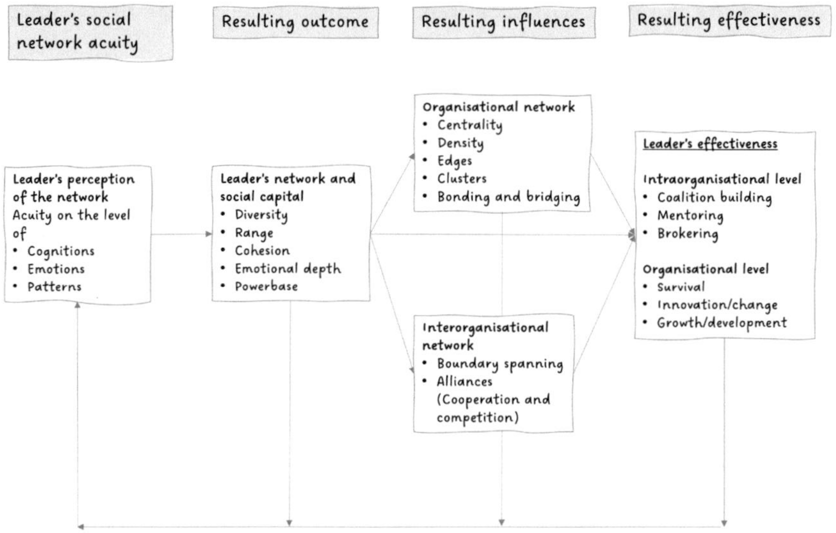

Figure 33: The three relevant networks for leaders (author's drawing)[247]

It might be difficult to focus on internal and external networks at the same time, so sometimes as a leader you must make choices with which come trade-offs. Yet your effectiveness as a leader depends, on the one hand, how well you understand the social network and its meaning and patterns from a cognitive as well as emotional perspective. On the other hand, it depends on your capability to transform your insights into a useful social network. Your personal social network then influences the organisational as well as the interorganisational network and hopefully leads to organisational survival, development, and innovation through different kinds of designing relationships. This sounds as if it were a linear process, which of course it is not, since we are talking about systems here. In Figure 33 (see above) you see the interconnectedness of the different building blocks of leadership effectiveness in social systems as well as the measures and characterising features.

Social network analysis can help to understand what is going on in an organisation where you think something is happening underneath the surface—for example, some hidden resistance or questionable activities—but you do not really know what. There are tools to do that qualitatively via ethnographic research or quantitatively via for example social media networks or email exchanges in a company. They produce maps or pictures that display the patterns of connections between the nodes of the network which represent people, whereas the links represent the relationships.

Leading for collaboration between organisational systems

The growing complexity demands that organisations work together to some extent. Similar to individuals as social actors, organisations do not exist independently of each other. They can engage with each other as buyer–vendor, as a loose network of information exchange to better understand the markets, etc., as joint ventures and the like.

To describe this working together, the literature has developed different technical terms from (social) networks as just discussed, as ecosystems, or as hybrid organisations. At the heart of the matter lies the question of how best to collaborate without giving up the respective organisational identity.

Business ecosystems

The notion of ecosystems in the context of systems leadership can be associated with business ecosystems as well as with the understanding of organisations being part of the natural overall ecosystem of our planet.

A business ecosystem is analogous to a biological ecosystem. A biological ecosystem is a community of living organisms with natural resources such as air and water. Yet they are not only assemblages of species, they also integrate organic and inorganic matter and entail natural forces that interact and change. It is also said that ecosystems are "the productive engines of the planet".[248]

Business ecosystems are social ecosystems which consist of firms and institutions, and not of people, as the word "social" could imply. A business ecosystem is an

> extended system of mutually supportive organizations; communities of customers, suppliers, lead producers, and other stakeholders, financing, trade associations, standard bodies, labour unions, governmental and quasigovernmental institutions, and other interested parties. These communities come together in a partially intentional, highly self-organizing, and even somewhat accidental manner.[249]

Moore[250] emphasises decentralised decision-making and self-organisation. The automotive industry is, for example, an ecosystem which has developed and shifted from car manufacturing and supply to larger ecosystems integrating IT systems, software platforms, artificial intelligence, batteries, chargers, and their producers, etc. Leading an ecosystem is comparable to leading a hybrid organisation. We will talk about that in more detail later in this chapter.

Eco leadership

Yet what is looked at differently is eco leadership. Over the last twenty or so years, different notions of eco leadership have been developed.

However, Bertalanffy, the founder of the general systems theory, already advocated for systems theory in pointing to endangered human survival. He noted a lack of ethical, ethological, and ecological criteria in human affairs. And as today, he believed it to be a matter of life and death, for us and for our planet. Advocating for a new morality that is not centred on the individual, but rather focuses on mankind adapting to the changing environment, he states: "We are dealing with emergent realities; no longer with isolated groups of men, but with a systematically interdependent global community."[251] It seems Bertalanffy heard the call much earlier than many other scientists.

A more recent understanding of eco leadership was developed by Wielkiewicz around the turn of the century. He proposed to understand organisations as complex adaptive systems and claimed that to be successful in today's environment organisations must draw on ecological principles to match the complexity of the environment in which organisations function.[252] By that he means diversity, feedback loops, increased organisational learning, and systems thinking.[253] This is not so removed from what we have discussed so far. More interesting is his proposition to rate leadership on two scales: one for hierarchical thinking (in procedures, rules, norms, hierarchies, and dependence on the leader), and one scale for systems thinking, or the ability to relate a variety of ideas and concepts to organisational success, such as ethics, the need for cooperation of all individuals to help the organisation accomplish goals, the need for long-term thinking, and the need for organisation learning (see Figure 34).[254]

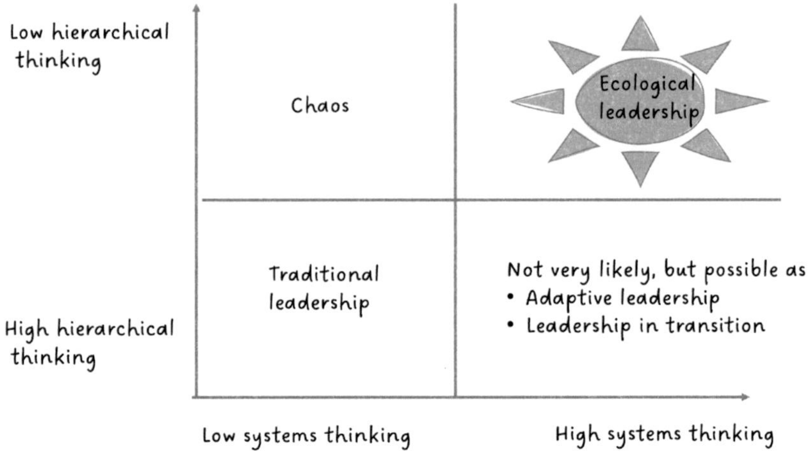

Figure 34: Leadership ranking depending on the level of hierarchical and systems thinking (author's drawing)[255]

Hierarchical thinking stands for power and control in the leadership of the organisation, so that failure and success are also attributed to the leaders and are attributable to them. Rules, procedures, and goals are part of the leadership system. In systemic thinking, leaders understand the connectedness and do not claim success for themselves only. The systemic perspective calls for ecological leadership, which emphasises long-term perspectives, sustainability orientation, and responsible decision-making.[256]

Eco leaders in the Western understanding reframe the form and the purpose of organisations. Whereas connectivity is at the heart of the eco leadership discourse, distributed leadership, ethics, sustainability, and leading adaptive networked organisations are all core to the task of eco leadership.

> Within an organisation there are interdependent parts which make up a whole, this goes for all stakeholder relationships, and in ever widening circles that eventually reach the air we breathe. It is about connectivity, interdependence and sustainability underpinned by an ethical and socially responsible stance.[257]

Eco leadership aims to focus on the interconnectedness of nature—between the human beings and the systems they have created. Western researchers claim it to be filled with human spirit, whether spiritual or not.[258] Whereas an Eastern perspective would include the spiritual side.

Hybrid organisations

The understandings of organisations as complex adaptive systems, social network systems, and ecosystems are all grounded in systems thinking and stem from the same paradigm with slightly different foci.

Yet, to understand business ecosystems which span different organisations and which are purposefully created, the term *hybrid organisations* brings additional value. These organisation types focus on the goal of different organisations working together by maintaining their respective values, artefacts, strategies, and cultures. These organisations then stem from at least two sectoral paradigms and their logic,[259] hence a *hybrid* organisation. The need and their will to work together necessitate a (temporal) organisation in which an interorganisation integration can take place. This working together can take place on a spectrum from fully fragmented to fully connected.

The different stages of working together develop from loose cooperation, to coordination, to full collaboration. They are also called the "3 Cs" (see Figure 35).[260]

Degree of horizontal integration

	Cooperation	Coordination	Collaboration
Time to establish	Short-term	Medium-term	Longer-term
Goals and perspective	Purpose: dialogue, information sharing, base of support Independent, autonomous	Purpose: align resources to meet predetermined goals Retains autonomy, but gives some element to joint effort, planning and programming, semi-autonomous	Purpose: synergise to create something new, systems change Highly interdependent with sharing of power
Structural linkages	Movement in and out by members , loose links, low intensity level	Some level of stability of membership, medium links	Members move outside traditional functional areas, tight/dense links
Formality	Informal	Informal/formal	Informal/formal
Risks and rewards	Low risk, modest reward	Increase in benefits and risks	High risk, high rewards

Figure 35: Degrees of horizontal integration[261]

As you can see from the different integration levels, from left to right, from cooperation to collaboration, the task of the leader is becoming more and more difficult and complex. The main difficulties lie in the integration of the intangible and rather hidden aspects such as culture, value systems, organisational identity, and suchlike. When two or more organisations are supposed to work together, several tensions are likely to arise which the leader(s) need(s) to deal with. These tensions result from cognitive, emotional, and unconscious conflicts regarding, role, task, relationships, and ideas about the respective other and their different levels of expression. They impact the emotions of people, since they feel challenged because of their different organisational backgrounds, their assumptions and expectations, the question of equality in the relationship, and the level of trust needed to work together. All these difficulties can be ascribed to the fundamental question of how to combine cooperation with competition. This paradoxical tension is also described with the notion of "co-opetition", which is depicted as an inherent paradoxical tension in situations of working together across organisational boundaries.

Figure 36 gives an overview of the levels of tensions and which areas they stem from. As in every other organisation, and even more so for a hybrid organisation, goal alignment and recognition of interdependence are essential and can only be achieved via open dialogue.

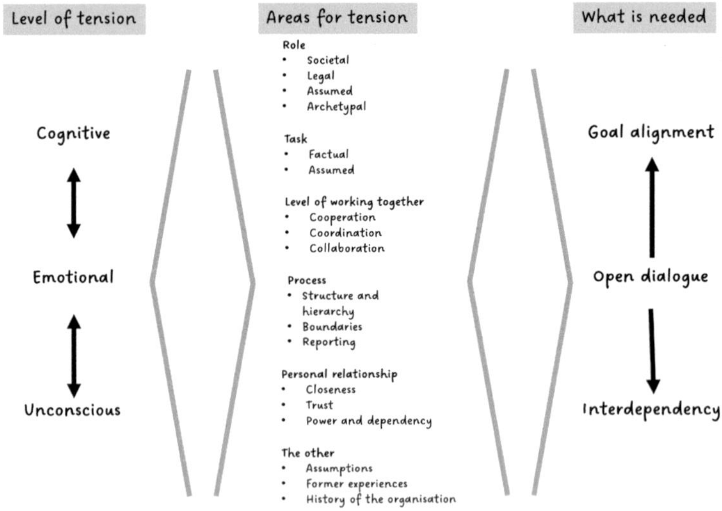

Figure 36: Tensions in situations of organisational "co-opetition" (author's drawing)

Tensions can come from role conflicts—different perceptions and expectations of what one's own role, the role of the organisation and the role of the other, and that of the other organisations, shall look like. The same accounts for task. The level of working together must be defined, but often the definition is blurry and causes irritation. When designing the process of working together, tensions can arise out of the possible structure, its formalisation and hierarchy, what to integrate and what not to (boundaries). Reporting and controlling lines also have potential to cause open and hidden conflict. Ideas about how relationships across organisational boundaries should be managed can vary—openly or hidden and implicitly: how close these relationships shall be, whether and which level of trust is needed to collaborate, and whether and how to admit and live up to the mutual dependence and the respective power to make the collaboration work. Fantasies and assumptions about the other organisation, its culture and identity, can create difficulty working closely together, especially if they are not seen as positive. These fantasies and assumptions can stem from the past, the perception of the organisational history, and reported experiences.

We can now summarise the key challenges for leaders:

- Establishing a collective goal for all organisations involved which is explored and aligned
- Clarifying together what level of working together/horizontal integration is needed
- Clarifying mutual (inter)dependence—is there a hierarchy between the partners or not? If so, how do you deal with it?
- Surfacing the hidden assumptions about how and what the other organisation is like
- Surfacing the hidden goals and agendas when working together, especially when designing the process of collaboration and the roles and tasks
- Establishing a climate of mutual trust
- Transcending the paradoxical tension to a new third with regard to the outcome of the collaboration.

These are difficult yet important tasks which are often underestimated, as the case study will show.

Whereas the task for the leaders seems to be rather clear in the *what* they should be doing, the *how* is also important to understand. We have looked at dealing with paradoxical tensions in Chapter 2. The spectrum ranges from differentiating over integrating to transcending.

In my research with my colleagues at the Vrije Universiteit Amsterdam, Prof Marcel Veejnswik, Prof Issy Drori, and Dr Timo Fiorito, we found three different ways of transcending the paradoxical tensions: behavioural, rhetorical, and emotional transcendence.[262] This means that when dealing with paradoxical challenges, overcoming them and creating something new can take place through speaking, behaving, and feeling about the cooperation which is experienced as co-opetition. The following case shows how we came to these research conclusions.

Case study

Living systems—dealing with paradoxes and emotional tensions

Claudia Nagel

Together with my colleagues at the Vrije Universiteit in Amsterdam (Professors Drori and Veenswijk, Dr Fiorito) we are researching how a public private partnership (PPP) in fighting large-scale financial crime in the Netherlands functions with respect to leadership and emotions.[263,264] We ask the question of what is it that makes the collaboration in a PPP difficult in a general and in this specific setting, and what is done to effectively deal with these challenges?

We know that to collaborate successfully despite and across different goals, mindsets, agendas, cultures, value systems, and expectations of the public and the private partners is demanding, but we want to find out what the challenge consists of, how it emerges, and how the different partners in the PPP react.

The PPP we're looking at is the SCTF (Serious Crime Task Force), a unique PPP for solving an important societal question and a pilot in its field about the way the collaboration works. In the SCTF, the national police, the Public Prosecutor's Office, the Financial Intelligence Unit (FIU), and the Fiscal Information and Investigation Service (FIOD) work together with several major banks (ING, Rabo Banken, ABN Amro, and Volksbanken) to find out how money laundering is executed via financial brokers who facilitate not just money laundering but fraud, corruption, and violent crime. The cooperation is set up to enable the police and the FIOD—in coordination with and under the authority of the Public Prosecution Service—to pass on to the participating banks the names of advisors or legal persons who are on the radar of the national police. The banks can then link these names to certain unusual transactions. When the data on these transactions are handed over to the police and the FIOD, these and similar transactions are analysed by the banks together with the FIU to determine whether or not they are suspicions, in which case they would be handed over to the public prosecutor who can start a case against the broker in question.

I will share here the results of the first phase of research in 2020. First, we found that several paradoxical tensions are inherent in the set-up of this PPP. They influence the perceptions and emotions of all parties involved and create mostly difficult feelings and result in emotional defences which most partners in the PPP are not actively aware of.

Second, we also found, on the level of the individual, different ways of dealing with these paradoxical tensions, which cover the broad spectrum described above (see Chapter 2), from differentiating to integrating and finally to transcending.

I will depict both sets of findings in detail to demonstrate the challenges and solutions to these tensions challenging people in this PPP phase. In the following descriptions I will have to simplify our findings; the actual situation is more complex, and the findings are more nuanced than is practical to describe here in this short overview of the case.

First findings

The set-up

In setting up the SCTF as a PPP, we have the public sector, which is represented by the FIU, the police, and the FIOD, all part of law enforcement, yet working under different ministries. Between the police, the FIOD, and the FIU we observed boundary and role confusion and, by that, competition between the different partners on the public side, especially between the FIOD and the police. The banks, together with the Dutch Banking Association (Nederlandse Vereniging van Banken, or “NVB”), belong to the private sector. There is a natural tension between the public side of law enforcement and the private side, with the banks being investigated for breaching the law.

The structural tensions

The Financial Expertise Centre (FEC) governs the SCTF and is a public partnership of supervisors and public authorities, under the roof of the Dutch National Bank, involved in supervision, control, detection, and prosecution in the financial sector. In doing so, a natural tension with the banks is inherent. In one of the steering committees the private banks are taking part, yet under a prevailing feeling that they do not belong there, that the real decisions are taken somewhere else. The following figure gives an overview of the kind of tensions to be expected due to conflicting and opposing agendas (see Figure 37).

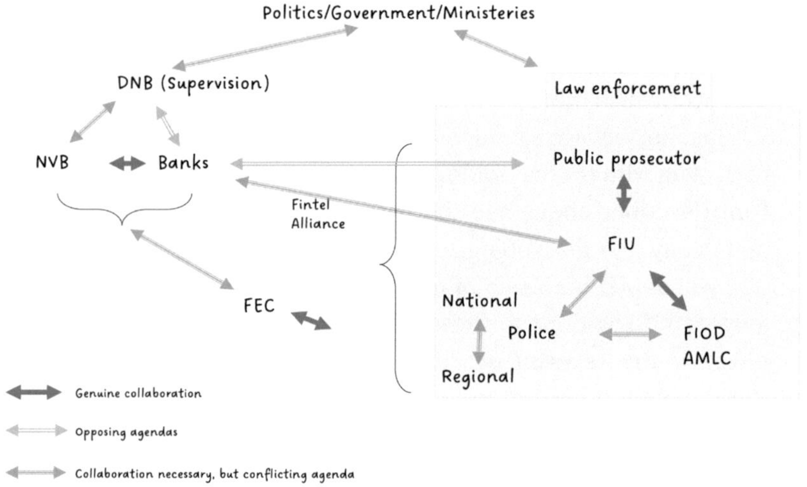

Figure 37: Collaborative tensions in the ecosystem for fighting financial crime (author's drawing)

The work process

The PPP itself and the work process are structured in a complex way which seems to hold the emotions and tensions at bay. It looks similar from the outside to the classical Dutch polder model, which is about integrating all parties at the table in a shared decision-making process. Yet under these circumstances we interpret it as a symbolic collaboration due to the over-complexity of the structure which functions as a defence against the anxieties—this defence, at the same time containing and holding, is also blurring the boundaries and hindering fast decision-making and open dialogue.

The structure goes as follows: at the top is the FEC board, which then manages the FEC PPS, the committee which the banks are also part of. On the next level we have the CP, the meeting of all institutional representatives, where managers of all partners come together to exchange information. Underneath is the *Klankboard*, the sounding board where the operational managers meet. And only then, on level 5, the work group level, does collaboration begin to take place. It consists of three process phases, yet only in one specific step is the real PPP executed. In the input phase, police, public prosecutor, and FIOD (all public side) decide which cases are to be looked at. In the next phase, the throughput phase, we find the only real collaboration between public and private, where the banks look into their transaction data under the guidance of the FIU to detect suspicious transactions—the FIU has no direct impact, it just consults the banks on whether or not they are on the right track. This group is also part of the so-called Fintel Alliance, another institutional structure. The next phase is the output phase, when suspicious transactions are handed over from the FIU to the public prosecutor, both public. The banks as private partners are only involved in that throughput phase. Once they have done this work they rarely hear anything back about their work results and whether their data regarding the transactions examined have contributed to catching criminals. We call the PPP a "symbolic collaboration", since the collaborative work does not take place anywhere other than this work group level, and even there it is actually more of an information exchange.

The emotional and the narrative level

The role and boundary conflicts between the public parties, and the genuine tensions and conflicts between the public and private side, have led to a broad array of emotions which are kept at bay via projections and splitting behaviours.

On the police level, the emotions towards the banks are characterised by feelings of superiority (only we know) and distrust (the banks are not really interested, they only want to make money). The banks feel devalued, inferior, and made dependant, despite their willingness to contribute to the process (they don't trust us, we've spent so much money, it is never enough, we never get any praise for our work). On the public side, a gang-like process in which the involved public institutions collude "against" the banks—a somewhat parallel process to what is happening on the criminal side. The banks are rather angry and looking for revenge for not being seen for what they are; they also see themselves as victims of the criminals, not as offenders. Yet they are also trapped in a dilemma regarding how much information they share—what kind of information is good enough and not making them vulnerable to the public prosecutor. Another dilemma is that they are profit-oriented, yet have to play the role given by law of a (public) gatekeeper, which impacts costs and profit because of business not pursued. A certain helplessness around what to do and how to best react can be observed. In addition, feelings of guilt and shame for not having better protected their clients and shareholders from criminals exploiting their systems are also part of the picture. Of course, most of these emotions are not openly discussed within the PPP.

The narrative level of the PPP is the light side that contrasts the shadow aspects I just described. Here the partners talk in public about the great success of the PPP; of working well together and having an important shared goal—catching criminals—to which every institution contributes its utmost possible (see Figure 38).

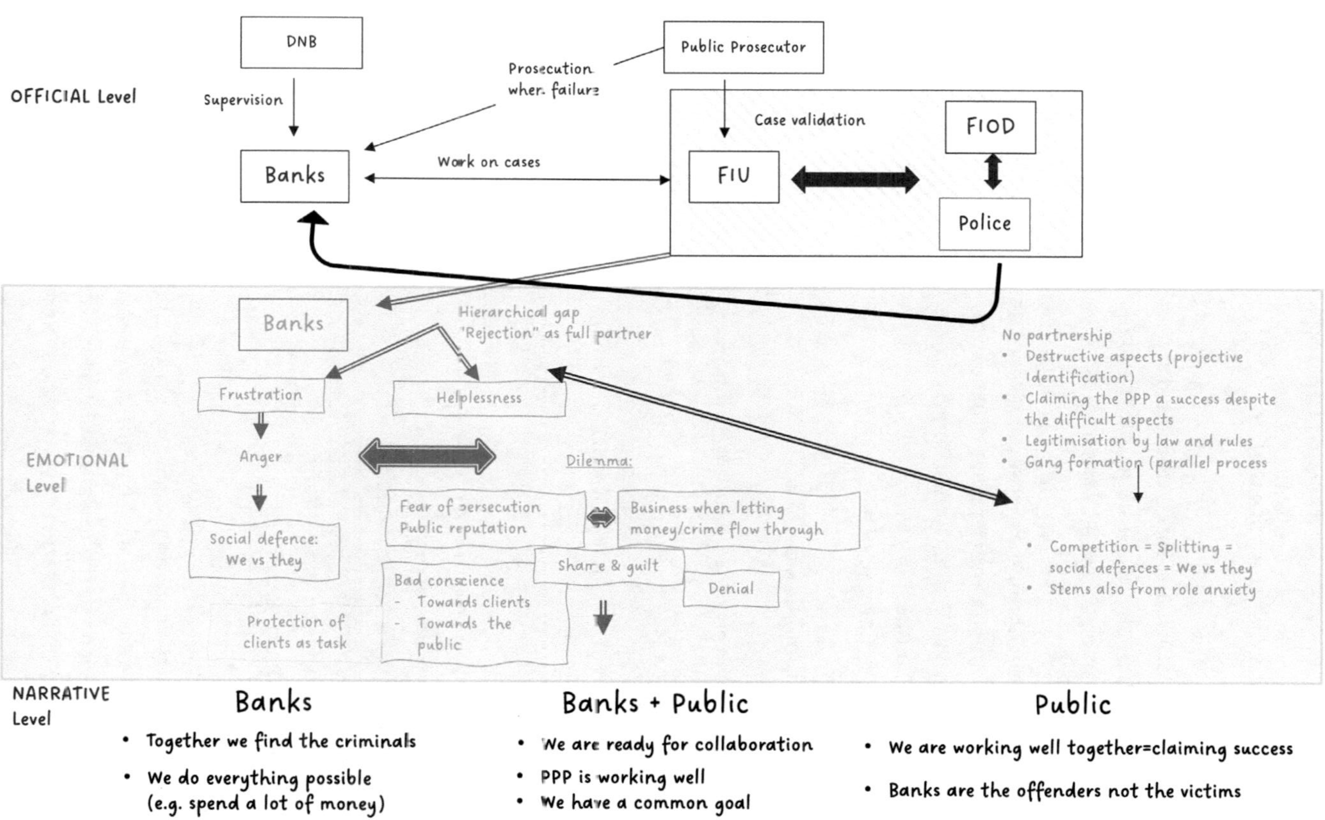

Figure 38: Overview of the findings on the emotional level (author's drawing)

Second findings

Transcending the paradoxical tension

The specific set-up of the PPP leads to several difficult to solve paradoxical tensions which are part of this legal set-up and situation—they have to be dealt with and, if possible, transcended.

For the banks, these tensions are:

- Information-sharing vs Protecting client data
- Information-sharing vs Public prosecution
- Reputation vs Profit (double-bind)
- Profit vs Gatekeeping
- Business vs Compliance

For the police/public side:

- Information sharing vs indirectly informing criminals
- Trust vs Control/distrust
- Support vs Persecution
- Reputation vs Duty

For all:

- Cat vs Dog (who is what?)
- Enemy vs Same ecosystem
- Hierarchy vs Interdependence
- Inequality vs Equality
- Cooperation vs Competition
- Control/Distrust vs Trust

The emotional reactions described are part of the first level of differentiating—for example, choosing one side of the paradox. We have observed emotional defences, but also a significant lack of transparency, which leads to the question of who is hiding what from whom?

One reaction is creating new narratives and, by that, a success works well and avoids exercising operational leadership. One line of defence is also that dealing with the other as a person is different in a positive way and less problematic since they are not the organisation.

The differentiation takes place in splitting, for example, the managerial level from the strategic level in this complex organisational structure set-up; in understanding the collaboration as a chess board and establishing it as a sequential process. Also, the banks talk about their dilemmas at the work group level in monthly meetings—yet this is not the main level where they should be discussed. This conversation should be had at the strategic level; however, there is not much discussion taking place.

The integration takes place when former public managers, for example, move to compliance on the banking side, and when then these connections are used to form constructive work relationships in the PPP. Furthermore, the establishment of the sounding board on the operational level is an attempt to integrate the paradoxical tensions. One can also understand the set-up of the work process and the integrated polder model as only differentiating, or as integrating in the sense of dealing with paradoxical tensions.

Transcendence efforts are the most mature way of dealing with paradoxical tensions. We have found here three methods of transcendence: rhetorical, behavioural, and emotional—the last is our new contribution to the theory.

Transcendence involves "moving towards a higher plane of understanding in which paradoxical poles are understood as complex interdependences rather than competing interests".[265] The management of paradoxical tensions in co-optative relationships requires "both sides to understand each other's perspectives and develop a shared perspective that transcends their differences".[266] It is about "moving towards a higher plane of understanding in which paradoxical poles are understood as complex interdependences rather than competing interests". Such transcendence, which involves the ability to think beyond paradoxes,[267] entails the realisation of the synthesis of two poles of a contradiction that "transcends or rises above them" and persists through "a higher level of abstraction".[268]

Rhetorical transcendence takes place when the PPP is understood as the only necessary tool to combat large-scale crime, despite the tensions and difficulties which have to be overcome. Understanding and talking about large-scale financial crime as societal crime which needs to be combatted together, as well as emphasising the complementarity of the partners and their interdependence, belongs to that form of transcendence. On the behavioural level we could observe aims to work towards exchanging information on a more abstract level with all parties involved. As it happens, the FEC has founded a new work group where line managers from both sides tackle the paradoxical tensions together.

Emotional transcendence takes place when some members, especially at a strategic level, actively embrace the opposing objectives and share this view within their organisation. Searching for and relying on positive former collegial relationships across organisational boundaries to solve problems together, which will often develop trust between partners and therefore is contagious in a positive sense, is a way of emotionally transcending the paradoxical tensions.

A way forward for the leaders

When aiming for a PPP the question of equality and admitted interdependence is crucial. For the PPP here it would mean a change in the collaboration culture. Only when aiming to become equal partners can acceptance and integration of mutual dependence lead to the development of real emotional trust and, by that, collaboration across boundaries that stays on track with the respective organisational agendas. This needs a suitable ambience and safe space for continuous open negotiations on what is possible and how it can be achieved together. This entails a process of aligning what the PPP means for the partners and what the purpose and goal of the PPP are. This process needs time and leaders should be realistic about what the partners can contribute—and what they cannot.

Talking about realistic goals, for this PPP it could be a focus on patterns of crime (something which other workforces are already doing). Integrating not only banks as gatekeepers, but also notaries, insurance companies etc., would take away the positioning of the banks as the criminals themselves. It would, of course, help if the public partners had done their homework with regard to institutional boundaries, roles, and responsibilities, as well as clarifying the role of the FEC in the whole set-up.

At the core for a successful hybrid organisation lies the need to create greater mutual understanding, which entails:

- Reflecting on dealing with inherent paradoxical tensions
- Reflecting on cultural and projected roles in the PPP
- Reflecting on real and projected responsibilities
- Reflecting on the limitations of the PPP
- Co-creating a shared narrative for the PPP.

The partners of this PPP are now on their way to integrating our research results and recommendations into the hybrid organisation set-up and back into their respective organisations.[269]

* * *

This case demonstrated very clearly the difficulties faced when working together across organisational boundaries. Yet these tensions and difficulties are similar for any organisations aiming for collaboration, also within systems. The insights gained here can hence also be applied also to intraorganisational collaborative efforts—the question is always around how to bridge differences while respecting and even using them for creative purposes.

KEY LEARNING

- Coming from a general system and a living system theory, today we understand organisations as complex adaptive systems. This means that they consist of changing relationships between human beings that demand continuous adaptation—a challenging task for leaders who can no longer rely on hierarchical management alone, and who must integrate different parts of larger systems in their decision-making.
- When integrating the world around us we can call that an ecological leadership approach.
- In a complex world, cooperation between organisations is a key competency, and one that is highly dependent on paradoxical thinking and emotional, behavioural, and rhetorical transcendence.

CHAPTER 15

Taking over and then?

Mergers and acquisitions (M&A) often fail to deliver what the involved parties were hoping for. The failure rate lies between 50 and 90 per cent depending on the research source. Some research has even found that the total returns of M&A are negative. So, the question is, why do these often-so-spectacular deals go wrong? And—before we can understand that—why are they agreed in the first place, despite their well-known failure rate?

The official or public reasons to buy a company are to improve performance by, for example, maintaining and improving your specific market position (e.g. buying a young and bullish start-up), leveraging synergies (e.g. buying an existing competitor) and by that lowering costs. The second reason is to renew and reinvent the existing business model,[270] which is often hidden behind the first reason, not wanting to admit the need for renewal. Another reason is to find a successor for the existing owner and then buying a more junior company so that the junior owner may take over the leadership one day.

The unspoken reasons are that an M&A deal sounds great and glamorous, feeds the CEO's vanity and boosts their ego. Furthermore, often, once the thought of a possible merger or acquisition has been mentioned by somebody on the board, it is like a train that, having left the station, cannot be stopped, while it gains more and more speed because all the future intermediaries involved—advisors and researchers, lawyers, bankers, and consultants—do not want to let go of such a great opportunity.

The reasons why M&A deals fail are multiple:

- Lack of a proper due diligence process, because of time pressure or because the wrong people are involved—being those who will leave after the deal is complete.
- False promises with regard to collaboration and synergies—the C-level suite says it wants to collaborate, yet shortly after the deal is signed off, the power struggle starts and the people of the acquired company always end up drawing the short straw; the proposed merger of equals never works out. In addition, mergers are very often disguised takeovers which are even more painful for the acquired organisation.
- Not understanding the real reasons behind the merger. Is it the value added? The technology? The business model? A vertical or horizontal integration? It could even simply be showing off, becoming bigger and more important by acquiring a larger company.
- Not involving the right people—people at lower levels who know about the day-to-day operations are more important than those at the top level—generally, the greater your say in negotiations, the further away you are from the shop floor and their managers, yet this is where the work has to be done.
- Involving intermediaries as well as the press too early puts pressure on the possible deal—from which it is difficult to withdraw.

In addition to these craft- and knowledge-oriented mistakes, more subtle yet very powerful reasons for failure emerge from interpersonal relationships. We can talk about a clash of cultures—companies often have very different ways of doing similar things, and people generally do not enjoy learning new tricks when they are happy with their current method of working. Power struggles, psychosocial defences and more will hence kick in.

The following case gives an overview of how a good idea is destroyed when the wrong people are chosen to execute it. Merging two cultures is particularly difficult as we can see; there is always one who does not want to give up their position to integrate.

Case study

A merger—crown jewel or poisoned chalice?

Ajit Menon

The tension in the boardroom was palpable. The room was filled with senior executives sitting on either side of a long boardroom table. On each end of the table was a CEO and I was positioned in the middle of the room. Both sides were angry, and I was awaiting the conflict to emerge. Jaspreet and Gordon, the two CEOs were there to negotiate the deal, the break-up of a partnership. In my career, I have worked with several conflict situations, but this came closest to a corporate divorce. Ambit Insurance and Ambit-Pioneer were in the room led by their respective CEOs. The meeting was to start a process of negotiation where the two companies would demerge and go their own ways. After years of pushing for integration, it was a turning point in their history that the two businesses now wanted to go their own way. This case is a description of the story of these two organisations and the paths that they carved out together and separately.

Ambit Insurance

Ambit is a 6,000-strong global speciality insurance firm headquartered in the City of London. The firm was founded by two entrepreneurs in the 1980s, Joseph Lamb and Daniel Levitt, and the name Ambit was created using a combination of both their surnames. Lamb and Levitt were known for their strong entrepreneurial spirit and their nose for opportunities. They each had invested £10,000 of their own personal wealth to form the company. In the late 1980s, when London was falling behind other global centres such as New York, the Thatcher government changed the stock market rules. This led to the Big Bang, a dramatic increase in market activity which made London the leader of financial services globally. Lamb and Levitt took advantage of this and built their business by adding new lines of speciality insurance for luxury goods, shipping, and aviation to their books. This exponentially changed their market cap and the presence they had in the UK market.

Though mainly London-centric, Ambit has been building a global presence in the speciality insurance sector and now has offices in

Australia, Singapore, and India. The influence of the two founders, Lamb and Levitt, on the business is very strong. The LL maxims as they are known, are the cultural boundaries of the organisation. These are maxims that the founders lived by and expected their employees and the organisation to adhere to. Lamb, in particular, was very passionate about culture and spent a lot of time reinforcing the message that the culture of Ambit was sacred. The founders were larger-than-life characters who used to roam the floors of the office; they knew almost every employee by name and were very present in organisational life. Unusually for insurance businesses in the 1980s they started speaking of a "flat structure" and created an environment of access, meritocracy, and dialogue. Most other insurance organisations in the City at the time were very hierarchical. They took their models from Lloyd's of London and the narrative that "underwriters were kings" was prevalent across the City. However, not at Ambit; Lamb and Levitt were very clear that the underwriters were nothing without the teams around them and a large part of the underwriters' remuneration was measured on how they built and managed their teams. This was highly unusual at the time, and they found out that it was hard to hold on to the old school underwriters. But they were not fazed by this. They were steadfast in their beliefs that by building a strong culture, they would build a strong organisation that would ensure longevity.

What was interesting was that whilst it was difficult for them to recruit senior underwriters at first, their open, egalitarian environment meant more opportunities for others to grow and those who came to work at Ambit usually stayed for many years. Being entrepreneurial, they always looked for opportunities and were keen to add other lines of business. In the early 2000s they decided that they wanted to expand their offering and have a more regional presence in the UK. Having done their research they concluded that instead of starting a whole new line of products they would simply acquire an existing firm. The thinking was that these products are not complex but what would differentiate Ambit was the customer experience. They were very proud of the organisation they had built and the culture that they were promoting. They were convinced that if they found the right firm to acquire, by integrating it into their culture, they could use the firm's existing product and networks set to build a successful nationwide business. This is how they encountered Pioneer.

Pioneer

Pioneer was a mid-size general insurer based just outside Liverpool with around 2,000 employees. It had a history that is over 100 years old. It had deep expertise in providing business insurance to businesses of all sizes and complexities. It provided commercial covers such as public liability insurance for several businesses across the UK. Its brand was well known in the North of England and in Scotland with thirteen offices; however, it had no presence in the South. Pioneer was also built on strong entrepreneurial values. Over the years, the business had been bought and sold several times and had gone through multiple changes. There was a strong sales culture in the organisation and the performance was driven hard. There was a distance between staff and management, including factors such as separate executive parking and dining rooms. Many individuals had grown up in the firm and had worked at Pioneer all their lives.

A general executive team ran the business from their headquarters; however, it was a federated model where each of the thirteen offices was run as an individual business and the MD of each of these offices had full control as to what happened in its patch. Hierarchy was strictly adhered to and respected and the business was tightly controlled by the executives. Underwriters were pandered to, and a lot of time and effort was spent in ensuring that the senior underwriters were always kept happy, even though at times their behaviour was questionable. Staff feared the senior underwriters and there was an unsaid rule that no one questioned what the underwriters said. There was a strong sense of camaraderie among the staff, they were happy and felt well treated by the organisation. The culture, while rigid and autocratic, had served a purpose as the business was very successful and had won many awards in its time. Pioneer had ambitions to grow, and its principals felt that they had reached a ceiling in the markets that they were operating in. They wanted a strategic partnership that would enable them to break out of their mid-market status and give them access to London.

The deal

In 2010, following weeks of discussions, the board of Ambit approved a decision to acquire a major stake in Pioneer. This would enable both businesses to pursue their growth ambitions. Ambit would get a vehicle to expand nationally and an additional business line. Pioneer would be able to leverage Ambit's presence in London and globally. Together the two businesses would benefit from the reciprocal arrangement. It was decided that Pioneer would not lose its heritage and history by being consumed by Ambit; instead the new company would be called Ambit-Pioneer and would be a subsidiary of the Ambit group. Several discussions were had about the culture of the two businesses, and it was decided that while there were several differences, the integration process would take this into account and work with it. The partnership was seen to be strategic and beneficial to both parties. The CEO of the newly formed Ambit-Pioneer company would together with the CEO of Ambit report into Lamb and Levitt in their role as group CEOs.

It was to be an eighteen-month integration process and there was a lot of buzz in both the businesses about the opportunity that this deal presented. Ambit's new CEO, Jaspreet, was selected from among the executive team. She was a fifty-year-old British Asian woman who had led Ambit's international business. She was close to the founders and had been selected because of her deep expertise in the business and her long tenure with the organisation. It was decided that Ambit-Pioneer's new CEO would come from within the Pioneer business. Lamb and Levitt did not want the Pioneer team to feel that their entire identity was being eroded and they felt that the business needed a leader who was familiar with the people to provide them with the containment they needed during this turbulent period of change. However, despite this, they decided to go external and appointed Gordon, a fifty-two-year-old Mancunian who was the finance director of a competitor, to be the CEO of Ambit-Pioneer. The reasoning was that they needed someone hard-hitting to build the business and work with integrating it into the Ambit Group.

The unfortunate pair

Gordan and Jaspreet set off on their individual journeys to build their part of the business. They were seen as siblings by Lamb and Levitt and treated as such. There was a strong push from Lamb and Levitt to create an integrated business and bring the two closer together. And, while Jaspreet tried her hardest, Gordon was reluctant to do so. Gordon set off by changing the entire management team at Ambit-Pioneer. He let go of many of the old hands and recruited a number of senior positions from the market.

At the end of the first year, he commissioned a consultancy to help them build their internal culture. He resisted calls from Group to work with building an integrated culture by saying that the Pioneer side of the business was different, and that Group was not taking into account these differences and was trying to annihilate their heritage by imposing a culture on them. He was extremely suspicious of Jaspreet and did everything he could to ensure that the two businesses were treated as separate entities. This led to a lot of confusion in the system. Ambit Group set out an objective for all the businesses and they labelled this "Universal Ambit". The idea was that they would create a more integrated business model especially in the support areas. Creating leveraged support areas meant that businesses could reduce duplication and receive a more cost-effective service. Jaspreet was very energised by this concept; she was very cost conscious and had for a long time suggested that the support services were very expensive as the group had duplicated them for the different business.

This was a real opportunity to rationalise this and bring the cost to income ratio down thereby increasing the profitability of the business. Gordon was very opposed to this and repeatedly said in many fora that the integration process must not discount the nuance of the individual businesses. He said that a centralised support function would not really understand his business's needs and given that his business area was smaller, (he said) that Ambit may not get the attention it needs. Gordon and Jaspreet's relationship became strained very quickly. And, in group executive meetings they would often be on opposing viewpoints and disagree with each other.

A fraught integration

Over a period of four months, Gordon slowly built his executive team. They were brought in from various businesses across the country and were strong players in the industry. Gordon ran Ambit-Pioneer completely differently to the other businesses in Ambit Group. He started introducing governance practices, structural changes, and even branding differences into the organisation. Jaspreet was very concerned, and she raised in group executive meetings that there was a "separatist" atmosphere in Ambit-Pioneer. Lamb and Levitt were not concerned; they told Gordon to respect the Ambit group brand and culture but were happy that he was creating a strong business. They asked Jaspreet to just concentrate on her own business line and that with time the group would bring it all together. Over this period, several duplicate processes started emerging within the organisation. Sitting floors apart, there were multiple compliance teams and HR teams that were servicing the same group. Ambit Insurance had its own client onboarding team, and this was different to Ambit-Pioneer's. Often clients would phone the office and be put through to the wrong team. Compliance teams would get the regulatory responses mixed up and on one occasion, a senior underwriter was issued the wrong employment contract. This started creating noise in the system that the integration between the businesses was not going well. Lamb and Levitt started asking questions about this. In one executive committee Gordon became enraged and said that his team was being stifled and not allowed to work with the freedom they needed to build their businesses.

At the year-end results, Ambit Insurance excelled and produced market leading results despite the economic conditions. However, Ambit-Pioneer was down 15 per cent on the previous year's results. The analysts were not sympathetic, and their analysis suggested that Ambit-Pioneer was a drain on the Ambit group. They blamed this on inflated costs and bad management; Gordon was held to account for this. It had only been a year since the acquisition; however, Lamb and Levitt decided that Gordon was not the person to lead the integration. They were disappointed with his separatist attitude and his unwillingness to integrate with the rest of the group. They were even more concerned with the losses made by the Ambit-Pioneer side of the business. What was seen to be a profitable initiative suddenly started to look like a bad investment and they started to distance themselves from this side of the business. Over a period, they started ignoring Gordon and conversations began to demerge Ambit-Pioneer. Jaspreet was tasked with the accountability to break up the business.

What was supposed to be the jewel in the crown for the Ambit Group ended up being the poisoned chalice. And over a period of six months the Pioneer part of the business was removed from the Ambit group.

* * *

The case shows well how the promises of getting together as two companies are not fulfilled if you do not pay enough attention to the possibly clashing two cultures of an organisation. Behind this clash are several psychological reasons which we will look at now.[271]

A merger brings two companies together to create a new third—something new is created and something existing is to be destroyed so that the new can come into being. A merger is just a paradoxical mixture of destruction and creation;[272] both take place at the same time, and that makes it difficult to understand and deal with. This is basically the major reason why mergers fail—the emotions connected with destroying something already existing and for a while working well enough, and at the same time creating something new and unknown. All kinds of fantasies, positive as well as negative emotional forces, often unconscious, are impacting the success of a merger—theses forces apply to the individuals and their relationships with others as well as to groups and teams and their intergroup relations.

The M&A journey

Brunning[273] talks about a migration, and a migrant's journey to the new organisation, which I think is a very strong picture for the emotional rollercoaster people go through in a merger process—on both sides, the acquiring as well as the acquired. The journey which consists of five stages starts, at least for some, with hope and for others with despair when they contemplate migration (see Figure 39).

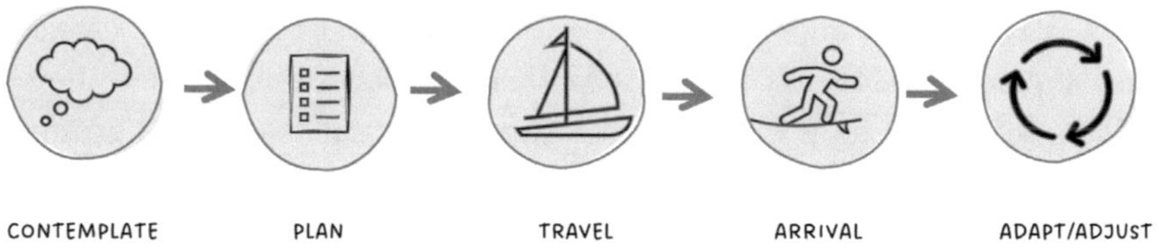

Figure 39: The M&A journey from an emigration perspective (author's drawing)

The contemplation in the organisations about the merger starts at latest when the merger is announced publicly and when the first conversations in the companies start about what will be happening during this merger.

Once the deal is signed the employees must get prepared for leaving the existing organisation. It is the time of a slowly approaching death for parts of the merging organisations. In this phase the uncertainty is high, the consequences are not yet thought through, people start to feel unsafe and insecure; it is frightening to leave the shore/the existing organisation and the questions come up: can we not stay, why do we have to migrate, what did we do wrong in the past, why us and not them?

The journey itself is the toughest part of the migration. One has to expect clouds, rain, strong winds and even storms, high waves, strong undercurrents, hidden reefs, shallow waters, but also sunshine and warm weather, good winds. In that phase, the psychological task is thus multilayered: one has to deal with expectations and disappointment, with letting go and leaving behind the familiar past, with embracing an uncertain future and learning to survive.

This phase of the real journey creates anxiety and fear of annihilation, of losing the job, role, the task, own authority, and identity. Also, the network of colleagues will be lost, which also means that attachment and close working relationships will not be the same afterwards. This loss is painful and threatening; the organisations as a whole disappear, in reality, but also in the mind. The latter is even more difficult to bear. This anxiety will cause individual and intergroup defences to develop and come out. Also, aggressive impulses, attacks combined with envy will be set free to fight for survival, as an individual as well as a group.

Both parties are fearful of being annihilated, one by being devoured and the other party being poisoned after having digested this party.

If the chaos and the changes are catastrophic and overwhelming, the ship starts sinking; people might leave and try to get onshore somewhere else with another organisation.

Sometimes fantasies can come up that only the good parts of two organisations merge—which is, of course, not reality but part of the hope that things will develop better.

It can also happen that not only the employees but also the leadership struggles with the journey; they are undergoing the same emotional journey and difficulties as everybody else and have in addition to manage themselves support their people to go through the necessary changes. New structures, new roles, new tasks, new processes will be created, and some will also be adapted from one or both former organisations. Some traditions will be destroyed and not changed in a rational way. We also observe attacks from the not-so-healthy organisation to the healthier one, out of envy and jealousy, that might lead to devaluing and destroying the respective other part of the organisation.

When this journey is survived, what we hope for, the arrival at the new shore can be celebrated. New organisational structures have been created, the formal ones; the informal ones need more time to develop, while new roles and tasks have been developed. The destruction of parts of the old is going on in the creation of the newly emerging organisation. Celebrating this arrival is important for creating a new and different organisational identity and culture; it is setting the tone for both.

The last phase, which will also need a significant amount of time, is the adjustment phase. The new roles and task have to be taken up and adapted as well as the authority coming with it. New boundaries and new structures will have to be managed, new relationships will be built, and, by that, a hopefully constructive and not neurotic culture will develop. The psychological task for the individual consists of readjusting to the upheaval of role, identity, status, and the impact on core values of the individual as well as of the new organisation created.

How to get it right?

Three main tasks have to be delivered by the leadership for the merger to be a success:

- You need to contain emotional experiences of a catastrophe happening
- You need to manage realistic and neurotic anxieties
- You need to identify and manage the primary risk.

At the core is working with the emotions, whether good or bad, difficult or positive, in an open way by sharing experiences. Instead of denying, repressing, or rejecting them, it makes more sense to address them openly as a natural way of reacting to this kind of profound change and transformation. First and foremost it means that you in a leadership role have to understand the emotional process, and you should start with yourself and manage your emotions accordingly. This is not only important for you, but also for the people you lead—bearing your own anxieties enables you to bear your followers' anxieties.

You as a leader need to be present and available for the people you work with; it is your task to create containment and a safe space for this open exchange. This means managing real and fantasised risks as well as the real and neurotic anxieties. By this you create connectedness and relatedness—best by using real communication, face to face, whenever possible. Often new structures must be created, maybe smaller teams, for connecting individuals. These new structures, together with new roles and responsibilities, are best worked out by the people most probably stepping into these roles later. This creates a feeling of being involved in the process and fosters a sense of attachment to the new design, as well as a sense of pride.

You should pay a lot of attention to integrating the work-level staff into journeying through the merger and not just handing them the decision about how things will be done in the future. In a merger, boundaries may become blurred and fluid, so that eventually everybody has to think about the role they need to and want to play. Beside these emotional tasks it is also important to identify the primary task and manage the primary risk of the new organisation.

All of what is mentioned here is more easily talked about than done—but it is worth the effort. Working with an organisation after a traumatising journey is very difficult—these wounds will stay with the organisation for a long time and settle in as organisational complexes, and the question then is, whether and how healing will be possible.

KEY LEARNING

- An M&A process is a painful clash of cultures which causes emotional upheaval and can be compared to emigrating to a new land.
- To fulfil expectations, the bereavement process and loss must be allowed for, experienced, and managed. This will take time, usually much more than you think. The new achievements should then be celebrated.
- Only a caring integration process may make this possible.

CHAPTER 16

Love and loneliness

Love can take many forms and is important for all of us throughout our lives—how you love a person can be romantic, *agape*, or brotherly love, *philia*, the loving friendship, or unconditional love for your children or your parents. Heartfelt or ambivalent, you can love not only people, but also your profession, your role, your job, your organisation—all this is part of the human condition. There is always an object of love—real or imagined, alive or dead, material or immaterial. The spectrum for love and loving is endless, I would say. Love is mostly about feeling close and connected, wanted, and appreciated.

In contrast, loneliness makes one feel disconnected. Loneliness means being alone and desolate, and is not to be mistaken for solitude, which is being with yourself without feeling lonely. Many people search for solitude to think deeply, to meditate, to daydream, or whatever feels good when being with yourself only. Nobody wants to feel lonely; it is a painful feeling, and it may even be accompanied and deepened by shame and guilt.[274]

Let us first have a look at what kind of love we can experience in general, and then how it applies in organisations, especially in leadership situations.

What is love?

There is no one definition of what love is and what loving means. It has so many facets and faces and is used in many different connotations and circumstances, not only in describing romantic love between partners (see Figure 40). However, we may find some common denominators. Love is a positive and, in general, pleasant emotional experience which is attached to someone or something. The aim of love is to become one, as in a romantic pair, or to become whole, as with a task or profession you really enjoy doing. It relates to self-realisation and an integration of what is loved. It also wants the other object, whatever it is, to be alive and to thrive. It results in creating something—giving new life to an idea, a child, a project, or even an organisation.

Love involves all our basic emotional systems (see Chapter 5). Love has its roots in LUST—in the sexual desire, which Freud translated as libido, and in CARE.

Desire as an aspect of love can be for sexual fulfilment but may also be used in the sense offered by Lacan—who uses the notion of desire slightly differently and more pessimistically in claiming that desire will remain unfulfilled; it cannot and shall not be satisfied because it is born of and revolves around an absence, something missing. The desire can also turn into craving and yearning and has a connotation with pain and longing for something. We can draw desire back to the infant's (pre-birth) experience of being one with the mother, the first object of love.

The CARE system is also engaged in love—caring and nurturing the helpless infant, the partner in need, physically and emotionally, are important aspects. It is connected to creating attachment relations which—when everything develops well—are full of love and care. It then includes tenderness, holding and containing. If that is not the case, we may find a person who has difficulty building lasting relationships—emotionally, socially, or even with physical objects.

This leads us to the next emotion, SEEKING—we seek what we need (food and shelter) and find useful for survival, or what we desire, love, and enjoy. Passion for an activity grows out of never-ending SEEKING, out of curiosity and wanting to know, out of wanting to be recognised for an achievement or talent. PLAY also has a role in love, because of the creative aspect. PLAY is about trying out and a "doing as if"—and, by that, leads to new behaviours, new insights, new relationships.

When love is withdrawn, PANIC/GRIEF sets in—a very painful emotion for both children and adults at any stage of life. Another reaction towards an unfulfilled need shows up in RAGE, which wants to destroy what frustrates us and stands in the way of us getting our needs met.

Love very often includes the FEAR of losing the beloved object—which could be not only life-threatening for an infant, but also the emotional threat of losing a beloved partner or friend, or even the cognitive threat of losing a theme or subject which fascinates you and makes you thrive. Love flows through all the emotional systems.

Love can also be understood as (psychic) energy directed at someone or something which is needed for survival (as a species) and self-preservation. This libido is, for Jung, a general creative energy and a willingness to be in the world. It grows out of oppositional pairs (good/bad, warm/cold, caring/destroying, etc.) and their differences which, according to his theory, tend towards wholeness. Through its repression, the energy can become attached to unconscious complexes which strive to come into consciousness via creativity. Symbols, which have a much broader meaning and many more connotations when compared to images, are an expression of this unconscious will to emerge into consciousness (see Chapter 13).

The life-creating energy is also an expression of the Greek god Eros, who was said to have created life on Earth, as well as joy, pleasure, and motion. Different mythological stories exist to recount his life and his meaning. One goes that he is the son of Aphrodite and Ares (Mars and Venus in Roman mythology), another that he was born at the birth of the cosmos itself. As the son of Aphrodite, he supports her with a golden bow, but having dark wings he also has some cruel, unruly, and cunning aspects to him. Only later did he become the little fat putto infant boy we see in the Renaissance. He stands for carnal love and lust, for creation, passion, and romantic love. Whereas Freud sees Thanatos, the death drive, as the opposite, Jung connects Eros with Logos, as Plato did, as opposing principles.

The platonic Eros is a well-known expression. Eros stands here for the principle of relatedness and now has little to do with sexual drive and desire. In Plato's teachings, Eros also represents the search for beauty/aesthetics, and the search for ideas in the sense of his Allegory of the Cave. Today, the platonic Eros is a non-sexually-desiring, somewhat tender and caring (although this is not always expressed) relationship with somebody that can also be found in male-only clubs and in general in organisations where people are unconsciously drawn towards each other.

This leads to another aspect of love—showing empathy and compassion for another human being. Putting yourself in the shoes of the other person is—if you think it through—a very intimate act of understanding the soul of another. This is almost impossible without any feelings of love, at least in the sense of either *agape* or *philia*. Compassion, as showing passionate suffering with another, is intimate in a similar way: you put yourself in another's shoes, feel as they do, and go through the pain together.

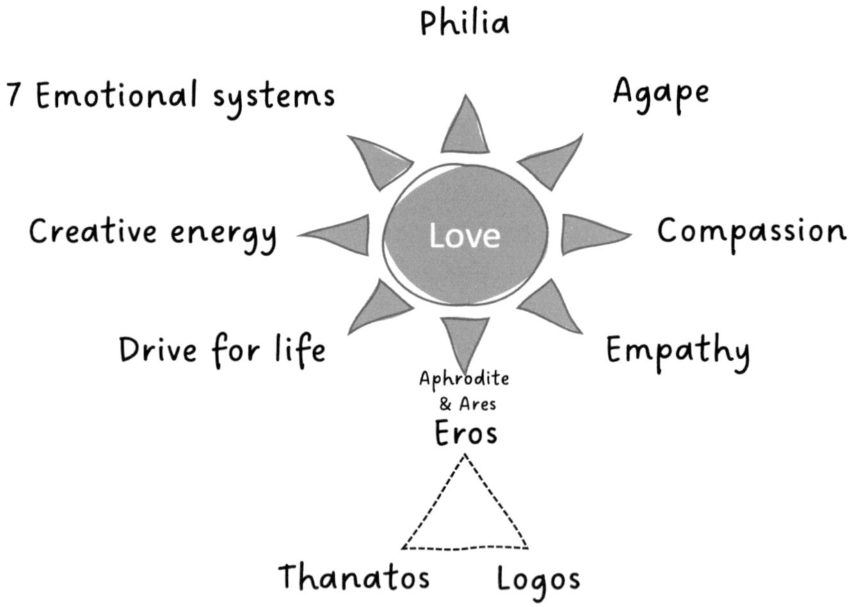

Figure 40: The multifaceted ways and expressions of love (author's drawing)

The final dimension which I want to mention here is the love for God, the highest being, or even love as a spiritual principle in itself. What we have not touched upon yet in detail is love's shadow—when love wants to possess, control, and have power over someone; when it leads to jealousy, deception, and revenge, to unrealistic projections, or when it turns into hate or, even worse, indifference.

How can we apply this broad network of meanings and set it in the organisational context?

Love in the workplace

Think about how your work takes place for you, as a leader, mostly via collaboration with other colleagues, whether on the board or middle management level or with your followers. In most organisations—except for during the very early days of a start-up, for example—organisational work has become so complex that you always need other people to complete a piece of work: you work on a project together, you develop strategy with others, you think about organisational development, about hiring, or about the problems on a production site. In these collegial relationships, pair-relationships stick out and become especially visible for others because of the importance of love as the central theme through life.

The working pair-relationships can be between the same or opposite genders, within a hierarchical level (board colleagues), or between hierarchies (client and consultant); there are formal pairs (director/secretary) or informal pairs. All kinds of pairs attract the attention of others, especially when they are working well together and show their pleasure in doing so. This invites attributions and projections which are sometimes far from reality or even acted out.

There can be a pair who, when working together, achieve better results, have more creative ideas, or offer a broader array of solutions than they would if they were working on their own. This creative pair can be so strong that it excludes others from its creative process, but for the two involved, it is often highly energising, sometimes also challenging and frustrating, but connected with pleasure and joy. Other pairs may have a shared task which is part of their role description; they have to work together to get the task done—two researchers in a lab, for example. Whether they will develop into a relationship as a creative pair depends on their chemistry. When the mutual sympathy is there they might also work on their relationship, and not only on the task. This kind of relationship may even become a friendship.

Friendship

When you are the leader and the other person is your team member, friendship is more difficult to develop—for both parties. As a leader you can never be sure why the other person is hoping or working for friendship, since it is not unusual that they might expect special attention or gain advantages from it, and you would want to avoid that. As a follower, you cannot be sure whether or not the leaders would like to (ab)use you as an informal informant checking the emotions in the team.

You need to exercise caution with regard to the projections of the other onto yourself and the seduction to live up to that projection, especially when it is connected with fantasies of greatness and uniqueness.

Over time and across cultures, the meaning of friendship has changed and shifted. In their book, Bonnerup and Hasselanger share the interesting insights of the British scholar Robert French, who explored ancient perspectives on friendship and their relevance to today's organisation. He states:[275]

> Put most simply, the modern view sees friendship as primarily, if not exclusively, a private affair—'it sets friendship within the realm of private relations and stresses personal values'—whereas the classical tradition emphasizes friendship as a public good—'[it] included some personal values like affection but was a public as well as a private relationship'.[276]

Our Western understanding sees friendship as part of relationships within the intimate sphere, which are the most important places for self-exploration, -discovery, and -fulfilment. Ethics link the public and societal sphere with the private sphere, being one of the major subjects looked at by Aristotle. He sees friendship as a *hexis*, which indicates the understanding of friendship as a state of mind or *Weltanschauung* instead of a pure affective relationship. According to Aristotle, friendships can be categorised depending on their motivation-utility, be that pleasure or the search for virtue. This is not so far from how we use our social networks or career networks—at least not with regard to utility—which we value ambivalently because for us this is not "real" friendship.

It is this level of friendship to which Aristotle applied the notion of utility, the most basic of the three levels:

> Now those who love each other for their utility do not love each other for themselves but in virtue of some good which they get from each other. … Therefore those who love for the sake of utility love for the sake of what is good for themselves, … And thus these friendships are only incidental; for it is not as being the man he is that the loved person is loved, but as providing some good or pleasure. Such friendships, then, are easily dissolved, if the parties do not remain like themselves; for if the one party is no longer pleasant or useful the other ceases to love him.
>
> Now the useful is not permanent but is always changing. Thus, when the motive of the friendship is done away, the friendship is dissolved, in as much as it existed only for the ends in question.[277]

Pleasure-based friendships have as their true object not a person, but the mutual enjoyment of similar likes: "Similarly, too, with those who love each other because of pleasure: people do not feel affection for the witty for their being of a certain character, but for the pleasure they themselves get from them."[278]

With true friendship, *vera amicitia* or *amicitia perfecta*, a different level is reached:

> However, it is the friendship between good people, those resembling each other in excellence, that is complete; for each alike of these wishes good things for the other in so far as he is good, and he is good in himself. And those who wish good things for their friends, for their friends' sake, are friends most of all; for they do so because of the friends themselves, and not incidentally.[279]

Apparently, it is always the other and the sharing with the other which is central to this notion of friendship as a state of mind, as well as not letting self-interest fall out of sight. Two practices are part of the ancient tradition—guest friendship and frankness of speech. The latter, especially, is avoided nowadays since conflicting opinions and opposition are understood as attacks, whereas in ancient times "opposition is true friendship" was held to be true.[280]

This interesting and, from an organisational perspective, new understanding of friendship could bring a different educated notion of how to create long-lasting work relationships. French proposes to understand friendship as an organising principle—which it could be from my understanding, but it would need some education of the heart and the mind to incorporate fully the ethical aspects of Aristotle.

A working pair is confronted with two different problems which stem from its "pairness". They can either enter into collusion, or their formation can be a reaction to a group dynamic and thus a group defence. We talked about the latter in Chapter 12. Collusion, on the other hand, is a widespread psychic phenomenon which appears when the internal conflicts of two people (or more) fit so well together that they appear as if they were meant for each other, like hand in glove. The collusion makes the involved individuals take over the respective opposite roles in their interaction.

We encounter this at the beginning of a love relationship, when two people fall in love and see in each other what has more to do with their own self-ideal. Normally, the collusion dissolves when the illusions of who the other is start to break and when the relationship develops on a more mature level—seeing the other not as a mirror of themselves, but as an independent human other. Yet, in neurotic couples the collusion remains, functioning to compensate for former frustrations and to repress fears of intimacy. This may develop into hugely dysfunctional interaction patterns.

In a working pair, a collusion could consist of, for example, one of the pair being the analytical decision maker, and the other being the more creative part. Both are doing what they prefer, and both parties are avoiding what they have difficulty with. This can be functional with regard to the completion of the task, yet their own individual development becomes stuck, and in the long run the relationship risks stiffening, which might then impact on fulfilling the task. Collusion may develop around four themes,[281] all of which may emerge together in a relationship:

- Affirmation—mutually affirming each other's complementary way of being, as in the just-mentioned example—this keeps insecurities and ambivalence out of the relationship.

- Nurturing—one is emotionally nurturing, supporting and caring for the other, whereas the other is being nurtured and supported because of, for instance, a personal crisis.
- Exclusivity—when the world of the pair consists only of the two and nobody is allowed to enter this small circle or break it, such as when job roles change.
- Domination and submission—one is dominant, claiming independence and autonomy, the other is dependent, with traits of jealousy and separation anxiety. This more often takes place in hierarchical pairs where both need the other for their specific role.

Love of (parts of) the organisation

The feeling of love can also develop towards a specific task, profession, or role. This love can be best described as emotional dedication, joy, and passion which arises when one is executing the task, profession, or role one really wants.

Work is an important part of our identity, and people who are very involved in their work often identify with it. This can be healthy, nourishing, fulfilling, and self-developing—until the moment that health, family life, or social relationships become so unimportant in relation to the work role that barely any time is given to them. This over-obsession can develop out of wanting to cover up "inner worm-holes"[282] which stem from a lack of appreciation, love, care, and containment in early social relationships. The detrimental effects of this kind of work addiction are obvious. However, they are often only realised when it is too late, when the first problems of the heart appear, the family has turned away, or the circle of friends has become practically non-existent. The feelings of emptiness and melancholia, or even sadness which had been avoided by overworking, are than rebounding with great force, and addressing this by investing time in other aspects of one's identity with fulfilling activities takes much time and energy.

We have also observed in recent years that, in the knowledge society we are in, passion is crucial for fast-moving and generative product development. Hirschhorn[283] argues that passion drives productivity. However, the irrational, excessive, and sometimes obsessive aspects can make it difficult for you, as a leader, to control—think about how difficult it is to control your own passion, let alone that of one of your employees. If you as a leader want to build a culture around passion, Hirschhorn recommends attending to two distinct issues: "They must create mechanisms that enable passionate people to sweep in others, and they must create mechanisms to monitor and control the progress of projects impelled by passion. In this way they can appropriate passion as an organizational resource."

Loving the organisation, its reputation, its values, and its products often comes with love for the task or the profession. Large and complex organisations which appear as if they were one, such as investment banks and consulting companies, social networks, etc., can be labelled as "giant subjects".[284] They represent an overarching ideal of meaning and purpose for the individual, and a community of like-minded people to which one wants to adhere. Often, they integrate new members through some kind of brainwashing-like onboarding events, where the organisational culture is explored and shared. Being part of a community, belonging somewhere is—as we have already discussed—identity-building and stabilises the ego as well as the self.

What we can also observe is that these kinds of communities also develop in different parts of the organisation; they form their own culture. In my research I observed, for example, that in a large automotive company the R&D department has a very different mindset and cultural code which they try to live up to. This culture often remains unconscious and can only be realised when leaving this communion or from a third-person perspective. When you are in it, you are part of the game, you know the specific rules and do not think about them as something you have to adapt to. By choosing the organisation and the profession you have already begun integrating these peculiarities.

Case study

A working couple—love, isolation, and survival

Annemette Hasselager and Birgitte Bonnerup

We have many years' experience in guiding organisations through critical phases. Overcoming, managing, or surviving critical phases is not merely about focusing on the bottom line, clarifying the primary task, trimming the use of resources and suchlike. There is always more at stake: relationships, emotions, meaning, and identity. Typically, a crisis reveals itself through conflicts, cooperation problems, stress, issues with the work environment, and feelings of abandonment or resignation. Over the years, in our practice as organisational psychologists, we are increasingly aware that it matters hugely that people are able to like one other in their professional relationships. This has led us to formulate the concept of what we term "love" within the context of organisations: love for the task, love for the organisation as a whole, and love in professional relationships.[285] "Love" can be defined as the ability to accept ambivalent feelings, empathy, and understanding of each other's weak points and less attractive attributes plus a willingness not to simply check out or quit when problems mount up.

Organisations are full of what can best be described as "working couples". There are both "formal" couples—defined by the organisational roles they play—and "informal" couples—colleagues who get together, for example, because they just happen to work really well together. In the following case, we will meet a working couple, who are formally a couple via their roles as CEO and CFO respectively. We shall see how, after an initial quarrelsome cat-and-dog period, they gradually developed a more loving and caring relation to one another—which in turn became decisive for the company's ability to overcome a crisis. Our thesis is that without any kind of loving relationships it is difficult for an organisation to survive, particularly when faced with surviving critical phases. The test case that follows is in fact a hybrid of real examples from our practice.

Expedit—love, isolation, and survival

Expedit is a major travel agency that sells high-quality travel products. The company was founded by someone we will call Albert, while still a young man. The vision for Expedit grew out of Albert's own passion for travel and his sense for class and quality. In the 1990s, the demand for Expedit's products increased, leading the company to substantially expand the workforce. Albert was thrilled when he then hired Robert as CFO; having no children of his own, Albert saw something like a grown-up son in Robert, on whom he could rely through thick and thin. Robert reciprocated Albert's trust and responded to his invitation to participate in almost all management decisions and tasks with loyalty and diligence. For Robert, work in fact became like a second home.

It was a source of great sadness for everyone at Expedit when Albert suddenly became seriously ill and died at roughly the same time the Covid pandemic broke out. Until then, Expedit had enjoyed a good and solid turnover with a substantial portfolio of loyal customers. The company had always wanted to stay on the safe side in terms of expansion, and subsequently there had been neither a desire nor the pressing need to substantially develop the organisation or the product range. Although Expedit still had decent financial reserves to draw on, the Covid pandemic unsurprisingly created new and unexpected problems.

Robert had assumed he would be taking over the role as CEO after Albert. Albert's sudden death only reinforced this conviction; now he would really be needed in this time of twin crises. Instead, to Robert's mortification and great surprise, the board chose Michelle, who came with experience from another travel agency with a somewhat different and more dynamic profile. As a consequence, Robert became silent and withdrawn in his job; he even considered resigning, but faced the incontrovertible truth that his heart was in Expedit and where his heart was, he wanted to stay.

Robert was forced to swallow that Michelle was the new chosen CEO, even though he found it difficult to see her as such when she came strutting in wearing high heels (really high heels) with the complacent air of someone offering hard and fast solutions. From her conversations with the board, Michelle had been primed for meeting a certain level of conservatism in the company and especially in dealings with Robert, but she was not prepared for the passive resistance she met when important decisions not only had to be taken, but also implemented.

Neither had chosen the other. Both had chosen the company, however, and so needed their collaboration to work, but neither could find much positive to say about the other; it was a corrosive state of affairs that gradually created a schism within the organisation. On the one hand were those who sided with Michelle and the new leadership style and then those who sided with Robert and the old ways. This dynamic between them proved debilitating, meaning much energy was squandered through their maintaining a profoundly negative view of each other. Michelle and Robert were in fact lacking what we refer to as libido invested in the relationship.[286]

Over time, real problems arose with cooperation. Robert felt that Michelle lacked respect for Albert's historical legacy and that she was too hard on the employees when she simply dismissed out of hand their suggestions for change. He especially thought she was unduly harsh when she dismissed both the youngest male employee—who had admittedly had a large number of sick days—but who also contributed with optimism and a positive mindset, and Bernadette, who had been with the company since the very beginning.

To start with, Michelle was just driven up the wall by Robert. His detailed and over-elaborate notes, his slow, laboured speech, and his infuriating desire to be party to every decision were simply too much. It set her teeth on edge to have to run with Robert's chronic lack of interest in developing new products, one of them trips for adults wanting to travel like young backpackers (but with high-class hotels, good beds, and good food). When Michelle and Robert discussed the problems they faced in Expedit, Michelle typically became loud and strident while Robert fell silent, repeating the same arguments over and over again. Outwardly, Robert might have seemed to be a man of few words, but this was due in reality to his feeling somewhat intimidated by Michelle's rather (to him) repulsive and bloody-minded attitudes whilst under pressure. Over time, however, Robert began to suspect that Michelle's behaviour was in fact a safety valve, a way of expressing the extent to which she was under pressure, even though she would never admit this explicitly. From her perspective, Michelle still found it difficult to see Robert as anything other than what in nautical terms is called a drift anchor—something dragging behind in the water—at the same time failing to see how a drift anchor in fact helps a boat maintain a suitable direction in rough water.

Gradually Robert understood how Michelle's behaviour was in fact communicating how she felt and was much more than just the unpleasant personality trait he had struggled with. The fact that Robert was now able to decode what was happening was a significant step towards better cooperation. Being able to respect the other as someone different from oneself while simultaneously appreciating that diversity as a strength and an asset is a crucial element in a well-functioning collaborative relationship.[287]

Robert and Michelle's strained relations and lack of cooperation was just one of the problem areas that plagued Expedit. The Covid pandemic plunged Expedit into an increasingly painful financial slump. Robert was forced to work longer hours dealing with budgets and contracts late into the night as well as having to scour the horizon for potential savings in overheads and to negotiate more favourable agreements with business partners. He noticed that Michelle also worked late and was typically engrossed in her computer. Late one Wednesday evening, Robert saw that Michelle had taken off her shoes, perhaps in the belief she was alone and unobserved in the office. Something moved him to get up and walk over to her and he was duly surprised when he saw how awkward this seemingly made her feel. This made Robert feel both uncertain and confused and something prompted him to say, "We appear to be in the same boat, Michelle; perhaps we should call it a day?" Michelle then looked up with an honest and vulnerable look that Robert had not seen before and replied, "Robert, OK this is awkward, I … um … actually have no idea how to manage this …" The situation was clearly painful for both of them and they quickly went their separate ways. A few days later, however, Michelle reached out to Robert and suggested that they spend an evening joining forces and putting their heads together. Robert sensed both his resistance and antagonism towards engaging and sharing ideas with this high-heeled battleaxe, but he also had the intuition or presence of mind to think this was probably the only right thing to do given the circumstances. The two duly got together one evening and it quickly became clear that the survival of Expedit was very dear to both their hearts. They agreed to try to pool their resources and attempt to put their collaboration back on track. To summarise: Robert had seen an opening and he had acted on it. Michelle had realised it was OK to be seen as vulnerable with her guard down. They had discovered how connected they were in their mutual love for the Expedit brand, and it now became possible to forge a (still) difficult and demanding yet much more trusting relationship within the company.

Some difficult months lay ahead for the company. Amongst other things, Expedit had to lay off a number of the workforce. When Robert cautiously suggested to Michelle that they slash their own wages by 30 per cent, she immediately agreed. When Michelle then suggested launching a brand new concept in readiness for when travelling became possible again, Robert, sceptical at first, found use for his newly acquired and hitherto unused optimism. He put his naturally critical approach to good use, finding and solving possible problems rather than routinely dismissing proposals. When it did become possible to travel again, Michelle's idea quickly became an attractive product. "Whoever would have thought that?!" Robert asked himself, knowing that now Expedit with Michelle and himself at the helm as CEO and CFO were the ones to do just that.

Michelle and Robert's relationship gradually became characterised by their acceptance of its ambivalence. Both were able to respect the other for their professionalism even while tacitly feeling irritated by the other's temperament. But there was also a shared joy in steering the company through the Covid crisis and in being able to adapt to a changed market. Gradually, they developed an acceptance, plus a feeling almost of tenderness towards each other's less flattering sides, and this was an important benchmark; just where someone needs to be nuanced, they can just as easily become myopic and narrow-minded. Cooperation can be faced off by different defence mechanisms against anxiety. It is vital that both parties in a working relationship try to comprehend precisely this dynamic in collaborating together, a dynamic that by the same token all too easily might cause division through employees taking sides and deciding which of the two they agree with the most.

There can be no doubt that both Robert and Michelle initially felt lonely and isolated in their work. With no one to reach out to they failed at first to reconcile their differences and to instead see each other's dynamic as a catalyst for growth—until it was almost too late. Had

Robert not spotted an opening offering a potential thaw in relations and had Michelle not seized the opportunity laid at her feet in an awkward moment, they might never have arrived at a fruitful collaboration driven by their shared passion for an organisation and its products. As we know, diversity is seldom problem-free and the friction and sometimes stormy waters it carries with it can be difficult to navigate through. Here, though, we saw how a deep and shared devotion to a task became the decisive and motivating factor for ensuring an organisation's survival. This was the old adage of two heads being better than one, with this central relationship in an organisation being the guiding force and primary agent for empowering change.

* * *

The rollercoaster this case depicts is not unusual in human relationships. Two very different pairs appear to show up. The first a beautiful and promising father–son relationship, the second a pair at first rejecting each other and later finding acceptance together—via the need for human beings to connect and love in some way. In the latter, the love for the organisation creates a first bond, and then, from a utility-oriented friendship in the second step, to taking care of this shared love-object—by which something deeper develops, more caring for each other and for the organisation. I find this a wonderful example of how we can learn from each other and develop by showing a bit of vulnerability and opening up to the otherness of the other. This helps to overcome the loneliness both characters must have felt before uniting their forces.

Loneliness

With the recent pandemic we have become more aware of what loneliness means for many and also where it stems from. The pandemic has functioned as a giant magnifying glass showing us the positive and negative effects of virtual connections of our network and platform society, while at the same time making the agony of the excluded or self-excluded in this world more visible. In addition, it has exposed us to the possible and actual shallowness of virtual conversations when they are not embedded in face-to-face encounters.

As *The Economist* reports,[288] two in five office workers feel lonely at work, a figure which has risen to three in five in Britain. Gig economy jobs can leave people with insecure incomes and without the companionship of colleagues. The pandemic has made it more difficult to make and maintain friendships, particularly for new employees. Recent developments have exacerbated this situation.[289] The internet has indeed led to more companionship, but also to the overuse of smartphones, fewer social activities, and much more cyber-bullying. The major trade-off is caused by technology which provides us with the possibility to work, relax, and be entertained from home—convenient, comfortable, but lonesome.

Some more painful numbers on loneliness: Gallup finds in a survey that 330 million adults globally go at least two weeks without talking to a single friend or family member.[290] Although we have yet to capture loneliness data globally since the pandemic, other studies suggest it is worsening. The Survey Centre on American Life, a think-tank project, found that 10 per cent of women reported having no close friends in 2021, up from 2 per cent in 1990. And it was worse for men: 15 per cent reported having no close friends in 2021, up from 3 per cent in 1990.[291]

Loneliness equals unhappiness, which makes you more vulnerable to stress, anger, and anxiety, and causes other mental and physical health problems. In contrast, we have also observed an unprecedented focus on emotions and our inner world connected with the need for self-optimisation and self-responsibility. Illouz spoke in 2007 about "homo sentimentalis".[292] She sees three factors having contributed to this development: economic growth, the women's liberation movement, and the spread of therapy. The latter could also be described as a therapisation of (Western) societies: people talk about psychology and therapy in the same way they talk and know about sports. Therapeutic language has invaded everyday language and many people consider themselves to be experts—which the case may be for their own psyche (but likely not for the psyche of others). We need to deeply question this development, due to the unconscious forces holding all of us in their grip. The self-help and self-development movements, books, and courses have not brought us more happiness, as we would have hoped, but more unhappiness and suffering in creating a constant awareness of our gaps, shortcomings, and failures. The outcome is more loneliness combined with shame and guilt, since we will never ever live up to the standards set by photoshopped beauties, influencers, celebrities, and PR-designed superheroes in business and politics. We're all aware of these unrealistic expectations, yet we still feel the pressure to be special individuals with special jobs, and special families and friends …

What is loneliness?

When thinking about how special we all must be I immediately get a feeling of loneliness. How can I be that special and what do I need to do to get there? Is just being yourself not good enough? And is that not already difficult enough? The pressing need for self-optimisation and at the same time for a special self is contradictory and seems to lead to a rather empty existence, where people cannot feel themselves anymore. This aspiration to be "special" does not allow you to be human, that is, to fail and to suffer, to have changing moods and changing feelings; on the other hand, the dictum of the homo sentimentalis asks for the opposite—you are continuously failing and suffering since you will never achieve your optimal self. This presents an unsolvable tension which is part of human life. It has a paradoxical nature and feels like a trap: optimising, suffering, and becoming part of the self-optimising mass—and becoming special and thus not suffer, because when you are special then you must enjoy it! Do we have to embrace this? Or is there a way out of this tension, out of the overwhelming helplessness and accompanying despair and loneliness?

The feeling of loneliness develops out of being different and not belonging to the respective context. Our inner world, the way we feel and perceive our fantasies, dreams, hopes, attachments, and ideas about other people, can be understood as the inner self. We also have an outer self which we call the persona. It is the way we are and behave consciously and unconsciously towards the people around us. When we feel that we are not allowed to show our inner self to the outside world or to connect the inner self with our persona, loneliness may develop out of that incongruence. Feeling lonely is part of life. We all know situations where we feel that we do not belong to the group of people around us—for example, at a party or a network event with lots of strangers. This feeling will not last and can be overcome by either leaving or making a step towards the other. Worse, is the feeling of being a stranger in the world as such, not knowing where to find people with whom to connect—at least temporarily. When this becomes a general mood or state of mind and one does not feel joy or pleasure in being alone, then it might be time to seek help.

Developing the capacity for being alone and finding pleasure in it depends largely on our inner world and with whom we are when we are alone with our self. One of my clients always thought he enjoyed being alone until he discovered that he could only be alone when in work mode. His inner voice was a strong parental call for efficiency, performance, and continuous improvement. If he could change that inner voice to a more benevolent one, he would then be able to discover how he could enjoy this mode. We can see in this little example how early relationships shape our inner world and our inner voice which tells us what to do, how to do it, and what not to do.

Another form of loneliness that can be felt in the workplace is the solitude that is inherent to the leader role. Hierarchy creates distance—it is difficult to be emotional friends (not in the platonic network friendship way we discussed earlier) and at the same time fulfil the roles of boss and subordinate. Emotional friendship is based on mutual recognition of equality, understanding, love, and care. Mutuality is the key word here. Yet in a leadership position, the leader needs to take decisions which do not always please the team, moreover not every plan can be discussed publicly; both endanger close friendship. Maintaining a distance to observe, reflect, and take action is a key part of the leadership role.

At the same time, as a leader you are a projection figure for many—for the positive projections of idealising and wanting to be like you, as well as for the negative projections of being overly dominant, critical, demanding, etc. There is a broad array of possible projections. Both positive and negative projections may induce the feeling of not being recognised for who you really are, and feelings of loneliness may result. These need to be dealt with through self-reflection and having a separate social life where emotional connection and recognition is given the needed containment.

When the projections do not emerge from the individual but from the group—as a social defence—the leader might be seen as part of a pair, or as a hero leading the group out of the storm, or the scapegoat having caused the crisis. We have seen the possible social defences helping or hindering work on the primary task. Yet you, as a leader and a human being, are not only a projection surface; you want and need to be recognised, liked, or even loved for the way you are. This is an almost impossible wish to fulfil. Be prepared.

KEY LEARNING

- Love and loneliness pervade the organisation as a whole and play an important role in all our lives, including our work life. Working pairs are common and can have an extremely positive but also detrimental impact on organisational success. As a leader you need to watch out for the latter whilst also exploring your own working-pair relationships.
- Loneliness, in contrast, is a feeling that you need to get used to.
- However, a solution could be found through a focus on work friendships as an organising principle. To this end it would be necessary to provision the organisation with the respective personal development required to educate the self in the sense of educating the heart and ethical thinking.

CHAPTER 17

Digitalisation of our world of work

One of the most important buzzwords to enter the discourse over recent decades is digitalisation. Every company and every organisation needs to take this step whether small or big, privately owned or public. It impacts our work life as well as our private life. Yet what exactly is digitalisation? And digitisation? And digital transformation? What does it mean for organisations as systems and for us individuals working in them from an emotional perspective? What are the dangers and how can we avoid them?

Let us start with some basic definitions:

- *Digitisation* is the process of changing from analogue to digital, also known as digital enablement. Digitisation takes an analogue process and changes it to a digital form without any different-in-kind changes to the process itself.[293]
- *Digitalisation* goes one step further. It is the use of digital technologies to change a business model and provide new revenue and value-producing opportunities; it is the process of moving to a digital business. An often-used helpful example is the move from

renting physical DVDs to online streaming of movies, watchable at any time from your computer.

- *Digital transformation* is the organisation-wide adaptation and change of the business, and especially the business processes, according to the new business model.

Digital transformation and the adoption of new technologies is not easy, especially if they not only automatise parts of the work process, but also go much deeper and change the way the entire organisation works together. Rethinking the value chain from the customer perspective is an often-applied approach in digitalisation and is shaking up former silos and business units—the new work processes flow over former business units—and everything that we know about (cultural) change and the difficult implementation of matrix organisations applies here.

A classic example of how digitalisation takes place in organisations is cooperation between a large organisation that has existed for quite some years—an incumbent, and a start-up—an innovative organisation developing new ideas for digital business models. This cooperation derives from the problem that changing an organisation from within to a completely new, digital business model while having to continue to work analogue creates an organisation of two speeds—think a big oil tanker alongside a small speedboat. This is complex to manage, and some organisations have therefore externalised their digital business into a separate unit. This is also complicated by managing the exchange between the two parts and overcoming destructive in-group–out-group dynamics, as well as (re)integrating the new way of working which has already been implemented in the speedboat organisation.

When an incumbent and a start-up work together it is by nature an asymmetric relationship resulting from the power differential of abundant vs constrained resources—in the sense of money, knowledge, and experience. In addition, these two kinds of organisation represent the two sides of the paradox of exploitation vs exploration—which is, of course, also the main reason to collaborate. This entails risks for both sides: the large corporation could end up wasting resources, whereas the start-up may face unfair appropriation of its intellectual property and an exploitative takeover.

The emotional effects of cooperation between an established organisation and a digital business start-up have been well researched,[294] particularly group emotions. Group emotions are the shared emotions of a like-minded group of people with a common ground, such as being in the same business unit, having similar backgrounds, or similar competencies. These group emotions may also develop from emotional resonance or even contagion. They are a similar concept to social defences, but entail all kinds of emotions, being a defence or not.

The cooperation goes through three basic emotional phases: anticipation and hope, anxiety, then adaptation. In the first phase, anticipation and hope, both see the cooperation as an important strategic intent, yet for the start-up the stakes are higher and the collaboration is more important since it presents a kind of litmus test for its product and thus for its existence. The enthusiasm in that first phase leads to high commitment and to intense exchange between the two partners. The start-up company's dream is to be bought out, as its goal, if it gets it right.

After a while, both parties start to recognise the hurdles and the challenges. Conflictual tensions arise, the rose-tinted glasses start to become clearer, or the opposite: they get darker as the first enthusiasm is turning into anxiety. In this second phase, anxiety prevails. This anxiety emerges from the tensions between different ways of working and decision-making and the level of complexity in the partnering organisations. Corporate managers are rather risk averse, whereas start-up founders are entrepreneurs, always looking for the big money and taking on risk while being highly flexible and adaptive in order to find a marketable solution. The clearer view of their differences is a source of fear for both sides. These conflictual tensions lead to anxiety, which in turn brings up typical defence mechanisms.

This is particularly the case on the corporate programme manager side, who is under pressure to rectify the use of resources for the start-up towards its own corporate managers. Also, both sides are afraid of losing face, which raises these defences even higher, showing as avoiding clear commitment, and rationalising and blaming the other in saying that the start-up is not yet ready. Hopefully, this phase can be dealt with so that in the following phase the differences are accepted and both parties find ways of working together while remaining two distinct businesses. An integration of the start-up and its product and knowledge is much harder to achieve and overall doesn't have a great track record.

Digitalisation is not only dealt with in an accelerator where start-ups develop new and digital business ideas. It also needs to take place within existent organisations where processes can be redesigned and adapted—to achieve a higher pace or better connection between units, or even deliver a new service or new approach to an existent service, as we will see in the following case study.

Case study

Digitalisation—in pursuit of better connections

Phil Boxer

Introduction

An orthosis is "an externally applied device used to influence the structural and functional characteristics of the neuromuscular and skeletal system".[295] Orthotic departments are typically found in acute hospitals supplying appliances in support of orthopaedic surgeons. From the point of view of hospital administrators, the orthotist is an overhead cost associated with fitting appliances that are part of the cost of a patient's treatment within the acute system.

This case study is about six projects undertaken for the Purchasing and Supplies Agency (PASA) within the United Kingdom's National Health Service (NHS). The NHS is a nationally funded healthcare service for UK citizens. The projects had established that over a period of five years, for every £1 spent on orthotics services, £4 would be saved in the larger healthcare system.[296] These potential benefits were never realised by the NHS.[297] This was despite proving the existence and feasibility of the benefits through the adoption of clinician-led services enabled by digital platforms supporting that leadership. This case study will examine how this digitally enabled change in leadership approach was able to establish these benefits.

Establishing the need for clinician-led leadership—the pilot studies

The UK's Audit Commission had published a report in March 2000 finding issues with the way orthoses were being made available to citizens. Patients' expectations and the demands on community care were increasing as the UK population aged. At the same time there were unacceptable variations in levels of service across the NHS. These were compounded by wasted expenditures on inappropriate or substandard orthoses, fragmented services, and a lack of integration with other services.

PASA was charged with addressing these issues and had commissioned three pilot studies to set up an approach to decentralising its services. Its aim was to extend its support beyond acute care trusts (ACTs) to include primary care trusts (PCTs). This focused on the continuation of care within the community in ways that integrated social and health care. At the heart of the change needed were patient referral pathways focused on the quality of final outcomes. Referral pathways define the forms of clinical delegation available to a clinician based on a diagnosis. This involved extending the focus beyond acute episodes of care to address care throughout the duration of a patient's condition.

The pilot studies proved the need for PASA to move from its current focus on the procured value of manufactured appliances to one that focused on the value delivered by the supply networks supporting patient care pathways. A care pathway defines a particular way in which treatments are provided to patients. This focus had to include how these care pathways could be organised to support the requisite referral pathways. For example, access to orthotic care could be sped up and the need for consultant assessment eliminated by enabling PCT clinicians to refer directly to orthotists for common conditions. This increased patient numbers accessing orthotic care, proving there was unmet demand from patients primarily aged sixty-plus. Early access to continuous care and review prevented falls, fractures, and loss of mobility, all major costs for ACTs. It also prevented patients from early entry into social care, a major cost for PCTs.

Working with clinical leadership—the pathfinder projects

Six pathfinder projects were set up within six sponsoring NHS trusts to learn how to bring about this decentralisation. While orthotic departments were the clients, the challenge each one faced was to show how the changes each project brought about could be made permanent by its sponsor. The projects had to change the way its clients managed the tension between the vertical needs of sponsors and the horizontal needs of their patients.

A focus on the quality of patient outcomes required clinical leadership, providing judgements about the alignment and cohesion of treatments being necessarily clinical. This focus on "throughout the duration of a condition care" (TTDoCC) involved setting up referral pathways for clinical delegation. This enabled associated medical professionals (AMPs) to orchestrate and synchronise care pathways around each patient based on agreed delegation protocols. The complex nature of this task meant that TTDoCC was impossible to sustain at scale without a supporting data platform. Such a platform enabled a clinician to take responsibility for patient outcomes while at the same time being held accountable for doing so within economic constraints.

The approach to establishing TTDoCC involved working through three phases: (I) changes within the orthotics clinic to improve efficiencies; (II) changes outside the clinic to the referral pathways for clinical delegation within ACTs; and (III) adding satellite clinics, dual funding, and extending the changes in referral pathways to the PCTs. The major challenges were met, and defences encountered as the work progressed are shown in Table 1. Meeting these challenges and overcoming these defences depended on the digitalisation of data and creating a platform architecture[298] that could support interoperability with the platforms supporting other parts of a healthcare ecosystem that spanned PCTs, ACTs, community trusts, and the private sector.

Table 1: The major challenges to establishing TTDoCC and the enabling role of digitalisation (Philip Boxer)

The major challenges			*The role of digitalisation*	*Defences encountered*
1	Phase I	Conflicting views of what actions were for "the good" of a patient where services outsourced to the private sector were involved.	Tracking total cost of treatment within an episode of care in order that outsourced costs could be related to episode outcomes.	The livelihoods of individuals and organisations were at stake. The overall goal of growing the service made it possible to find ways of acknowledging these interests.
2		A lack of patient-centric data through which joined-up data could enable a clinician to "see" the patient's condition(s), treatment history, and clinical outcomes.	Tracking the relation between patients' conditions, treatments, and outcomes across the variety of conditions being met within the clinic.	Individuals and departments felt that the data belonged to them and their practices. Its release was made part of a two-way process where both they and patients could benefit.
3	Phase II	A lack of agreement between clinical specialisms, including the AHPs such as orthotists and physiotherapists, as to how conditions should be defined to enable effective clinical delegation.	Outcome-data relating conditions and treatment protocols that enabled clinician peer review, supplying a basis for clinical delegation protocols to be set up and kept under review.	The clinicians built trust by sharing relevant clinical histories from which delegation protocols and review processes were created. This was inhibited by historic power relationships between their clinical silos.

(Continued)

Table 1: (*Continued*)

The major challenges			*The role of digitalisation*	*Defences encountered*
4		Funding of patient care not following TTDoCC outcomes for patients but distributed via annual budgets and “block contracts” fixing the volume of treatments within clinical silos.	Supplying the basis for challenging existing budget allocations while also setting up a basis of accountability for delivering TTDoCC outcomes.	New output formats based on TTDoCC data on outcomes enabled the value of these changes to be proved. Top-down budgetary controls sometimes made changes impossible.
5	Phase III	Control of healthcare expenditures dominated by the focus of ACTs on the cost of treatments that extended to their “discharged” patients, further complicating (3) and (4) above.	Making it possible to show the potentially significant savings through implementing TTDoCC both within the ACT and across the healthcare ecosystem.	At stake were commissioning practices between primary and acute care systems. The UK’s Treasury Department validated the potential savings, but changed relationships between silos had to be negotiated on a local basis.

Digitalisation as enabling clinical leadership

The ACT sponsor of each pathfinder project agreed to its being clinician-led, to implementing the first two phases, and to evaluating the potential for implementing the third phase. Each project lasted eight months, the first two months working to establish a shared base of understanding, the remaining six months working through the phases.

> The inclusion of myself as the clinician at the front line of care within the orthotic service, or "appliance clinic", as it was still referred to, was the starkest difference between any action, before or since, to effect change within it.
>
> The Pathfinder was not reliant on the standard NHS processes of "steering committees". Helped greatly by the proactive line manager within the Trust, it was able to take on suggestions by both service users and those working within the service. It made use of information taken from both historic prescription records and a specially developed data collection platform.[299]

The project approach enabled a transitional space to be created,[300] supported by a consultant, in which new possibilities could be explored under the leadership of the clinician. This involved in-person and virtual meetings in which the challenges and defences in Table 1 could be worked through. The approach used was adapted from systemic family therapy. It involved working with individuals and teams "behind the mirror" to create a reflective space not identified with the sponsors.[301] This enabled the focus to be kept on the dynamics of the clinic and the leadership of the clinician in pursuit of improved patient outcomes. The process of digitalisation involved supporting relations between five distinct kinds of data dispersed across patient notes, NHS administrative records, and suppliers. Much of this data was on paper or in the minds of clinicians during the course of their practice:

1. The patient's details
2. The referral pathway by which the patient had come to the clinic, including the nature of the clinical delegation
3. The details defining the current episode of care

4. The details of any orthoses used in support of an episode of care
5. The timing and duration of clinical sessions within and between episodes.

To achieve this, the projects built supporting platforms using agile methods for rapid prototyping of outputs from the available data.[302] This made it possible to stay close to the clinician's judgements of what would be useful as the phases progressed. The prototyping involved building a relational database that could absorb data from multiple sources, could hold the relationships between the distinct kinds of data, and could present outcomes in ways that were useful to clinicians. This agile approach, making rapid iterations in outputs tightly coupled to project developments, both empowered the project team and maximised shared learning.

Key to the work was supporting the interpersonal dialogues for building trust not only within the transitional spaces but also in meetings between clinicians. This involved coming together around rationales for making changes that focused on progressing and improving clinical strategy in pursuit of improved patient care. The developing output-based reporting enabled clinicians to review the impact on clinical performance of such things as referral pathways, episode characteristics and intervals between episodes. The projects generated a Phase I 25 per cent improvement in a clinic's capacity utilisation and a Phase II saving of about 20 per cent of the cost of a service in released acute consultant appointments for the existing numbers of patients. Phase III showed the potential to save 100 per cent of the cost of a clinic through prophylactic effects and mobility gains for older patients in the community, every £1 spent on orthotics services saving £4 in the larger healthcare system over time.

The further benefits of working in this way became clear when about one hundred health professionals from acute, community, and primary care trusts came together in one region to start the changes necessary to securing Phase III outcomes:

> Pathfinder moved the responsibility of care from the referring clinician, normally an orthopaedic consultant, to the treating physician, in this case the orthotist. Following the Pathfinder and after discussion with the commissioning

manager, all referrals into orthopaedics were triaged by a GP with special interest in orthotics and an increasingly large team of Allied Health Professionals. This group triaged, arranged diagnostic tests and treatment for the referred patients and provided follow-up reviews. This new service therefore extended the AHP role to that of the primary carer, mirroring that of the Pathfinder within the Acute Trust.[303]

Conclusions

Key to a pathfinder's successful outcome was setting up and supporting clinical leadership, the empowering use of digitalisation using agile methods, and the steady building of trust through the joint development and delivery of evidence-based changes. The shared focus had to be on a commitment to working in the gaps in outcomes as they became apparent to the projects.[304] A great deal of the work took place remotely and/or virtually, making this shared focus critically important to sustaining the working together. This in turn enabled the sources of authorisation to come not from the consultants but from a shared working through of the challenges and anxieties arising when gaps were recognised.[305] From the patient's perspective, gaps in outcome were obvious. Joined-up platform data on a patient's interactions with both primary and acute care systems made this TTDoCC perspective visible to clinicians. Working in these gaps meant clinicians seeing them as symptoms of existing ways in which the work of the clinic was being organised and funded. The approach of working from "behind the mirror" supported the change of focus needed, setting aside anxieties about "doing things right" to be able to focus on asking "what are the right things to be doing?"

By the end of the pathfinders, it had become clear that the service would require dual funding by both sponsoring ACTs and PCTs, reflecting the benefits gained by both. The NHS approach to governance was not able to sustain this change.[306] It lacked the capability for creating digitalisation processes that could enable budgets to be coordinated at local levels between ACTs and PCTs based on TTDoCC patient outcomes. Neither did the use of such processes fit with its top-down approach to commissioning within the healthcare ecosystem as a whole,[307] rendering the NHS unable to realise the full potential benefits identified by the pathfinders:

> As had always been the case, Orthotics in the Acute Trust, run by another manager who was unaware of the Pathfinder, was reduced in terms of patient choice of number of available clinic slots and locations and even of footwear colour. Having become more efficient, cost-effective and having influenced change throughout the Acute Trust, Orthotics returned to being the Cinderella service.[308]

In the end, the future of the clinic was decided neither by its clinical outcomes nor by the superior economics of TTDoCC, but by the interests of managements marching to the tunes of separate silos.

* * *

In this case, an important process could have been digitalised, reducing costs and making the patient's life easier. For that, several defences had to be and were managed through a project approach, creating a safe space for reflection and reflexion.

Yet, due to bureaucratic constraints and organisational inertia, the advantages could not be played out, although it would have become a perfect pilot for further development in that area. It shows perfectly well how other social defences hinder this constructive development, certainly also because of the then eroding power base of the involved management.

New work modes

Digitalisation is not only about digital transformation and changing the business model, it brings about two main additional components:

- Working together (hybrid) in continuously changing teams, which is part of agile management and was derived from software development techniques

- Working together with robots, machines, artificial intelligence, or whatever you call non-human work counterparts.

Working (hybrid) in continuously changing teams in the realm of agile management also means that new forms of leadership, such as leading from the side, are developing and that, compared to the past, teams will be more autonomous.[309] Individuals will have to take on more responsibility and continuously learn to broaden and deepen their skill set. Yet this development is in conflict with the human need for a clear leader in a group giving direction. If there is no formal leader, a group will always work out the informal leader—and this person will have the advantage and disadvantage of being the optimal projection figure for the issues of that group.

Whether the group can stay on task depends on the issue, the intensity, and how much the leader identifies unconsciously with that projection. In these putative autonomous teams we will observe power struggles as well as boundary issues. When you are neither chosen to be the formal or the informal leader, how you influence the direction of the team depends on your empathic collaboration and your own power needs. An often-used strategy of asserting power is withholding information. In addition, if these teams change very often, there may be too little time to develop a feeling of belonging and trust.

At the end stands the big question: who will trust the de facto leader—and how can one collaborate without trust? Furthermore, in-group–out-group dynamics with all the social group defences we have discussed are highly likely to develop, since the general ambience is uncertainty and ambivalence. Rotating and changing autonomous teams is a tricky task and requires a lot of containment and presence from the leadership.

People working in autonomous teams with shifting positions, roles, and teams need to possess well-developed psychological skills if they are to manage themselves well. One of the key tasks of leaders is to enable and empower people to act accordingly. As a leader you are not only role model for the group, but you need these skills as well to manage the group—everything we talk about in this book is crucial to the task of guiding teams in the work of the future. Leaders are becoming more important because of their human and humane qualities. It is also to be assumed that the more (unpleasant) work processes become automatised, the more time we need to spend on learning and development—the new life model might be divided as one third for work, one third for learning, and one third for private life and taking care of your own community, that is, family and friends. In the next chapter we will take a further look at hybrid working models.

Working together with machines will be the second big change. One of the first things that comes to mind when we talk about machines is the robot. What are your first associations to a robot? A humanoid steel apparatus? A human being like a large living doll, such as that shown in the movie *Ex Machina*? Or do you think of large multiple-armed devices supporting manufacturing and assembly in, for example, the automotive industry?

Robots exist for many different purposes:[310]

- Manufacturing: industrial robots handle various tasks like arc welding, material handling, steel cutting, and food packaging.
- Health care: robots can do everything from assisting surgery to physical therapy, to delivering essential supplies such as meds or linens.
- Home life: cleaning, lawn mowing, or answering our day-to-day questions.
- Logistics: stacking warehouse shelves, retrieving goods, and conducting short-range deliveries.
- Space exploration: Mars explorers such as Sojourner and Perseverance; the Hubble telescope is classified as a robot, as are deep-space probes like Voyager and Cassini.
- Military: dangerous tasks associated with war, disabling mines and IEDs, the MUTT, which follows soldiers around and totes their gear, and SAFFiR, which fights fires that break out on naval vessels.
- Entertainment: toy robots, robot statues, and robot restaurants.
- Mobility: self-driving vehicles.

They have advantages in that they work in dangerous environments, increase productivity, are cost-effective, and they offer better quality assurance. Yet they incur deep start-up costs. The biggest problem is, however, that they might take the jobs of unskilled or less skilled workers, jobs which cannot easily be replaced, whereas at the same time, more skilled support staff are needed, such as programmers, operators, and repair personnel.[311] The risk of social upheaval is therefore very high, and what we observe all around the globe is that people who feel left out or incapable vote for populist leaders who promise them a land of milk and honey. Whether proposed solutions such as unconditional basic income will be the answer remains to be seen.

Other robots we have not yet talked about are the humanoid type that imitate human beings. In the film *You Are My Man*, we can observe how the feelings of creepiness of a woman going out with a male robot are changing during the time she is with him until she develops some feelings of affection. This is psychologically understandable, since this humanoid robot acts like a human being—in the film. In reality we are still far away from any such closeness between us and them.

I do not, however, think that humans being replaced by robots is our major problem at the moment. There is another risk which is much more evident and dangerous. As Konrad Zuse, the inventor of the modern computer, said: "The danger of computers becoming like humans is not as great as the danger of humans becoming like computers." The threat lies in our human nature to innovate and improve—not only the outer world but also ourselves. With that comes the risk of losing our inherent, human capacity for moral judgement and behaviour. If we were to become like computers, we might also lose sight of the risks of artificial intelligence (AI).

Digitalisation and AI are not per se good or bad; the issue is how they are used, and that depends, as with any other technology, on the creator and the user. Losing our moral judgement and moral behaviour will pose a significant problem and could lead to a world revolving around performance optimisation, with, finally, money being the only measure for performance. If we manage to act before that problem arises, AI could be manageable.

There is some way to go yet before we achieve AI that comes even close to human intelligence; the AI of today is known as weak or narrow AI, it does not have sophisticated cognitive capacities, artificial consciousness, or emotions. It is not yet clear whether strong AI, that which is close to the human brain or mind, or even superintelligence, machines which have a superior intelligence to humans, can or will be developed.

Examples of weak AI are self-driving cars, Facebook, Siri, or Alexa. The latter two are also understood to be software robots. They are computer programs that perform tasks without human intervention, such as web crawlers or chatbots. These robots are entirely virtual and not considered actual robots since they have no physical characteristics. Chatbots can simulate natural language and can answer questions. One application is replacing psychotherapy, for example, for people with depression.

Since AI is dangerous if it is abused, to keep the development and the danger of its use at bay, twenty-one principles[312] were developed at the 2017 Asilomar Conference which were signed by Ray Kurzweil, the late Stephen Hawking, Elon Musk, and several AI experts. In 2019, forty-two countries adopted the new OECD Principles on Artificial Intelligence. In 2021, all 193 UNESCO states adopted a similar document on the ethics of AI—Recommendation on the Ethics of Artificial Intelligence.[313] One can say that the danger of the use of AI for non-benevolent purposes is recognised, but that does not mean that all countries and companies will follow these recommendations and rules.

KEY LEARNING

- The requested digitalisation of businesses and their processes is more complex and more anxiety-provoking than one thought. For leaders, it is difficult to stand with one foot in the analogue world and one foot in the digital world. It requires strength and flexibility at the same time.
- In addition, the use of AI, which was once seen as a major force in democratising, proves to be more dangerous than expected. The question of whether AI will become superintelligent, more intelligent than human beings, and will merge into one with us, as Ray Kurzweil predicts, or supplant us, as science fiction films imagine, is not yet solvable. We will see.
- But in the meantime, we must take measures to ensure that AI and deep learning is not used for nefarious purposes. Our humanness and our moral compass are the means for that. As a leader you need to create a frame in the organisation allowing for this moral compass to develop and be applied to manage the use carefully and to focus on beneficial and not harmful applications.

CHAPTER 18

Leading by the screen: how to do online and hybrid right

The pandemic saw the slowly approaching changes to the way we work together pick up pace. Videoconferencing has been available for some years now, but until recently was mostly used in the high-end corporate sphere, or by distant friends and family who needed to keep in touch.[314] The pandemic was an accelerator for this change, ushering the majority of the business world (that wasn't there already) online. This had a lot of advantages: people could work from home, social contacts and business contacts could be kept alive, coordination and collaboration was made possible without physical meeting—all of which has been discussed at length.

For leaders, this change has been positive, mostly in the sense that it has allowed us to overcome time, space, and pandemic-set boundaries and made us stay connected. Yet, it has also revealed some challenges which we will explore here. We want to understand how to react towards hybrid and online working in the future.

Zoom fatigue

So, what happens to you as an individual when you take part in an online conference? We all know the feeling of being exhausted after a day of Zoom meetings; we're often even more tired than we would be after an ordinary business day in the office. This is so apparent, in fact, that it has even been given a name—Zoom fatigue. There are a number of psychological factors behind this fatigue.

One has to do with the "flatness"—literally and symbolically—that's felt when working online. This flatness, the two dimensionality of the screen we are immersed in, leaves out the third dimension of depth—the depth of the facial features as well the possible emotional depth of a conversation. It results from not being able to see the micro-signals—those subtle indicators that we react to with our whole mind–body system—for example, the movement of little wrinkles around the eyes and mouth. Switching on the wrinkle reduction or image enhancing feature makes it even more difficult, and when looking at several small tiles on the screen this becomes almost impossible. Yet, we are always trying to figure out what is happening on the other side of the screen, and doing this with limited micro-signal feedback is cognitively and emotionally demanding, and, by that, exhausting. Some people say they don't mind, they can still work as well online as face-to-face, but I have my reservations—instead of tuning in, in this set-up we may well be projecting our own ideas onto the other person.

While we perceive each other as flat tiles, we are staring at each other constantly and, not only that, but we are also staring each other in the eye. This continuous eye contact happens much more than it would under normal social situations, where we break eye contact, intermittently, rhythmically. When in an elevator with others, we mostly avoid close eye contact and look elsewhere. Research has found that when we Zoom with one other person, their face appears as if it is only 50 cm away from our own—this is extremely close and invades our intimacy boundary (everything closer than 65 cm is perceived as invading).[315] This boundary invasion and the unusual amount of eye contact may also cause us to put our guard up and initiate protection mechanisms which likely hinder openness and mutual understanding, and contributes to this feeling of exhaustion.

A third important contributor to Zoom fatigue is continuously staring at yourself in a mirror. Although you can close the self view, many people choose not to. This continuous "self-behavioural-facial-outfit-background control" puts us in competition with the other tiles (faces)—which are more (or less) beautiful, competent, professional, etc. Competition, which is not publicly admitted, and the necessary self-management and self-control, are also a drain on our energy. Furthermore, you have to invest thought into what kind of image and persona you wish to design and present and which kind of ideal self you want to sell on the screen. Is it any surprise that the cosmetic surgery industry has seen a boom in recent years? I think that this speaks volumes about the feelings many people experience when spending so much time in front of the screen—anxiety about not looking or being good enough, feeling that they need to be more—more beautiful, more expressive, more professional…

Self-mirroring is thus closely linked to the important question of our identity. This question emerges also in our case—who are we, a flat little tile only? And how do we want to be seen? With whom do we belong in one group? We will come back to that later.

A fourth factor is limited mobility—sitting still in front of a computer for several hours without moving is neither healthy nor good for creativity. You certainly know how beneficial getting up and taking a walk is when you hit a mental brick wall. Also, the immobility in front of a screen where you are continuously observed is different to how we behave when we are, for example, on the phone.

Fifth, it also seems that coordinating groups needs more time investment and, by that, extra work becomes another contributor to exhaustion and fatigue.

A sixth point refers to cases when one gives a presentation to people who have turned off their camera—it feels like talking to a big black hole of nothingness which, again, sucks away our energy.

Emotional effects[316]

Working online has affected us all emotionally as well. Some of these emotional reactions have contributed to the Zoom fatigue just discussed, but much more was and is going on beyond that fatigue. We also have to say that, despite the negative effects we experience, it was and is possible to form new relationships with people we did not know prior to the pandemic. Clicking with others, experiencing sympathy and warmth, is possible, and when you later meet the person face-to-face, most of these positive emotional reactions are proven right.

Before we dive into the emotional difficulties, it is worth noting that it does seem to be better to meet online than not at all. Despite all the negative effects, the positives do outweigh the negatives in times when one cannot meet physically.

It makes sense to look at the emotional aspects, however, especially when we know that hybrid working is here to stay, hence we need to improve the way we work as much as we can.

Technology fosters a focus on the tool rather than the relationship; it allows us to hide our emotions and withdraw from the group or the other—when we turn off the camera, or the volume, or do other things online while we are looking at the screen. The feeling of being in a box (which is at least still three-dimensional) or a flat tile (two-dimensional only) affects our sense of self and identity. This identity struggle is concerned with the questions: Who do I want to be online? What is my best self I want to present? How do I look my best? What is the respective in-group I want to belong to? How do I feel that I belong to the group? Is the other person, when, for example, smiling, addressing me? Is it about me, or somebody else?

This struggle leads to continuous self-reflection and elicits the need to "curate" your image. This "curation" also includes your backdrop when on camera: do you choose something artificial, use your own real background as it is, show your (carefully arranged) bookshelf, plain white walls, empty corners, blur it out? What might stand out, what do you not want others to see? Choosing defences against being seen (the unwanted, ugliness, the shadow) or desires to be seen (the good, positive, kind, and professional aspects) is the tension we are all in and are struggling with. These defences make us withdraw, intellectualise, or hide within the role of being overly task-focused. On the other hand, I have the impression that working online in small groups is such a joy for many who have been deprived and are now able to connect, that they completely forget the task at hand.

When you are meeting people in the office, you rely more on how the person behaves: you read the body language, you see the whole body and person—and artefacts do not play such an important role. Online is less personal and intimate, but at the same time more focused on talking with each other. This lack of bodily encounter creates a sense of loss and grief around the online work and makes emotional connections more difficult. A loss of genuine dynamic interaction is another part of working together online. Real dialogue, where people in a group are engaged and talking actively, is almost impossible to achieve online, where we must speak one after the other. This loss can be experienced as flat interaction or even as stultifying or stilted discussion.

It also seems that in this environment the containment of negative emotions is less effective, since the other is not as easily experienced as a kind and caring human being. Negative emotions feel rather amplified, and the feeling of isolation can be reinforced. These difficulties to contain engender also difficulties in exploring conflict—it is mostly avoided since you can never be sure how the other perceives feedback which is not so positive. So, better to not give feedback and avoid any potential for conflict. And when there is no conflict, creativity and new ideas are more difficult to develop—the creative tension you need cannot be felt as well when together online, unless you knew each other well before the pandemic. This leads us to the question of trust—it takes longer and is more difficult to establish trust, one has to work harder for it.

The following case study will share the results of a recent research project on the effects of virtual work. It amplifies and also adds new perspectives to what we have just discussed.

Case study

The effects of hybrid work—leading by the screen

Kalina Stamenova

The vignettes below come from three explorations in which we tried to investigate the impact of the Zoom field on the emotional experience of people working online. For the purposes of the study, we designed a temporary online organisation with the primary task of studying the impact of the online platform on the participants' thoughts, feelings, and perceptions. Participants were invited to self-organise and explore, share, and reflect on their experiences in the online space. Each exploration lasted three hours and included working in small groups (teams) in breakout rooms as well as opening and closing plenaries with all participants. This design of the explorations allowed the creation of a sort of simulation of an organisation working online with participants from across the globe, and in this way it approximates an international company working in a virtual world. The temporary online organisations we co-created were also learning laboratories in the sense that the task was to learn from the experience of the people taking part in such organisations. The participants were predominantly systems psychodynamic practitioners and consultants and partners in the explorations.

As we were interested in exploring the hidden dynamics of such work, we used an adaptation of the method of observing organisations,[317] and the three of us—Kalina Stamenova, Irene O'Byrne-Maguire, and Bryan Maguire—tried to observe the interactions on the screen with free-floating attention while also noticing our subjective experiences in the field to help us understand what was going on beneath the surface of these temporary organisations. After each exploration, we wrote observation reports in the form of reflective notes. Themes related to identity emerged from the observations and the vignettes below present some of them.

Struggle with identity

Throughout the three explorations, the observers and the participants all experienced various difficulties related to asserting one's identity online, finding one's voice, and dealing with the sense of feeling diminished or almost invisible on the screen.

There was an interesting and rather paradoxical occurrence in the second exploratory event in one of the breakout rooms where participants were trying to reflect on their experience of being together online. This was a rather small group, and the participants were trying to get to know each other. One could find many parallels with a new team in an organisation coming to work together online. And here is what happened in this group.

> There was some talk about a storm in Rwanda where one of the participants was. Then one of the participants said she was worried as someone joined the event with their mobile phone only, so the face was hidden. People somewhat agreed and nodded, then an elderly woman said she was feeling confused as she was not sure if the name of one of the participants was a woman's or a man's name. I [the researcher] found it really strange as the woman was in the room with her camera on and she was obviously a woman. A man asked the woman if she had any problems with her sight, she replied she didn't, and then the man added that the woman with the peculiar name was in the room and asked the other woman if she could see her. The elderly woman still looked confused. Another woman participant suddenly said she was challenged by the researchers about curiosity, and she was going to follow her curiosity and go and see what is happening in the other groups. And she left immediately. This did not seem to evoke any response in the group.
>
> The woman with the peculiar name said she suddenly felt like she wanted to go online and look up information about the participants there—check their LinkedIn profiles etc. A man asked her what stopped her from asking people in the room such information. I felt there was some challenge, but the interaction was lively. (Exploration 2)

The vignette seems to illustrate rather vividly the difficulty and the palpable struggle around identity and presence online. It seems that the online environment makes it more difficult for people to emerge with their own identities and stimulates a peculiar sense of invisibility. Being unable to see well someone's face on the screen seems to affect the mind of the people in the group. One participant has turned their camera off. This seems to start a chain reaction in the team. A second participant, a woman, is then unable to differentiate the gender of another woman, as if the inability to see one member affects the perception of another who is paradoxically clearly visible. There is somewhat strange confusion about the gender of the woman from Rwanda and she also seems to have become invisible! As if she has disappeared from the mind of the other woman. The misperception is challenged by a male member but still, the difficulty persists, and a member suddenly leaves the group claiming she will follow her curiosity. The experience is perhaps rather painful and leaving the room is a way to avoid it. Yet the curiosity somewhat remains but it is now directed at finding information about others online, that is, who they are and what their professional identities are. It is as if the Zoom environment stimulates more individual technical satisfaction of curiosity rather than a lively interaction between people. This seems to be picked up by the male participant and challenged again and he suggests that the participants can ask each other about who they are rather than researching identities online.

There seems to be some palpable struggle with asserting one's identity but also with connecting and getting to know one another through the medium of technology.

The need to assert one's identity online was expressed and shared again in the plenary discussion with the whole temporary organisation. Below is another short vignette from the plenary where people reflected on and shared their emotional experiences.

> There was some recognition that we connect differently in person than online. One needs to assert one's identity more. There was a feeling of "loss of senses" and while able to meet people from everywhere on Zoom there is a difficulty: "We talk, then we disappear!" This evoked a question: "Am I being ghosted?" There seemed to be confusion as to what this might mean. (Exploration 2)

The loss of senses and its impact on the emotional experiences of people working online seems to indicate that it is more difficult to connect to others, and to work as a team, as some of the underlying concerns might be that one could easily disappear from the minds of the other members and become "ghosted". The anxiety seems vividly expressed by one of the participants who reflects, "We talk, then disappear!", pointing at the fragility of the link in the virtual space both between the participants and in their minds. It seems difficult to keep things in mind when one works online.

Another difficult experience that was identified relates to being a small box on the screen. The vignette below is from the third exploration. In this temporary organisation, the participants were working together in small teams and their task again was to reflect on what is going on inside them as well as what is going on on the screen. This was a very small group of three participants—an Iranian woman, a Pakistani man, an American man, and a female researcher.

> The Pakistani participant commented that now the configuration of the boxes on his screen was different and his box was the smallest, the two women (myself [the researcher] and the Iranian participant) had equal-sized boxes and the American had the biggest box. The American said one can adjust the size of the boxes by adjusting the view and we all started checking the setting very carefully. The American then said he was not interested in the technological side and was more interested in finding out more about the people in the room and continuing the conversation. (Exploration 3)

Again, we can see the impact of the screen on the minds of the participants. Perhaps being a small box on the screen diminishes one's sense of identity and evokes feelings of inequality. People seem preoccupied with what is happening on the screen. It also seems to affect how people connect to each other and the American suggests that they can easily fix that by adjusting the view on the screen and the difficulty seems to be denied by shifting the focus of the reflection on the people and finding out more about them. But it is also an acknowledgement that the screen seems to interfere with the way people connect and relate to one another.

Stateless mind, feeling homeless, and feeling like a refugee

Other important themes which emerged in the explorations relate to the feeling of being without a home and to the inability to find a home. The participants expressed particular feelings which they described by the use of metaphors of feeling like refugees, feeling homeless and stateless when working online.

The vignettes below are from the plenary reflection with all the participants in the second temporary organisation after people had worked in their small groups. People were invited to share their thoughts, reflections, and experiences of working in this temporary online organisation.

> A man from group 6 spoke about what they had discussed in his group. They felt like refugees and as if they had no country or state to which they belonged. They spoke in the group that it seems as if in this digital world there are no nations and physical things. No one stayed in this group; after talking for a while they all left the breakout room and joined other groups.
>
> A woman said she felt it was an exercise to leave the home group and go and visit other groups; being like a refugee, maybe the motivation is curiosity; something good is out there but when you go to other groups you feel like a stranger. You have to wait and see what people changing countries feel.
>
> Another participant said that the experience felt like being homeless or stateless. She added everybody should do this exercise, particularly politicians so they can experience what it means to be stateless. I [the researcher] felt there was some blurring between the virtual world and the physical world, and I was not sure what the woman meant.
>
> Someone mentioned that living on Zoom made them feel stateless, like a refugee. This resonated with some others who talked about the lack of evidence to prove that a Zoom group was a group vs an in-person group. (Exploration 2)

The reflections from the plenary indicate quite clearly the way the online platform impacts one's emotional experience and one's sense of identity online at a deeper level. Moreover, people find it really difficult to connect to the group and feel that they belong to a group. It seems very easy to disconnect and leave a space when one is working online but such fragility of linking perhaps resonates with something in the mind and evokes feelings that one does not belong anywhere in the virtual world. The lack of physical boundaries online does indeed seem to affect one's thinking, and the subjective experience of the researcher is one of confusion and blurring the boundaries between the physical and the virtual world. Moreover, the inability to create robust links with the group and the organisation seems to be expressed by the participant who doubts that a Zoom group is really a group.

The online space, the interactions among people through the screen, do seem to have an impact on one's sense of identity—in some cases perhaps diminishing it and creating a palpable struggle to assert oneself and one's authority online, and in other cases leading to a peculiar experience of feeling like refugees. And refugees with accompanying feelings of displacement find it difficult to assert themselves in foreign countries. Perhaps the online space does feel like a foreign country in which it is difficult to find oneself, one's group, one's voice, and authority.

So, *Who am I online?* Technologies are never just tools; they are evocative objects, and they cause us to see ourselves and the world differently. These are important questions for managers, leaders, consultants, and in general everyone leading and working online. A deeper understanding of how the online platform affects one's emotional experience and one's sense of identity online has implications for the way we work online. It can provide some explanation for the phenomenon of Zoom fatigue and has implications for employees' efficient work and well-being. The understanding can then be used to design interventions for teams and organisations that work with these online platforms.[318]

* * *

In this research study a new aspect comes to the forefront: the feeling of being homeless, stateless, and being a refugee when living on Zoom. It means that you have lost your physical home and entered a state of being a Zoom refugee. "Being lost in Zoom-transition" comes to my mind as well. This is a strong metaphor which I find interesting and explicable.

What to do to improve online collaboration

As a leader, you need to focus on three key points:

- How do you create containment as a leader?
- How do you create connection to and between the people?
- How do you integrate emotions into the setting?

Containment and connection are mutually influencing each other, yet for containment you need to create boundaries, and that works best with good preparation, clear structures and processes, more time for interrelatedness, and more time for checking-in in between. You can also create containment by individually checking-in with people before and after the meeting (preferably not online, but personally or via the phone). It is also important to maintain focus on your own emotions while simultaneously being aware of the needs of those around you. Tuning in to worries and fears is an important part of creating good containment.

Working with small break-out groups creates connection and connectivity between the people; it has a greater positive impact if you establish this way of working from the outset. Your own connection to others grows when you expose yourself and show your own vulnerability as a leader (although it is, of course, a balancing act) and when you are able to allow yourself to make mistakes—not everything needs to be planned in detail—giving space and time for questions and ideas to evolve and be discussed is as important as structure and focus.

Some aspects are obvious. When working together, everybody should keep their cameras on (to stay with each other) and their microphone on mute (to avoid background noise and unexpected interruptions), and when wanting to speak to ask for using the electronic hand-up function in the larger meeting group. In a smaller group of three or four people, the conversation can also flow more naturally without the electronic hand.

Integrating emotions works here by carefully asking for feedback and sharing reflections at the end of a session or a task. Asking explicitly for emotions, the emotional energy, and the way people feel right now can also be helpful at times. Yet, you should stay attuned to hidden or partly exposed emotions—try to focus more on the emotions of others without losing track of your own.

And please do not forget to allow for breaks—we need a moment of detachment and privacy to refresh and to recharge.

Group size also impacts efficacy, and by that the joy of working together and the outcome. You will thus have to craft your meetings, the size of these meetings, and the people you involve much more carefully. The effects of unplanned, boring, exhausting, one-way meetings are detrimental to the emotional willingness to contribute in a demanding environment.

Hybrid working

The next step for many organisations post-pandemic is hybrid working—the combination of online and on-site working is at the centre of the actual conversation around the future of work. Online working will not disappear, that we can be sure of. In addition to what I wrote previously, a hybrid work environment needs to be carefully crafted.

There exist several more considerations emerging when combining online and on-site work. These mainly have to do with the fact that not all members of the organisation will be present in the office at the same time. There may even be two groups—the office workers, and the online workers. Parallel development of two separate cultures would be detrimental—the on-site work culture will likely be much stronger, due to the fact that being and working together in one real space enables more connection and shared values.

The culture of those working remotely might then be characterised by impressions such as feeling abandoned/isolated, disenfranchised, or even refugee-like (as in the case study). What would be lost is the sense of common purpose and a shared identity, a feeling of belonging. The only way to create a successful shared culture is to create situations in which all members of the organisation or team inhabit a shared physical space. The two groups should not be working in isolation but interwoven and regularly connecting face-to-face.

Another big question is who shall be allowed to work online, and whose work can be executed more efficiently in the office? It very much depends, of course, on the job and the task, on processes and workflows, as well as on personal preferences.[319] "Hybrid arrangements should never replicate existing bad practices, as when firms began automating work processes, decades ago ..."[320]

When the task is more thinking focused, where undisturbed time is needed, online could be a good solution (e.g. strategic planner). This also applies for more coordination-focused tasks like those of a team manager. Coordination can be done on-site and online when everybody needed is present. Yet, collaboration tasks where you need to share your thoughts and ideas, for example, when developing a new product or product features, where you need to be freer in your communication, are better suited to on-site working.

You also need to take into account that people have individual preferences: some can work at home because they have an office and can work alone in peace, whereas others have no choice but to sit at a kitchen table together with their children doing their homework—the latter not being an ideal setting for efficient and productive online work.

Reimagining workflows and work processes is a good exercise after the disruptive impact of Covid. It also helps to determine which tasks are more suited for online vs off-site working.

An important aspect, which Gratton brings up, is the question of fairness and inclusion. In difficult times of change—and going hybrid is a huge change—people tend to split as a social defence. They might easily feel excluded, unwanted, or unfairly treated, impacting work performance and retention. The trick to get over that feeling is creating an inclusive, company-wide process in designing the work. When this design takes place piecemeal, department by department, team by team, for example, a fragmented landscape may develop, and this will be emotionally difficult for people to manage.

How do you get there?

A company-wide process to design hybrid work is at the core of this change. Different employees from different parts of the organisation need to work together via interviews, surveys, focus groups, and workshops to figure out the key processes and tasks and also what drives them. As in every other change process, open and continuous communication is key, but also important is to let people figure it out together.

It is also helpful to train change agents in understanding the difficulties and the drivers of this process—regularly checking the pulse of the organisation supports this. It also includes questions around the value set of the organisation and its purpose; the hybrid work model needs to fit in with what is important to the organisation and the people working in it—it needs to prepare for the future as well.

Hybrid working can only succeed when people have the right technical/software tools to seamlessly collaborate online and on-site without loss of information, time, or energy. This might entail some additional investment, but it is absolutely necessary to reduce the additional frustration which could come up from a technology which does not work—we all have had the experience that IT processes are not always fulfilling our hopes or wishes when focusing on cost instead of technology.

KEY LEARNING

- Hybrid working is challenging and requires careful planning and structuring—on the one hand, by giving autonomy and (a limited or framed) freedom of choice over where to work, and on the other, more empathy and tuning in to others' emotions.
- The virtual work arrangement seems to threaten the identity of individuals as well as organisations and creating space for both reflection and reflexion is your key task as a leader.

And now? Some final reflections with an outlook

Quite a while ago, before the idea of this book developed in my mind, I began to think about how we need to rethink what leadership means and what you as leaders might need to do differently. The changes in the world of work and business have been obvious, although not everything which is sold as a big change is a big change—some of the developments, such as agile management and teamwork, innovation and design thinking, etc. are just old wine in new skins. Yet, the situation has indeed changed, and obviously the three years of the pandemic (2019–22) have accelerated changes in unforeseen ways. The world is more interlinked and at the same time more disparate; individuals are more connected yet further apart from each other, we are over-informed and feel under-represented, we have to be politically correct, yet we lose our compassion and empathy for the other. Some political certainties, such as the bipolar split between the West/NATO and the East/Russia, we thought had lost their meanings, until Putin attacked Ukraine, and now we see many more difficult developments where civilisation and democracy are under threat.

The context for leadership now spans an active democratic understanding of how we want to live and work together, and the more defensive retreat to populistic and nationalistic endeavours in an attempt to keep our anxieties at bay. At the same time, we live between a digitalised world and a hope to withdraw to nature and grow our own potatoes. These paradoxical tensions impact the ideas of leadership and the roles of leaders in organisations.

I am convinced that the further we march into this new world, which is rather more aptly characterised by the acronym BANI (brittle, anxious, non-linear, and incomprehensible, which together stand for chaotic unforeseeable situations) than by the formerly important VUCA (volatile, uncertain, complex, and ambiguous), the more we need leaders characterised by humaneness and humanness. This is what makes us distinct from machines and at the same time contributes to what we all need in this world—to be seen and understood as a human being with an inner world of emotions that has (good) relationships with others.

This is one reason why I wanted to write this book—to create awareness of the need to develop an understanding of how emotions and relationships always and ever impact our work, our performance, and the other. To realise the constant interplay of (your)self and (the) other and to explore and dive into it is a basic new leadership skill set. Only when your understanding of yourself/your self incorporates at least some of your shadow, abyss, vulnerabilities, and defences, and, of course, also your successful behavioural and emotional patterns, will you be able to understand what it is that moves another person.

The most important character trait which holds the idea of this book together, a virtue in the Aristotelean sense, is *courage*. Courage has two faces. It entails being the hero, superman or superwoman, throwing yourself into the water to save a drowning child, fighting for other people's rights, attacking the evil to protect the good, taking a bold (strategic) decision—that is certainly one aspect of courage. The other form of courage I want to point to is not visible from the outside, but it is more important in the realm of contemporary leadership: it is the courage to bite the bullet or to do something despite yourself. By that I mean doing something even though you are afraid of doing it: looking into your own abyss, having the courage to show your vulnerability and your weakness, allowing yourself to feel your fear and sometimes even share it, changing your behaviour although you are afraid of the consequences, trying out new ways of communicating beyond the existent patterns—it is about giving space for something new within yourself and by that allowing a change in your emotional behaviour without knowing how both you and the other will react to it. This new inner place might change your leadership style completely—taking it in a direction from which you, your colleagues, and the organisation will benefit.

Finally, I would like to advocate for a healthy mixture of reflexion and reflection—only at their interplay will the quality of your leadership and its results be decided. Reflexion in the sense of self-reflection, tuning in to your own emotions, emotionally linking with others (I would like to create a new English word to fit this definition: *reflextion*—the *t* shall indicate that it is not only yourself you think about, but also the other) to connect with them, and reflection in the sense of cognitive analytical thinking. Both are needed and neither can replace the other. This in itself is a very interesting topic, but that would make for another book.

Enjoy your reflex(t)ions and be courageous. The first step is made by reading this book until the end!

Notes

Overview

1. The authors of the case studies have the consent of the person depicted in the case, have anonymised the case, or have compiled a single case from several cases of their own experiences.

Introduction

2. Aristotle (384–322 bc) was the first who developed the difference between philosophy and psychology.
3. For a short overview of the historical development of the notion of the unconscious, please have a look at my book: Nagel, C. (2020). *Psychodynamic Coaching: Distinctive Features*. New York: Routledge.
4. Lütkehaus, L. (Ed.) (2005). *Dieses wahre innere Afrika: Texte zur Entdeckung des Unbewussten vor Freud*. Giessen, Germany: Psychosozial.
5. In the work of Johann Friedrich Herbart. He taught Theodor Meynert, who went on to become one of Freud's teachers.
6. Hartmann, E. von (1869). *Die Philosophy des Unbewussten*. Berlin: Duncker.

7. Rohde-Dachser, C. (2005). Konzepte des Unbewussten. [Lecture] *Festvortrag zum 40-jährigen Bestehen des Lehrinstituts.* November 5.
8. Kahneman, D. (2011). *Thinking, Fast and Slow.* New York: Farrar, Straus and Giroux.
9. Kahneman, D., & Tversky, A. (1979). Prospect theory: An analysis of decision under risk. *Econometrica, 47*(2): 263–291.
10. Gigerenzer, G. (2007). *Gut Feelings: The Intelligence of the Unconscious.* New York: Penguin.
11. Dane, E., & Pratt, M. G. (2007). Exploring intuition and its role in managerial decision making. *Academy of Management Review, 32*(1): 33–54.
12. a. Khatri, N., & Ng, H. A. (2000). The role of intuition in strategic decision making. *Human Relations, 53*(1): 57–86.
    b. Ray, M., & Myers, R. (1990). Practical intuition. In: W. H. Agor (Ed.), *Intuition in Organizations* (pp. 247–262). Newbury Park, CA: Sage.
13. Damasio, A. R. (1999). *The Feeling of What Happens: Body and Emotion in the Making of Consciousness.* New York: Harcourt Brace.
14. Haidt, J. (2006). *The Happiness Hypothesis.* New York: Basic Books.
15. Ibid., p. 4.

Chapter 1

16. Lester, B. M., Conradt, E., & Marsit, C. (2016). Introduction to the Special Section on Epigenetics. *Child Development, 87*(1): 29–37.
17. Oberlander, F., Weinger, J., Papsdorf, M., Grunau, R., Misri, S., & Devlin, A. M. (2008). Prenatal exposure to maternal depression, neonatal methylation of human glucocorticoid receptor gene (NR3C1) and infant cortisol stress responses. *Epigenetics, 3*(2): 97–106.
18. Most of the research has been done on the mother–infant relationship, and despite some natural differences because of the antenatal stage, it is today understood as the relationship to the caregiver is important, which can be any parenting person.
19. Hughes, D. (2006). *Building the Bonds of Attachment: Awakening Love in Deeply Traumatized Children* (2nd edn). Lanham, MD: Rowman and Littlefield, p. ix.
20. Trevarthen, C. (2019). The psychobiology of the human spirit. In: G. Apter, E. Devouche, & M. Gratier (Ed.), *Early Interaction and*

Developmental Psychopathology, Vol. I: Infancy (pp. 1–20). Cham, Switzerland: Springer Nature.

21. Hobson, P. (2002). *The Cradle of Thought: Exploring the Origins of Human Thinking*. London: Pan.
22. Cohen-Baron, S. (2002). I am loved therefore I think. *Nature, 416*(6883): 791–792.
23. Tyson, P., & Tyson, R. (1990). *Psychoanalytic Theories of Development: An Integration*. New York: Yale University Press.
24. Bowlby developed these styles together with his post-doc Margaret Ainsworth, based on his work with adolescent thieves, whom he observed as having had disruptive relationships with their mothers.
25. Quirin, M., Gillath, O., Pruessner, J. C., & Eggert, L. D. (2010). Adult attachment insecurity and hippocampal cell density. *Social Cognitive and Affective Neuroscience, 5*(1): 39–47.
26. Gillath, O., Karantzas, G. C., & Fraley, R. C. (2016). *Adult Attachment Theory: A Concise Introduction to Theory and Research*. London: Academic Press.
27. Nagel, C. (2014). *Behavioral Strategy: Thoughts and Feelings in the Decision-Making Process. The Unconscious and Corporate Success.* Bonn, Germany: Unternehmermedien. Inspired by Bartholomew, K., & Horowitz, L. M. (1991). Attachment styles among young adults: A test of a four-category model. *Journal of Personality and Social Psychology, 61*: 226–244.
28. Own compilation, inspired by Cozolino, L. (2014). *The Neuroscience of Human Relationships: Attachment and the Developing Social Brain* (2nd edn). New York: W. W. Norton.
29. Adapted from Cozolino (2014, p. 133). See note 28.
30. Ibid., p. 134.
31. Ibid., p. 138.
32. It was C. G. Jung who developed the shadow concept.
33. a. Erikson, E. H. (1950). *Childhood and Society*. New York: W. W. Norton.
    b. Erikson, E. H. (1968). *Identity: Youth and Crisis*. New York: W. W. Norton.
34. Knight, Z. D. (2017). A proposed model of psychodynamic psychotherapy linked to Erik Erikson's eight stages of psychosocial development. *Clinical Psychological Psychotherapy, 25*(5): 1047–1058.

Chapter 2

35. Sadun, R., Fuller, J. B., Hansen, S., & Neal, P. J. (2022). The C-suite skills that matter most. *Harvard Business Review, 100*(4): 42–50.

36. King, A. J., Johnson, D. D., & Van Vugt, M. (2009). The origins and evolution of leadership. *Current Biology, 19*(19): R911–R916.

37. Van Vugt, M. (2006). Evolutionary origins of leadership and followership. *Personality and Social Psychology Review, 10*(4): 354–371.

38. Ibid.

39. de Waal-Andrews, W., & van Vugt, M. (2020). The triad model of follower needs: Theory and review. *Current Opinion in Psychology, 33*: 142–147.

40. Both notions, holding and the good enough mother, stem from Winnicott:
    a. Winnicott, D. W. (1953). Transitional objects and transitional phenomena. *International Journal of Psychoanalysis, 34*: 89–97.
    b. Winnicott, D. W. (1958). *Collected Papers: Through Paediatrics to Psycho-Analysis.* London: Tavistock.
    c. Winnicott, D. W. (1960). The theory of the parent–child relationship. *International Journal of Psychoanalysis, 41*: 585–595.

41. This is a concept which was developed by Heinz Kohut, a self-psychologist who was particularly interested in how a child develops a sense of self.

42. You can find the best overview of what negative capability means for leaders in Simpson, P., French, R., & Harvey, C. (2002). Leadership and negative capability. *Human Relations, 55*(10): 1209–1226.

43. Keats, J. (1970). *The Letters of John Keats: A Selection.* R. Gittings (Ed.). Oxford: Oxford University Press, p. 43.

44. Eisold, K. (2000). The rediscovery of the unknown: An inquiry into psychoanalytic praxis. *Contemporary Psychoanalysis, 36*(1): 57–75.

45. Ibid., p. 65.

46. Simpson, P., French, R., & Harvey, C. (2002). See note 42.

47. Erikson (1968). See note 33b.

48. Kast, V. (1991). *Joy, Inspiration, and Hope.* College Station, TX: A&M University Press.

49. a. Bowlby, J. (1988). *A Secure Base: Parent–Child Attachment and Healthy Human Development.* New York: Basic Books.
    b. Grossmann, K., & Grossmann, K. E. (2004). *Bindungen: Das Gefüge psychischer Sicherheit.* Stuttgart, Germany: Klett-Cotta.

50. Hopper, E. (2001). On the nature of hope in psychoanalysis and group analysis. *British Journal of Psychotherapy, 18*(2): 205–226.
51. Ibid., p. 210.
52. Nussbaum, M. C. (2018). *The Monarchy of Fear: A Philosopher Looks at Our Political Crisis*. New York: Simon & Schuster.
53. Petriglieri, G., & Petriglieri J. L. (2020). The return of the oppressed: A systems psychodynamic approach to organization studies. *Academy of Management Annals, 14*(1): 411–449.
54. Ybema, S., Yanow, D., Wels, H., & Kamsteeg, F. (Eds.) (2009). *Organizational Ethnography: Studying the Complexities of Everyday Life*. London: Sage, p. 306. They suggested that what makes an identity more or less real, more or less actual, is the "continuing capacity to enact [it]".

Chapter 3

55. If you want to get an overview of basic leadership theory, you might want to check out Northouse, P. G. (Ed.) (2021). *Leadership: Theory and Practice* (7th edn). Thousand Oaks, CA: Sage, p. 3.
56. Senge, P. M., Scharmer, C. O., Jaworski, J., & Flowers, B. S. (2004). *Presence: Human Purpose and the Field of the Future*. Cambridge, MA: Society for Organizational Learning, p. 186.
57. Kets de Vries, M. F. R., & Cheak, A. (2016). Psychodynamic approach. In: P. G. Northouse (Ed.), *Leadership: Theory and Practice* (7th ed.) (pp. 363–396). Thousand Oaks, CA: Sage, p. 391.
58. Senge et al. explore these ideas deeply in their book *Presence: Human Purpose and the Field of the Future* (see note 56). It is full of anecdotes and stories and a worthwhile read.
59. Scharmer, C. O. (2007). *Theory U: Leading from the Future as It Emerges. The Social Technology of Presencing*. Cambridge, MA: Society for Organizational Learning.
60. Adapted from Goleman, D., & Boyatzis, R. (2017). Emotional intelligence has 12 elements. Which do you need to work on? *Harvard Business Review, 84*(2): 1–5.
61. Riemann, F. (1961). *Grundformen der Angst* (*Basic Forms of Fear*). Munich, Germany: Reinhardt.
62. Kernberg, O. F. (1984). *Severe Personality Disorders: Psychotherapeutic Strategies*. New Haven, CT: Yale University Press.

63. Nagel, C. (2021). On the psychodynamics of hope and identity in times of crisis: Why they are needed when basic assumption victimism/supremacism prevail. *Organisational and Social Dynamics, 21*(1): 56–77.
64. Kets de Vries, M. F. R., & Miller, D. (1984). *The Neurotic Organization.* San Francisco, CA: Jossey-Bass, pp. 5–6.
65. Ibid.
66. Kets de Vries, M. F. R., & Engellau, E. (2010). A clinical approach to the dynamics of leadership and executive transformation. In: N. Nohria & R. Khurana (Eds.), *Handbook of Leadership Theory and Practice* (pp. 183–222). Cambridge, MA: Harvard University Press.
67. Kets de Vries, M. F. R., & Miller, D. (1997). Narcissism and leadership: An object relations perspective. In: R. P. Vecchio (Ed.), *Leadership: Understanding the Dynamics of Power and Influence in Organizations* (pp. 194–214). Notre Dame, IN: University of Notre Dame Press.
68. Maccoby, M. (2004). Narcissistic leaders: The incredible pros, the inevitable cons. *Harvard Business Review, 82*(1): 92–107.
69. Kets de Vries & Engellau (2010). See note 66.
70. a. Kernberg (1984). See note 62.
    b. Maccoby (2004). See note 68.
    c. Rosenthal, S. (2006). *Narcissism and Leadership: A Review and Research Agenda.* [Working paper.] Cambridge, MA: Centre for Public Leadership, Harvard University, p. 44.
71. Kernberg (1984). See note 62.
72. Kets de Vries & Engellau (2010). See note 66.
73. Kets de Vries, M. F. R. (2004). Organizations on the couch: A clinical perspective on organizational dynamics. *European Management Journal, 22*(2): 183–200.
74. Rosenthal (2006). See note 70c.
75. Kets de Vries (2004). See note 73.
76. Kernberg (1984). See note 62, p. 56.

Chapter 4

77. a. Damasio, A. R. (1994). *Descartes' Error: Emotion, Rationality and the Human Brain.* New York: Putnam, p. 352.
    b. Damasio (1999). See note 13.

c. LeDoux, J. (1998). *The Emotional Brain: The Mysterious Underpinnings of Emotional Life*. London: Weidenfeld & Nicolson.

d. Panksepp, J. (1998). *Affective Neuroscience: The Foundations of Human and Animal Emotions*. Oxford: Oxford University Press.

78. Schiller, D., Alessandra, N. C., Yu, N., Alia-Klein, N., Becker, S., Cromwell, H. C., Dolcos, F., Eslinger, P. J., Frewen, P., Kemp, A. H., Pace-Schott, E. F., et al. (2022). *The Human Affectome*. HAL Archives 03728066.

79. Panksepp (1998). See note 77d.

80. Panksepp, J., & Biven, L. (2012). *The Archeology of Mind: Neuroevolutionary Origins of Human Emotions*. New York: W. W. Norton.

81. Ibid., p. 9.

82. Ibid., pp. 13–16.

83. My understanding and my description of these processes derive from Schiller et al. (2022). See note 78.

84. Cromwell, H. C., & Lowe, L. J. (2022). The Human Affectome project: A dedication to Jaak Panksepp. *Neuroscience & Biobehavioral Reviews*, *138*(104693).

85. a. Dennett, D. (2017). *From Bacteria to Bach and Back: The Evolution of Mind*. New York: W. W. Norton.

b. Solms, M. (2015). Depression: A neuropsychoanalytic perspective. In: M. Solms (Ed.), *The Feeling Brain: Selected Papers on Neuropsychoanalysis* (pp. 95–108). London: Karnac.

86. Damasio, A. R. (2010). *Self Comes to Mind: Constructing the Conscious Brain*. New York: Pantheon/Random House.

87. See, for example, Panksepp & Biven (2012). See note 80.

88. a. Kihlstrom, J. F. (2013). Unconscious processes. In: D. Reisberg (Ed.), *Oxford Library of Psychology: The Oxford Handbook of Cognitive Psychology* (pp. 176–186). New York: Oxford University Press.

b. Kihlstrom, J. F., Tobias, B. A., Mulvaney, S., & Tobis, I. P. (2000). The emotional unconscious. In: E. Eich, J. F. Kihlstrom, G. H. Bower, J. P. Forgas, & P. M. Niedenthal (Eds.), *Counterpoints: Cognition and Emotion* (pp. 30–86). New York: Oxford University Press.

89. Kihlstrom et al. (2000). See note 88b.

90. Kihlstrom (2013). See note 88a, p. 176.

91. Solms, M. (2018). The scientific standing of psychoanalysis. *British Journal of Psychiatry—International, 15*(1): 5–8.
92. For example, Panksepp (1998). See note 77d.
93. Based on:
   a. Panksepp, J. (2006). Emotional endophenotypes in evolutionary psychiatry. *Progress in Neuro-Psychopharmacology and Biological Psychiatry, 30*(5): 774–784.
   b. Watt, D. F. (2005). Panksepp's common sense view of affective neuroscience is not the commonsense view in large areas of neuroscience. *Consciousness and Cognition, 14*(1): 81–88.
94. Taylor, S. E., Klein, L. C., Lewis, B. P., Gruenewald, T. L., Gurung, R. A. R., & Updegraff, J. A. (2000). Biobehavioral responses to stress in females: Tend-and-befriend, not fight-or-flight. *Psychological Review, 107*(3): 411–429.
95. This case is based on a paper that was discussed in a seminar on the seven emotional systems with Mark Solms and other participants, initiated by C-Lan (Gry Osnes). We owe much of our learning to that seminar, to Mark Solms, and to the other participants. The case was also presented at the ISPSO Annual Meeting 2019 with a different focus as a paper by Susan Long, Fiona Martin, and Christine Owen under the title "The shadow side of learning, leadership and culture in emergency services organisations".
96. AFAC Australasian Fire and Emergency Service Authorities Council: Climate report, 2018–2019.
97. See, for example:
   a. Fraher, A. (2011). *Thinking Through Crisis: Improving Teamwork and Leadership in High-Risk Fields.* London: Karnac.
   b. Owen, C. (Ed.). (2014). *Human Factors Challenges in Emergency Management: Enhancing Individual and Team Performance in Fire and Emergency Services.* Farnham, UK: Ashgate.
   c. Weick, K. E., Sutcliffe, K. M., & Obstfeld, D. (2008). Organizing for high reliability: Processes of collective mindfulness. *Crisis Management, 3*(1): 81–123.

Chapter 5

98. Shapiro, E. R. (2020). *Finding a Place to Stand: Developing Self-Reflective Institutions, Leaders and Citizens.* Bicester, UK: Phoenix, Kindle position 723–724.

99. Interestingly, Oedipus was an only child, whereas Freud had very complicated relationships with a brother who died at the age of one, and elder half-brothers and sisters, so that he would have preferred to have been the only child. Sibling relationships were excluded from his theoretical work even though they are full of negative emotions such as rivalry and hatred. See Prophecy Coles' work on this subject, including (2015). Sibling rivalry at work: from family to groups. *Psychodynamic Practice*, *21*(3): 254–263.
100. Richardson, R. W., & Richardson, L. A. (1990). *Birth Order and You*. North Vancouver, BC, Canada: Self-Counsel Press.
101. Visholm, S. (2021). *Family Psychodynamics in Organizational Contexts: The Hidden Forces that Shape the Workplace*. Abingdon, UK: Routledge.
102. Coles (2015). See note 99, p. 262.
103. Adler, A. (1928). Characteristics of the first, second, and third child. *Children: The Magazine for Parents*, *14*(3): 14–52.
104. Adam-Lauterbach, D. (2013). The psychic and clinical significance of sibling experiences. *Nordic Journal of Child and Adolescent Psychotherapy*, *28*: 40–49.
105. Kets de Vries (2004). See note 73, p. 190.
106. Ibid.
107. Laplanche, J., & Pontalis, J.-B. (1973). *The Language of Psychoanalysis*. D. Nicholson-Smith (Trans.). London: Hogarth.
108. Jung, C. G. (1916). The psychology of dreams. In: C. E. Long (Ed.), *Collected Papers on Analytical Psychology*. London: Baillière, Tindall & Cox.
109. Klein, M. (1946). Notes on some schizoid mechanisms. *International Journal of Psychoanalysis*, *27*: 99–110.
110. Ferenczi, S. (1909). Introjection and transference. *Sex in Psychoanalysis*. New York: Dover, 1956, pp. 30–79.

Chapter 6

111. Ely, R. J., Stone, P., & Ammerman, C. (2014). Rethink what you "know" about high-achieving women. *Harvard Business Review*, *92*(12): 100–109.
112. https://grantthornton.global/en/insights/women-in-business-2021/ (last accessed March 15, 2023).
113. https://fortune.com/2021/08/02/female-ceos-global-500-fortune-500-cvs-karen-lynch-ping-an-jessica-tan/ (last accessed March 15, 2023).

114. Gender Statistics Database (2021). Largest listed companies: CEOs, executives and non-executives. Vilnius: European Institute for Gender Equality.

115. Edwards, R., Guzzo, R., Jackson, C., Knoepflmacher, A., & Nalbantian, H. (2020). *Let's Get Real About Equality: When Women Thrive. 2020 Global Report*. https://www.uk.mercer.com/our-thinking/global-research-when-women-thrive-2020.html (last accessed March 15, 2023).

116. *Women in Management: Quick Take* (2022). Catalyst. See: https://catalyst.org/research/women-in-management/ (last accessed March 15, 2023).

117. Valerio, A. M. (2009). *Developing Women Leaders: A Guide for Men and Women in Organisations*. Chichester, UK: Wiley.

118. https://implicit.harvard.edu/implicit/takeatest.html (last accessed March 15, 2023).

119. Diverseo Women's Forum Leadership IAT June–October 2012.

120. Latu, I. M., Stewart, T. L., Myers, A. C., Lisco, C. G., Estes, S. B., & Donahue, D. K. (2011). What we "say" and what we "think" about female managers: Explicit versus implicit associations of women with success. *Psychology of Women Quarterly, 35*(2): 252–266.

121. Braun, S., Stegmann, S., Hernandez Bark, A. S., Junker, N. M., & van Dick, R. (2017). Think manager—think male, think follower—think female: Gender bias in implicit followership theories. *Journal of Applied Social Psychology, 47*(7): 377–388.

122. Player, A., Randsley de Moura, G., Leite, A. C., Abrams, D., & Tresh, F. (2019). Overlooked leadership potential: The preference for leadership potential in job candidates who are men vs. women. *Frontiers in Psychology, 10*: 755. doi: 10.3389/fpsyg.2019.00755.

123. Rudman, L. A., & Heppen, J. B. (2003). Implicit romantic fantasies and women's interest in personal power: A glass slipper effect? *Personality and Social Psychology Bulletin, 29*(11): 1357–1370.

124. Eden, A. (2006). Coaching women for senior executive roles: A societal perspective on power and exclusion. In: H. Brunning (Ed.), *Executive Coaching: Systems-Psychodynamic Perspective* (pp. 79–94). London: Karnac.

125. Valerio (2009). See note 117.

126. Desvaux, G., Devillard, S., de Zelicourt, A., Kossoff, C,, Labaye, E., & Sancier-Sultan, S. (2017). [Report.] Women Matter: Ten years of insights

on gender diversity. McKinsey. https://www.mckinsey.com/featured-insights/gender-equality/women-matter-ten-years-of-insights-on-gender-diversity (last accessed March 15, 2023).

Chapter 7

127. Guastello, S. J. (2009). Evolutionary game theory and leadership. *American Psychologist, 64*(1): 53–54.

128. Guastello, S. J. (2007). How leaders really emerge. *American Psychologist, 62*(6): 606–607, p. 607.

129. Ibid.

130. Weber, M. (1958). *The Protestant Ethic and the Spirit of Capitalism.* New York: Charles Scribner's Sons.

131. Trist, E. L. (1981). *The Evolution of Socio-Technical Systems, Vol. 2.* Toronto, Canada: Ontario Quality of Working Life Centre.

132. Trist, E. L., & Bamforth, K. W. (1951). Some social and psychological consequences of the longwall method of coal-getting: An examination of the psychological situation and defences of a work group in relation to the social structure and technological content of the work system. *Human Relations, 4*(1): 3–38.

133. Taggar, S., Hackew, R., & Saha, S. (1999). Leadership emergence in autonomous work teams: Antecedents and outcomes. *Personnel Psychology, 52*(4): 899–926.

134. Barker, J. R. (1993). Tightening the iron cage: Concertive control in self-managing teams. *Administrative Science Quarterly, 38*(3): 408–437, p. 411.

135. Northouse (2021). See note 55.

136. de Waal-Andrews & van Vugt (2020). See note 39.

137. From our perspective of focusing on the unconscious it is yet worthwhile to look at Otto Kernberg's five personality characteristics desirable for rational leadership, which are universal and still apply. Rational is meant here as the opposite of irrational and mentally unhealthy.
    1. Intelligence
    2. Honesty and incorruptibility
    3. The capacity to develop and maintain intensive relationships with other people
    4. Healthy narcissism

5. A healthy, justified, and anticipatorily paranoid attitude, as opposed to naivety.

Source: Kernberg, O. (1998). *Ideology, Conflict and Leadership in Groups and Organizations.* New Haven, CT: Yale University Press.

138. Joseph, D. L., Dhanani, L. Y., Shen, W., McHugh, B. C., & McCord, M. A. (2015). Is a happy leader a good leader? A meta-analytic investigation of leader trait affect and leadership. *Leadership Quarterly, 26*(4): 557–576, p. 560.
139. Kets de Vries, M. F. R. (2013). The eight archetypes of leadership. *Harvard Business Review.* https://hbr.org/2013/12/the-eight-archetypes-of-leadership (last accessed November 11, 2022).
140. Kragh, U. (1960). *The Defense Mechanism Test.* Lund, Sweden: Gleerup.
141. Jaques, E. (1996). *Requisite Organization: A Total System for Effective Managerial Organization and Managerial Leadership for the 21st Century.* Orange Park, FL: Cason Hall.
142. Zenger, J., & Folkman, J. (2019). Women score higher than men in most leadership skills. *Harvard Business Review, 92*(10): 86–93.
143. French, J. R. P., Jr., & Raven, B. (1959). The bases of social power. In: D. Cartwright (Ed.), *Studies in Social Power* (pp. 150–167). Ann Arbor, MI: University of Michigan Press.
144. Gilbert, D. T. (2006). *Stumbling on Happiness.* New York: Random House.
145. von Oetinger, B., von Ghyczy, T., & Bassford, C. (Eds.) (2003). *Clausewitz: Strategie denken.* Munich, Germany: Carl Hanser, p. 208.
146. Clausewitz, C. von. (1973). *Vom Kriege: Hinterlassenes Werk.* Bonn, Germany: Ferdinand Dümmler, p. 208.
147. Tzu, Sun (*c.* fifth century BC). *The Art of War.* Radford, VA: Wilder, 2008.
148. Based on: Bennis, W. G. (2004). The seven ages of the leader. *IEEE Engineering Management Review, 32*(2): 45–51.
149. Based on: Lester, D. L., Parnell, J. A., & Carraher, S. (2003). Organizational life cycle: A five-stage empirical scale. *International Journal of Organizational Analysis, 11*(4): 339–354.

Chapter 8

150. Csikszentmihalyi, M. (1990). *Flow: The Psychology of Optimal Experience.* New York: Harper & Row, p. 3.

151. Aristotle, *The Nicomachean Ethics* (Aristotle II.6). See Bartlett, R. C., & Collins, S. D. (2011). *Aristotle's Nicomachean Ethics*. London: University of Chicago Press.
152. Obholzer, A. (2006). Foreword. In: H. Brunning (Ed.), *Executive Coaching: Systems-Psychodynamic Perspective* (pp. xi–xxiv). London: Karnac.
153. Motowildo, S. S., Borman, W. C., & Schmitt, M. J. (1997). A theory of individual difference in task and contextual performance. *Human Performance, 10*(2): 71–83.
154. Ibid.
155. Beck, U. C. (2012). *Psychodynamic Coaching: Focus and Depth*. London: Karnac, p. 15.
156. Fromm, E. (1947). *Man for Himself. An Inquiry into the Psychology of Ethics*. New York: H. Holt.
157. Jung, C. G. (1921). *Psychological Types*. Definitions: Self. *C. W.* 6, par. 789. Princeton, NJ: Princeton University Press.
158. Goleman, D. (1995). *Emotional Intelligence: Why It Can Matter More Than IQ*. New York: Bantam.
159. a. Jung (1921). See note 157.
   b. Jung, C. G. (1966). *Two Essays on Analytical Psychology. C. W. 7.* Princeton, NJ: Princeton University Press.
160. Ibid. See note 159b.
161. Müller, L., & Müller, A. (Eds.) (2003). *Wörterbuch der Analytischen Psychologie*. Düsseldorf, Germany: Walter.
162. Stein, M. (2006). *The Principle of Individuation: Toward the Development of Human Consciousness*. Asheville, NC: Chiron.
163. Jung (1966), par 291. See note 159b.
164. Most elements have been changed so as not to allow identification of the client or the system around her. The purpose of this chapter is to illustrate a likely coaching scenario while not divulging any real details.
165. Annabel Green is a fictitious name given to the client.
166. The national move of patients infected with Covid-19 from the NHS (National Health Service) hospitals to care homes at the start of the pandemic was later criticised as shortsighted and dangerous as it shifted the site of infection from hospitals to care homes. This decision resulted in excess deaths. See Nuffield Trust report, Death of Care Home Residents, https://nuffieldtrust.org.uk/news-item/covid-19-and-the-deaths-

of-care-home-residents?gclid=CjwKCAjwvsqZBhAlEiwAqAHEle0wCIMlilQ-2w93W8oYJHi4gnQ4NcMUv35kNSDRIbzkWKFP1mo_xBoCfk4QAvD_BwE (last accessed September 27, 2022).

167. Nuffield Trust Report (2022). See note 166.

168. a. Brunning, H., & Khaleelee, O. (Eds.) (2023). *The Covid Trail: Psychodynamic Explorations*. Bicester, UK: Phoenix.
  b. Tabish, S. A. (2020). https://academia.edu/42625081/Covid_19_the_worst_health_calamity_of_the_world?email_work_card=abstract-read-more (last accessed September 28, 2022).

169. a. Brunning, H. (2001). Six domains of executive coaching. *Journal of Organisational and Social Dynamics*, *1*(2): 254–263.
  b. Brunning, H. (2014b). *From Entry to Ending—8 Stages of Executive Coaching. Manual of Executive Coaching*. Krakow, Poland: Prorozvoyovo.
  c. Brunning, H., & Khaleelee, O. (2021). From here to eternity? Work, coaching, and consulting in a post-Covid world. *Organisational and Social Dynamics*, *21*(1): 171–188.

170. Taken from Brunning (2001). See note 169a.

171. CQC stands for Care Quality Commission, which regularly inspects all health and social care institutions in the United Kingdom.

172. PPE stands for personal protective equipment such as high grade masks, gloves, and gowns.

173. Brunning & Khaleelee (2023). See note 168a.

174. a. Brunning (2001). See note 169a.
  b. Brunning (2006). *Executive Coaching. Systems-Psychodynamic Perspective*. London: Karnac.
  c. Brunning (2014a). *Psychoanalytic Essays on Power and Vulnerability*. London: Karnac.
  d. Brunning (2014b). See note 169b.
  e. Brunning & Khaleelee (2021). See note 169c.
  f. Brunning & Khaleelee (2023). See note 168a.
  g. Brunning, H., & Roberts, V. Z. (2007). Psychodynamic and systems-psychodynamic coaching. In: S. Palmer & A. Whybrow (Eds.), *Handbook of Coaching Psychology* (pp. 253–277). Hove, UK: Routledge.
  h. Nuffield Trust Report, Death of Care Home Residents (see note 166).
  i. Tabish (2020). See note 168b.

175. Searles, H. F. (1955). The effect of the structure of the therapeutic situation on the process of therapy. *Psychiatric Quarterly*, *29*(3): 193–208.

Chapter 9

176. Long, S. (2008). Organizational defenses against anxiety: What has happened since the 1955 Jaques paper? *International Journal of Applied Psychoanalytic Studies*, *3*(4): 279–295, p. 288.
177. Larry Hirschhorn developed the concept of primary task and primary risk. See, for example, Hirschhorn, L. (1999). The primary risk. *Human Relations*, *52*(1): 5–23.
178. Brown, A. D., & Starkey, K. (2000). Organizational identity and learning: A psychodynamic perspective. *Academy of Management Review*, *25*(1): 101–120.
179. Ibid.
180. Janis, J. (1972). *Victims of Groupthink: A Psychological Study of Foreign-Policy Decisions and Fiascoes*. Boston, MA: Houghton Mifflin.
181. Chapman, J. (2006). Anxiety and defective decision making: An elaboration of the groupthink model. *Management Decision*, *44*(10): 1391–1404.
182. However, more recent research questions the details of this theory and the test results. See Chapman (note 180) and Rose, J. D. (2011). Diverse perspectives on the Groupthink theory: A literary review. *Emerging Leadership Journeys*, *4*(1): 37–57.
183. Schein, E. H. (2010). *Organizational Culture and Leadership*. Hoboken, NJ: John Wiley & Sons, p. 12.
184. Bion, W. R. (1961). *Experiences in Groups and Other Papers*. London: Tavistock.
185. Ibid., pp. 143–144.
186. Kets de Vries (2004). See note 73.
187. Author's compilation based on Nagel, C. (2014). *Behavioral Strategy: Thoughts and Feelings in the Decision-Making Process. The Unconscious and Corporate Success*. Bonn, Germany : Unternehmermedien, p. 108, with a recently added new basic assumption mode, called victimism/supremacism. In: Nagel (2021). See note 63.
188. Ettin, M. F., Cohen, B. D., & Fidler J. W. (1997). Group-as-a-whole theory viewed in its 20th-century context. *Group Dynamics: Theory, Research, and Practice*, *1*(4): 329–340, p. 332.

Chapter 10

189. Gilbert, D. (2007). *Stumbling on Happiness.* New York: Vintage.
190. Ibid., pp. 52f.
191. Ibid.
192. Holzkamp-Osterkamp, U. (1975). *Grundlagen der Motivationsforschung.* Frankfurt, Germany: Campus.
193. Hirschhorn (1999). See note 177.
194. a. Ashford et al. (2010). Ambivalence in organizations. Presentation at the annual meeting of the Academy of Management, Montreal.
     b. Ashforth et al. (2014). Ambivalence in organizations: A multilevel approach. *Organization Science, 25*(5): 1453–1478.
195. Friedman, M. (1970). A Friedman doctrine: The social responsibility of business is to increase its profits. *New York Times Magazine, 13*: 32–33.
196. Yoder, K. J., & Decety, J. (2018). The neuroscience of morality and social decision-making. *Psychology, Crime & Law, 24*(3): 279–295, p. 281.
197. Ibid.
198. Kohlberg, L. (1976). Moral stages and moralization: The cognitive-development approach. In: T. Lickona (Ed.), *Moral Development and Behavior: Theory and Research and Social Issues* (pp. 31–53). New York, NY: Holt, Rienhart, and Winston.
199. Gilligan, C. (1982). *In a Different Voice: Psychological Theory and Women's Development.* Cambridge, MA: Harvard University Press.
200. Schad, J., Lewis, M. W., Raisch, S., & Smith, W. K. (2016). Paradox research in management science: Looking back to move forward. *Academy of Management Annals, 10*(1): 5–64.
201. Smith, W. K. (2015). Dynamic decision making: A model of senior leaders managing strategic paradoxes. *Academy of Management Journal, 1015*(1): 58–89.
202. Smith, W. K., & Lewis, M. W. (2011). Toward a theory of paradox: A dynamic equilibrium model of organizing. *Academy of Management Review, 38*(2): 381–403.
203. Lewis, M. W. (2000). Exploring paradox: Toward a more comprehensive guide. *Academy of Management Review, 25*(4): 760–776.
204. Ingram, A. E., Lewis, M. W., Barton, S., & Gartner, W. B. (2016). Paradoxes and innovation in family firms: The role of paradoxical thinking. *Entrepreneurship Theory and Practice, 40*: 161–176.

205. a. Lewis (2000). See note 203.
b. Smith (2015). See note 201.

206. Lewis (2000), p. 764. See note 203.

207. Smith, W. K., & Tushman, M. L. (2005). Managing strategic contradictions: A top management model for managing innovation streams. *Organization Science, 16*: 522–536.

208. a. Rothenberg, A. (1979). Homospatial thinking in creativity. *Archives of General Psychiatry, 33*: 17–26.
b. Lewis (2000). See note 203.
c. Schad et al. (2016). See note 200.

209. Schreyögg, G., & Kliesch-Eberl, M. (2007). How dynamic can organizational capabilities be? Towards a dual-process model of capability dynamization. *Strategic Management Journal, 28*(9): 913–933.

Chapter 11

210. Winnicott, D. W. (1971). *Playing and Reality*. London: Tavistock.

211. Matches at the four Grand Slam tournaments (Roland Garros, Wimbledon, Flushing Meadow, and the Australian Open) are all played in five sets, that means three winning sets.

212. Please have a look at the following titles:
a. Amado, G. (2009). Potential space: The threatened source of individual and collective creativity. In: B. Sievers (Ed.), *Psychoanalytic Studies of Organizations* (pp. 263–283). London: Karnac.
b. Amado, G., & Ambrose, A. (2001). *The Transitional Approach to Change*. London: Karnac.
c. Amado, G., & Vansina, L. (2005). *The Transitional Approach in Action*. London: Karnac.

213. Eisenman, R. (1997). Creativity, preference for complexity, and physical and mental health. In: M. A. Runco & R. Richards (Eds.), *Eminent Creativity, Everyday Creativity, and Health* (pp. 99–106). Norwood, NJ: Ablex.

214. Runco, M. A., & Yoruk, S. (2020). Conflict and creativity. In: E. Carayannis (Ed.), *Encyclopedia of Creativity, Invention, Innovation and Entrepreneurship* (2nd edn). Cham, Switzerland: Springer Nature, p. 243.

215. Peter Senge in: H. von Pierer, & B. von Oetinger (1999). *Wie kommt das Neue in die Welt?* Hamburg, Germany: Rowohlt Taschenbuch.

216. a. Moldaschl, M. (2006). Innovationsfähigkeit, Zukunftsfähigkeit, dynamic capabilities: Moderne Fähigkeitsmystik und eine Alternative. *Managementforschung, 16*: 1–36.
   b. Runco & Yoruk (2020). See note 214.
217. Yong, K., Sauer, S. J., & Mannix, E. A. (2014). Conflict and creativity in interdisciplinary teams. *Small Group Research, 45*(3): 266–289.
218. Guilford developed them when researching intelligence:
   a. Guilford, J. P. (1950). Creativity. *American Psychologist, 14*: 469–479.
   b. Guilford, J. P. (1967). *The Nature of Human Intelligence*. New York: McGraw-Hill.

Chapter 12

219. Critchley, B., & Casey, D. (1984). *Second Thoughts on Team Building: Management Education and Development, 15*(2): 163–175.
220. For in-depth descriptions of the phenomenon of thinking space and the related reflective space see the sources of the case contributor below:
   a. Ringer, T. M. (2002). *Group Action: The Dynamics of Groups in Therapeutic, Educational and Corporate Settings*. London: Jessica Kingsley. [In particular Chapter 10.]
   b. Ringer, T. M. (2007). Leadership for collective thinking in the work place. *Team Performance Management, 13*(3/4): 130–144.
   c. Ringer, T. M. (2017a). What's wrong with being open minded? The role of opinion blocks in thinking in groups and teams. *Gruppo: Omogeneità e Differenze* (*Group: Homogeneity and Difference*): 92–104.
   d. Ringer, T. M. (2017b). Opinion blocks: Some dynamics of collective self-righteousness. *Organisational and Social Dynamics, 17*(1): 19–31.
   e. Ringer, T. M., Gordon, R., & Vandenbussche, B. (Eds.) (2022). *The Collective Spark: Igniting Thinking in Groups, Teams and the Wider World*. Gent, Belgium: Grafische Cel.
221. The main researcher in this field is David Teece. See his most important papers:
   a. Teece, D. J. (2007). Explicating dynamic capabilities: The nature and microfoundations of (sustainable) enterprise performance. *Strategic Management Journal, 28*: 1319–1350.
   b. Teece, D. J., Pisano, G., & Shuen, A. (1997). Dynamic capabilities and strategic management. *Strategic Management Journal, 18*: 509–533.
222. Kahneman & Tversky (1979). See note 9.

223. Teece (2007). See note 221a.
224. Hodgkinson, G. P., & Healey, M. P. (2011). Psychological foundations of dynamic capabilities: Reflexion and reflection in strategic management. *Strategic Management Journal*, *32*: 1500–1516.
225. Teece (2007). See note 221a.
226. Kets de Vries, M. F. R. (2005). Leadership group coaching in action: The Zen of creating high performance teams. *Academy of Management Perspectives*, *19*(1): 61–76.

Chapter 13

227. Schein, E. (1984). Coming to a new awareness of organizational culture. *Sloane Management Review*, *25*(2): 3–16, p. 3.
228. Ibid.
229. a. Müller, L., & Knoll, D. (1998). *Ins Innere der Dinge schauen*. Düsseldorf, Germany: Patmos/Walter, p. 223.
 b. See Nagel (2021), note 63.
230. Rose Mersky is the owner of these photos:
 a. Mersky, R. R. (2017). Social dream-drawing (SDD): Praxis and research. [Doctoral dissertation, University of the West of England, Bristol.]
 b. Mersky, R. R. (2022). *The Social Dream-Drawing Workshop: A Handbook for Professionals*. London: Routledge.
231. a. Gabriel, Y. (2015) Narratives and stories in organizational life. In: A. de Fina & A. Georgakopoulou (Eds.), *The Handbook of Narrative Analysis* (pp. 275–292). Hoboken, NJ: Wiley-Blackwell, p. 277.
 b. Mitroff, I. I., & Kilmann, R. H. (1975). Stories managers tell: A new tool for organizational problem solving. *Management Review*, *64*(7): 18–28.
232. a. Moxnes, P. (1998). Fantasies and fairy tales in groups and organizations: Bion's basic assumptions and the deep roles. *European Journal of Work and Organizational Psychology*, *7*(3): 283–298.
 b. Moxnes, P. (1999). Deep roles: Twelve primordial roles of mind and organization. *Human Relations*, *52*(11): 1427–1444.
233. Adapted from Moxnes (1999). See note 232b.
234. Corlett, J. G., & Pearson, C. S. (2003). *Mapping the Organizational Psyche: A Jungian Theory of Organizational Dynamics and Change*. Gainesville, FL: Center for Applications of Psychological Type.
235. Based on Corlett & Pearson (2003). See note 234.
236. Adapted from Corlett & Pearson (2003). See note 234.

Chapter 14

237. von Bertalanffy, L. (1969). *General System Theory: Foundations, Development, Applications.* New York: George Braziller, p. 12.

238. a. Miller, J. G., & Miller, J. L. (1990). Introduction: The nature of living systems. *Behavioral Science, 35*(3): 157–163.
   b. Vancouver, J. B. (1996). Living systems theory as a paradigm for organizational behavior: Understanding humans, organizations, and social processes. *Behavioral Science, 41*(3): 165–204.

239. Parent, E. (1996). The living systems theory of James Grier Miller. Retrieved from https://web3.isss.org/primer2/asem14ep.html (last accessed November 19, 2022).

240. See Kant § 65: Things regarded as natural purposes are organised beings. In: Kant, E. (1914). *Critique of Judgement.* New York: Cosimo, 2007.

241. Stacey, R. D. (2010). *Strategic Management and Organisational Dynamics: The Challenge of Complexity.* Upper Saddle River, NJ: Pearson.

242. Neuberger, O. (2002). Führen und führen lassen. *Ansätze, Ergebnisse und Kritik der Führungsforschung, 6*: 197–203.

243. Stacey (2010). See note 241.

244. Petriglieri & Petriglieri (2020). See note 53.

245. See: NS Networking Sciences. https://ins-netgroup.com/globalcomm-oy/institutes/ns-networking-sciences/ (last accessed March 15, 2023).

246. Balkundi, P., & Kilduff, M. (2006). The ties that lead: A social network approach to leadership. *Leadership Quarterly, 17*(4): 419–439.

247. Based on Balkundi & Kilduff (2006), p. 422. See note 246.

248. Peltoniemi, M., & Vuori, E. (2004). Business ecosystem as the new approach to complex adaptive business environments. *Proceedings of eBusiness Research Forum, 2*(22): 267–281, p. 269.

249. Moore, J. F. (1998). The rise of a new corporate form. *Washington Quarterly, 21*(1): 167–181, p. 168.

250. Ibid., p. 168.

251. von Bertalanffy (1969), p. 252. See note 237.

252. Wielkiewicz, R. M. (2002). Validity of the Leadership Attitudes and Beliefs Scale: Relationships with personality, communal orientation, and social desirability. *Journal of College Student Development, 43*: 108–118.

253. https://journalofleadershiped.org/jole_articles/relationships-between-eco-leadership-and-problem-solving-styles-of-gifted-and-talented-youth/ (last accessed March 15, 2023).
254. Wielkiewicz, R. M. (2000). The Leadership Attitudes and Beliefs Scale: An instrument for evaluating college students' thinking about leadership and organizations. *Journal of College Student Development, 41*: 335–347.
255. Ibid. Also Wielkiewicz (2002). See note 252.
256. a. Allen, K. E., Stelzner, S. P., & Wielkiewicz, R. M. (1999). The ecology of leadership: Adapting to the challenges of a changing world. *Journal of Leadership Studies, 5*(2): 62–82.
    b. Henry, J. C. (2022). *Wisdom from the Wild: The Nine Unbreakable Laws of Leadership from the Animal Kingdom*. Austin, TX: Greenleaf.
    c. Rost, J. C. (1997). Moving from individual to relationship: A postindustrial paradigm of leadership. *Journal of Leadership & Organizational Studies, 4*(4): 3–16.
257. Western, S. (2019). *Leadership: A Critical Text*. London: Sage, p. 315.
258. Ibid.
259. Doherty, H., Doherty, B., Haugh, H., & Lyon, F. (2014). Social enterprises as hybrid organizations: A review and research agenda. *International Journal of Management Reviews, 16*(4): 417–436.
260. a. Fine, M. (2001). The New South Wales demonstration projects in integrated community care. In: M. P. Mandell (Ed.), *Getting Results through Collaboration: Networks and Network Structures for Public Policy and Management* (pp. 206–219). Westport, CT: Greenwood.
    b. Keast, R., Brown, K., & Mandell, M. (2007). Getting the right mix: Unpacking integration meanings and strategies. *International Public Management Journal, 10*(1): 9–33, p. 12.
261. Based on Keast et al. (2007). See note 260b.
262. Fiorito, T., Nagel, C., Veenswijk, M. B., & Drori, I. (2023). Navigating paradoxical tensions in the context of competition: Emotional transcendence in a Dutch public–private partnership. *Journal of Change Management*, 23(2): pp. 1–22.
263. Author's research results, unpublished.
264. Fiorito et al. (2023). See note 262.
265. Jarzabkowski, P., Lê, J. K., & Van de Ven, A. H. (2013). Responding to competing strategic demands: How organizing, belonging, and

performing paradoxes coevolve. *Strategic Organization*, *11*(3): 245–280, p. 249.

266. Gnyawali, D. R., Madhavan, R., He, J., & Bengtsson, M. (2016). The competition–cooperation paradox in inter-firm relationships: A conceptual framework. *Industrial Marketing Management*, *53*: 7–18, p. 8.
267. Lewis (2000). See note 203.
268. Abdallah, C., Denis, J.-L., & Langley, A. (2011). Having your cake and eating it too: Discourses of transcendence and their role in organizational change dynamics. *Journal of Organizational Change Management*, *24*: 333–348, p. 335.
269. Please watch out for the next paper about the second phase of research which will be published in 2023 or 2024.

Chapter 15

270. Christensen, C. M., Alton, R., Rising, C., & Waldeck, A. (2011). The new M&A playbook. *Harvard Business Review*, *89*(3): 48–57.
271. Jinette de Gooijer has written an excellent book about the psychological and psychodynamic aspects of a merger:
    de Gooijer, J. (2009). *The Murder in Merger*. London: Karnac.
    I would like to highly recommend that book. It presents an in-depth analysis of a merger and I draw on the theory she presents there.
272. Brunning, H. (2003). Organisational mergers—a dance of constructive and destructive elements. *Organisations & People*, *10*(1): 2–8.
273. Ibid.

Chapter 16

274. I owe the inspiration for this chapter to a book written by two very dear colleagues: Bonnerup, B., & Hasselager, A. (2019). *Love and Loneliness at Work: An Inspirational Guide for Consultants, Leaders and Other Professionals*. New York: Routledge.
    They give a very thorough and detailed overview of all aspects of this subject with illustrative cases in much more depth than I can touch on here. I have also used this book as one of my main references for this chapter.
275. a. Fiore, B. (1997). The theory and practice of friendship in Cicero. In: J. T. Fitzgerald (Ed.), *Friendship, Flattery, and Frankness of Speech:*

Studies on Friendship in the New Testament World (pp. 59–76). Leiden, the Netherlands: E. J. Brill.

b. French, R. (2007). Friendship and organization: Learning from the western friendship tradition. *Management & Organizational History, 2*(3): 255–272.

276. Fiore (1997). See note 275a, p. 59.
277. Aristotle, *The Nicomachean Ethics*, Book 8, 1156a10.
278. Ibid., 1156a13.
279. French (2007). See note 275b.
280. Ibid., 1156b7.
281. Jür, W. (1975). *Couples in Collusion*. New York: Jason Aronson.
282. Bonnerup & Hasselager (2019). See note 274.
283. Hirschhorn (1999). See note 177.
284. Visholm (2021). See note 101.
285. Bonnerup & Hasselager (2019). See note 274.
286. Ibid.
287. Ibid.
288. Bartleby: You'll often walk alone. Loneliness is a widespread problem with complex roots. *The Economist*, January 28, 2021.
289. According to Hertz, N. (2020). *The Lonely Century: A Call to Reconnect*. London: Sceptre.
290. Gallup Global Emotion Report (2022). https://gallup.com/analytics/349280/gallup-global-emotions-report (last accessed June 17, 2022).
291. Measuring misery. Unhappiness is soaring around the world, laments Jon Clifton. The head of Gallup says the problem began long before the pandemic. *The Economist*, June 17, 2022.
292. Illouz, E. (2007). *Cold Intimacies: The Making of Emotional Capitalism*. Cambridge: Polity. See also Bonnerup & Hasselager (2019), note 274.

Chapter 17

293. https://gartner.com/en/information-technology/glossary (last accessed March 15, 2023). All explanations and definitions of the terms used in the text stem from that glossary if not stated otherwise.
294. Wojcik, P., Obłój, K., Wąsowska, A., & Wierciński, S. (2020). Corporate acceleration process: A systems psychodynamics perspective. *Journal of Organizational Change Management*, *33*(6): 1163–1180.

295. See ISO 8549-3:2020.
296. Hutton, J., & Hurry, M. (2009). *Orthotic Service in the NHS: Improving Service Provision*. York, UK: York Health Economics Consortium.
297. Boxer, P. J. (2004). Facing facts: What is the good of change? *Journal of Psycho-Social Studies*, *3*(1): 20–46.
298. Tiwana, A. (2014). *Platform Ecosystems: Aligning Architecture, Governance, and Strategy*. Waltham, MA: Morgan Kaufmann Elsevier.
299. A trust's lead orthotist, private communication, September 26, 2022.
300. Winnicott, D. W. (1971). Transitional objects and transitional phenomena. In: *Playing and Reality* (pp. 1–25). London: Tavistock.
301. Cronen, V. E., & Pearce, W. B. (1985). Toward an explanation of how the Milan Method works: An invitation to a systemic epistemology and the evolution of family systems. In: D. Campbell & R. Draper (Eds.), *Applications of Systemic Family Therapy: The Milan Approach*. London: Grune & Stratton.
302. Lines, M., & Ambler, S. (2018). *Introduction to Disciplined Agile Delivery* (2nd edn). Newtown Square, PA: Disciplined Agile.
303. A trust's lead orthotist. See note 299.
304. Naylor, D. (2023). *Speaking Up in a Culture of Silence: Changing the Organization Activity from Bullying and Incivility to One of Listening and Productivity*. New York: Routledge.
305. Roth, P. (2004). Mapping the landscape: Levels of transference interpretation. In: E. Hargreaves & A. Varchevker (Eds.), *In Pursuit of Psychic Change: The Betty Joseph Workshop*. Hove, UK: Brunner-Routledge.
306. Hoggett, P. (2006). Conflict, ambivalence, and the contested purpose of public organisations. *Human Relations*, *59*(2): 175–194.
307. Boxer, P. J. (2014). Leading organisations without boundaries: "Quantum" organisation and the work of making meaning. *Organizational and Social Dynamics*, *14*(1): 130–153.
308. A trust's lead orthotist. See note 299.
309. Autonomous work teams are not an invention of today. We have been talking about and aiming for them since Mayo's Hawthorne experiment of 1933, ninety years ago. This subject was intensely discussed in the 1970s and 1980s under the notion of lean production and lean management.
310. Terra, J. (2023, February 7). The future of robotics: How robots will transform our lives. https://simplilearn.com/future-of-robotics-article (last accessed March 15, 2023).

311. See for example my paper on victimism: Nagel (2021), note 63.
312. The 21 principles, 2017 Asilomar Conference. See https://futureoflife.org/open-letter/ai-principles/ (last accessed March 15, 2023).
313. see https://unesdoc.unesco.org/ark:/48223/pf0000373434 (last accessed March 15, 2023).

Chapter 18

314. I use Zoom as a synonym for all video and online conferencing tools, whichever brand name is behind them—to Zoom has become an expression in its own right over the last three years.
315. Bailenson, J. N. (2021). Nonverbal overload: A theoretical argument for the causes of Zoom fatigue. *Technology, Mind, and Behavior, 2*(1): 1–6.
316. Thank you to all the Melbourne Regional Meeting participants in October 2022—we worked out some of these aspects together in a workshop during that meeting.
317. Hinshelwood, R. D., & Skogstad, W. (2000). *Observing Organisations.* London: Routledge.
318. Further sources:
    a. Dent, N. (2019). A reflexive account. In: H. Weinberg & A. Rolnick (Eds.), *Theory and Practice of Online Therapy.* London: Routledge.
    b. Grotstein, J. S. (1978). Inner space: Its dimensions and its coordinates. *International Journal of Psychoanalysis, 59*(1): 55–61.
    c. Isaacs Russell, G. (2018). *Screen Relations.* London: Routledge.
    d. Olson, G., & Olson, J. (2000). Distance matters. *Human-Computer Interaction, 15*(2–3): 139–178.
319. Gratton, L. (2021). How to do hybrid right. *Harvard Business Review, 99*(3): 66–74.
320. Ibid., p. 7. I have used her article as an inspiration for the next paragraphs as well.

Index